W9-CRL-952

JAMES PATTIE'S WEST

JAMES PATTIE'S WEST

WEST

The Dream and the Reality

(Published in hard cover as *American Ecclesiastes: The Stories of James Pattie*)

BY RICHARD BATMAN

UNIVERSITY OF OKLAHOMA PRESS
NORMAN AND LONDON

W
F
800
P33
B382
1986

Maps by Anita Karl and Jim Kemp

Library of Congress Cataloging-in-Publication Data

Batman, Richard.
  James Pattie's West: the dream and the reality.

  Originally published: American ecclesiastes. 1st ed. San Diego:
Harcourt Brace Jovanovich, © 1984.
  Bibliography: p.
  Includes index.
  1. Pattie, James O. (James Ohio), 1804?–1850? 2. Southwest,
New—History—To 1848. 3. Indians of North America—South-
west, New—History. 4. Fur traders—Southwest, New—Biography.
5. Southwest, New—Biography. I. Title.
F800.P33B382   1986   979'.02'0924   [B]   85–40937
ISBN 0–8061–1977–2 (pbk.)

University of Oklahoma Press paperback edition published by
arrangement with Harcourt Brace Jovanovich, Publishers. Copy-
right © 1984 by Richard Batman. Manufactured in the U.S.A.
All rights reserved. No part of this publication may be reproduced or transmitted in any form or by any means, electronic
or mechanical, including photocopy, recording, or any information storage and retrieval system, without permission in writing
from Permissions, Harcourt Brace Jovanovich, Publishers, Or-
lando, FL 32887. Hard-cover edition published by Harcourt
Brace Jovanovich under the title *American Ecclesiastes: The
Stories of James Pattie.* First printing of the University of Oklahoma Press paperback edition, 1986.

5-6-88

To Ann, Dayle, and Denise

CONTENTS

MAPS AND ILLUSTRATIONS

MAPS

ILLUSTRATIONS

SECTION I (following pp. 112)

Landscape with Cattle
The Mill Boy
Bellevue Trading Post
Interior at Bellevue
Petalesharo, Generous Chief, Pawnee Tribe
The Buffalo Bull, Grand Pawnee
Grand Pawnees
Beaver Dens
Herd of Buffalo
The Mountain of Rocks, Comanche
The Little Spaniard, Comanche
Comanche Village
A Packtrain to Santa Fe, 1820
View of Santa Fe and Vicinity
Pima Indian Country

Group of Apaches
Presidio at the Copper Mines
View of the Copper Mines

Vanity of vanities, saith the Preacher,
  vanity of vanities;
  all *is* vanity.
What profit hath a man of all his labor
  which he taketh under the sun?
One generation passeth away, and another generation
    cometh:
  but the earth abideth for ever.

                        —Ecclesiastes 1: 2–4

If any one of my years has felt, that the fashion of this world
passeth away, and that all below the sun is vanity, it is I.

                        —JAMES PATTIE in *The Personal
                        Narrative of James O. Pattie*

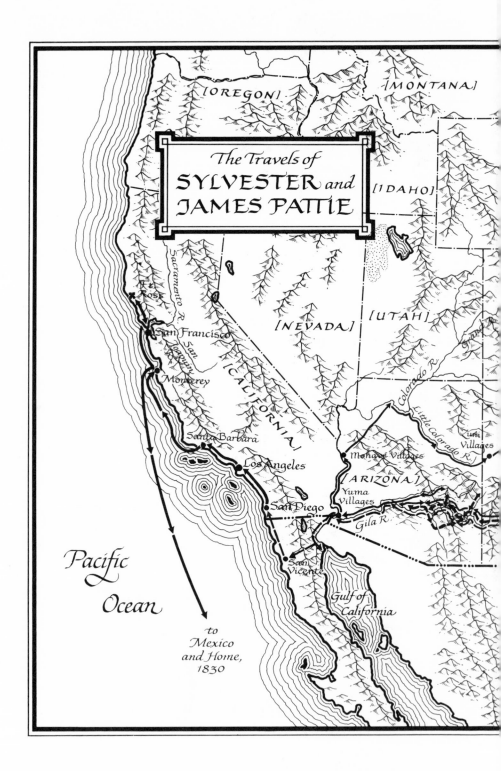

The Travels of SYLVESTER and JAMES PATTIE

[OREGON]

[MONTANA]

[IDAHO]

[NEVADA]

[UTAH]

Sacramento R.

Ft. Ross

San Francisco

San Joaquin R.

Monterey

[CALIFORNIA]

Santa Barbara

Los Angeles

Colorado R.

Little Colorado R.

Zuni Villages

Mohave Villages

San Diego

[ARIZONA]

Yuma Villages

Gila R.

San Vicente

Gulf of California

Pacific Ocean

to Mexico and Home, 1830

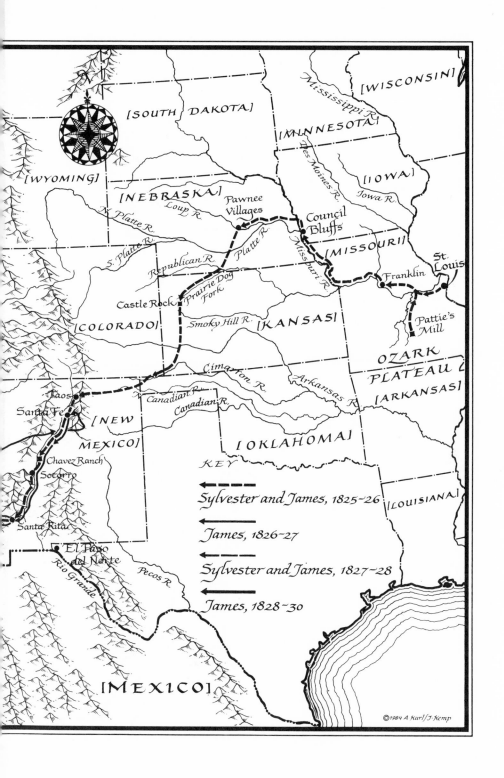

[WISCONSIN]

[SOUTH DAKOTA]

[MINNESOTA]

Mississippi R.

[WYOMING]

[IOWA]

Des Moines R.

Iowa R.

[NEBRASKA]

Loup. R.

Pawnee
Villages

Council
Bluffs

N. Platte R.

Platte R.

Missouri R.

[MISSOURI]

St.
Louis

S. Platte R.

Republican R.

Franklin

Prairie Dog
Fork

Castle Rock

Pattie's
Mill

[COLORADO]

Smoky Hill R.

[KANSAS]

OZARK

Cimarron R.

PLATEAU

Arkansas R.

[ARKANSAS]

Taos

Canadian R.

Santa Fe

[NEW

Canadian R.

[OKLAHOMA]

MEXICO]

KEY

Chavez Ranch

Socorro

Sylvester and James, 1825~26

[LOUISIANA]

Santa Rita

James, 1826~27

El Paso
del Norte

Sylvester and James, 1827~28

Rio Grande

Pecos R.

James, 1828~30

[MEXICO]

©1984 A. Karl/J. Kemp

JAMES PATTIE'S WEST

PROLOGUE

A SCENE FROM *Peer Gynt.*

AASE *(Peer's mother):*
   Oh, you bloody story-teller! How you can lie!
   I remember now, I heard all this rubbish
   Before, when I was a girl of twenty.
   It happened to Gudbrand Glesnë, not to you,
   You—!
PEER:
   To both of us.
   Such a thing can happen twice.
AASE:
   . . . Yes, a lie can be stood on its head,
   Smartened up and put in new clothes,
   So its own mother wouldn't know its skinny carcase,
   That's what you've done, letting on wild and great,
   Tricking it out with eagle's back
   And all that humbug, lying right and left,
   Yarning away and scaring me dumb
   So I couldn't recognise a story
   I'd heard in my mother's lap.

T WAS EARLY AUGUST 1830 WHEN JAMES
Pattie, after five years of wandering in the West,
found himself broke and stranded in New Orleans. Since the previous May he had been on his
way home from the other side of the continent,
traveling by ship from California to Mexico, by land
across Mexico, then by another ship from Mexico to the
United States. When he reached New Orleans, he was still a
long way from his home in Kentucky, but his money had
run out, and he could not even afford deck passage on a
steamboat bound upriver. He had all but given up hope, and
in desperation was thinking of taking a job as clerk on a ship
bound back to Mexico, when, almost by accident, he met
Josiah Johnston, the United States senator from Louisiana.
It was one of the few lucky breaks he had gotten in all his
years of travel, since Johnston, who knew several members
of Pattie's family, was willing to pay the forty dollars for
cabin passage on the steamboat *Cora*, which was leaving for
Cincinnati the next day.

For Johnston, it was money well spent as the price of stories he might hear during the long trip upriver. He was planning to travel on the *Cora* himself, and once the boat was
underway he often asked Pattie questions about his travels
in the West. Pattie later said he feared he was too much
preoccupied to give satisfactory answers, for he found it difficult to keep his mind off the fact that after five years of

•

fortune hunting he had left his father buried in a foreign land and was returning to his brothers and sisters empty-handed. Still, Pattie liked to tell stories, particularly about himself, and it is hard to imagine him passing up the chance to spin a few yarns.

All the years of travel had given him a formidable collection of tales, but he and the senator had plenty of time to talk. It took the *Cora* almost a month to wind its way up the Mississippi, then enter the Ohio and ascend it as far as Cincinnati. During that time Pattie could have told virtually every story he later included in his book. There were stories of crossing the plains from the Missouri River to the Rocky Mountains; stories of trapping on wild, untouched rivers in New Mexico; stories of life in California, which few Americans other than James Pattie had ever seen. And Josiah Johnston, United States senator from Louisiana, a state that sat right on the edge of the western country, would have been interested in them all. He also would have been interested in tales of American trappers in the West, for like many of them, he was a native of Kentucky. And certainly he would have liked stories involving James's father, for Johnston had known Sylvester Pattie during earlier days in Kentucky, when they both lived near Maysville.

A story that included almost all these elements was one Pattie told about his first real trapping expedition on the Gila River back in early 1826. His father was still alive then, and the two of them were part of a band of trappers traveling down the Gila. They were all seething with anger, for some weeks earlier several of their companions had deserted the party and pushed ahead to trap on their own. Those left behind found nothing but trapped-out streams, and they were angry enough to invoke God to bring disaster on their former friends in the form of an Indian attack or dismemberment by a grizzly bear.

It was enough to make a true believer of a man when, one cold day in January, they met six of the seven deserters coming back upstream. They had been robbed of all their fur by

.

3

Indians, and one of the men had been wounded by an arrow. The seventh man was dead, but the others had fled without stopping to bury the body. The main group, despite the curses they called down upon the deserters, offered to join them in attacking the Indians. The survivors, however, had seen enough, and instead of seeking vengeance they took food and horses and left the Indian country for good. The rest headed down the river toward the place where the Indians had attacked, but before they could reach it a storm broke, bringing high winds and heavy snow. It was impossible to travel, and they camped in a large cave in the riverbank until the storm blew itself out.

Finally, after three days, they rounded up their horses and began moving down the Gila again. Two days below the cave they found the seventh man's body among the mesquite trees in the wide river bottom. It had been butchered like the carcass of a hog. The severed head had been put on a stake and arrows fired into it. The Indians, with sardonic humor, had carefully replaced the man's hat on top of his head. Those who found the body paused long enough to gather up the various pieces and bury them. They wasted little time over the body, however, for they knew that this was as far as the others had come. They had reached un-trapped waters, and they quickly had their traps in the river.

IT WAS A hard, violent world that James had lived in, and one that was totally alien to those living farther east. Once, fifty years before, settlers there had also faced the danger and violence of Indian attack, but that had long since disappeared. Now, the Indians had all been pushed beyond the Mississippi, and most white men lived peaceful, settled lives on small farms or in quiet towns. The pursuit of wealth on a strange river more than a thousand miles from home, the place to begin trapping marked by the severed head of a human being, was something almost beyond their compre- hension.

•

4

Yet, it was also intriguing, and Senator Johnston, after listening to James's stories, apparently decided they would make a good book. For when the *Cora* arrived in Cincinnati, he gave Pattie a letter of introduction to his old friend, the well-known writer Timothy Flint. Since Pattie was broke, and since his stories were the only thing he had to show for all his years of travel, he called upon Flint almost immediately.

Flint's office in those years was a bookstore at 160 Main Street, "nearly opposite the Presbyterian Church." The store itself carried classical, medical, theological, and scholarly books as well as "all new works, as soon as published." It also was possible to buy stationery, blank books, and sheet music, and to subscribe to any number of current publications, ranging from the *Christian Examiner* to the *Transylvania Journal of Medicine.* Over this presided a clerk who, upon request, would usher an inquirer into the back room where Timothy Flint had his office.

In 1830, when Pattie met him, Flint was quite pleasant. In earlier years, when he was first a minister in Massachusetts and then a missionary in Missouri, he was disliked by almost everyone who knew him. In more recent years he had given up religion to become a writer and, by 1830, was a well-known author with seven books to his credit. He was also fifty years old, and the aging process, the finding of a congenial occupation, and his success as a writer had mellowed him into a pleasant, intelligent conversationalist. Even Frances Trollope, bitter and critical toward everything in Cincinnati, liked Timothy Flint.

James Pattie's story would have interested Flint, for five years before he himself had written *Francis Berrian,* a novel about a young man's adventures in New Mexico. Since then he had edited the *Western Monthly Review,* which had often carried stories about those in the West. The review had suspended publication a few months before Pattie arrived, but by then Flint was preparing another book, *The History and Geography of the Mississippi Valley,* which, despite its title,

•

would range as far afield as California. Pattie was an ideal source of information, and beyond that there was the possibility of making a book out of his experiences. The two men, however, could have done little more than talk briefly and arrange to meet again, for Pattie stayed in Cincinnati for only a day or two before continuing on to Augusta, Kentucky, to see his family. At the same time Flint, who had been in the West long enough to know the dangers of an uncritical acceptance of any story, needed time to do some checking.

James Pattie left Cincinnati and traveled the forty miles up the Ohio River to the small town of Augusta. He had been gone long enough to notice changes in his home. The stream that ran through his grandfather's farm had dried up; the deep grove of trees that shaded it had been chopped down; the fruit trees in the orchard had begun to decay. Even worse were the changes in the people he had left behind.

Five years before, his seven brothers and sisters had remained in Augusta, but now most of them were gone. James, when he asked about them, found that "one is here, and another is there, and my head is confused, in listening to the names of the places of their residence." Although Pattie had worried about explaining his return home without a fortune, his brothers and sisters apparently had had little faith in that promise.

Possibly what destroyed their faith was the news that reached Kentucky sometime in 1829. The Patties heard that James and Sylvester were among a group of Americans who were in a California prison. Instead of making a fortune, they clearly needed the help of those left behind, and the Kentucky Patties had gotten in touch with their congressman, Nicholas Coleman. He in turn had asked the State Department for help, and Secretary of State Martin Van Buren had personally asked Anthony Butler, the American chargé d'affaires in Mexico, to look into the case. It was all very official, but it was also very slow, and the next news the Patties received was when James himself arrived in Augusta.

•

If James's brothers and sisters were gone, his grandfather and grandmother were still there. Both were now old and feeble, and James had trouble recognizing his grandfather, whom he remembered as a vigorous man. Still, the old man was alert enough to listen to James's story of the death among strangers of his son Sylvester. In fact, he was not satisfied until he had pressed his grandson for detail after detail of Sylvester's last days. This story, and others like it, were all that Pattie had salvaged from his five years in the West. It was sometime after his discouraging homecoming that he decided to capitalize on these stories by turning them into a book.

By then Timothy Flint had checked on Pattie's story and what he discovered had convinced him that it was true. One thing that spoke well for Pattie was that he had been introduced by Josiah Johnston, not only a United States senator but an old and trusted friend of Flint's from Louisiana. Flint also knew of the Pattie family in Augusta and of the news they had received while James was in the West. Flint's years in Missouri also helped, for he remembered the respect with which those in St. Charles spoke of Sylvester Pattie. Finally, he had found people in Cincinnati who actually had seen James Pattie in various parts of New Mexico.

Flint did not mention their names, but one of them was certainly Rowland Willard, a druggist and later a physician in Cincinnati. Like Pattie, Willard had gone to New Mexico in 1825, traveling with the Santa Fe caravan that left Missouri in May and reached Taos in July. He found a place to board, established himself as a doctor, and thus was in Taos when Pattie arrived a few months later. Willard spent the next years traveling through Mexico, as did Pattie, then returned to Cincinnati, where he permanently settled. Like Pattie, he approached Flint with a written narrative of his adventures, which he hoped to see published. Not only could Willard verify Pattie's presence in New Mexico, but having been in the same place at the same time, he could provide a check on some of Pattie's stories.

•

Another man who could do the same was James Glenn. In 1830 he lived in Cincinnati, but four years earlier he had spent some time in New Mexico as a trader. He not only saw Pattie there but also did business with him, for on August 19, 1827, a trading permit was issued in Santa Fe to "Santiago Glen con Santiago O. Patis."

There was enough evidence, then, to convince Flint that Pattie had made such a trip, and he agreed to edit Pattie's book. Thus, James Pattie brought his collection of adventure stories to Flint's Cincinnati office, and from there they emerged, in 1831, as *The Personal Narrative of James O. Pattie.*

What began as no more than a young man's attempt to make a few dollars by telling the thrilling story of his trip into the West has survived surprisingly well. Most reminiscences, however well received initially, have a limited life-span—usually short—after which they fade away to reappear only rarely as a minor footnote in an obscure work. Each time Pattie's narrative showed signs of dying, however, it somehow attracted the attention of a writer or editor willing to revive it in one form or another. Such ability to survive can hardly be accidental, for accidents usually happen only once, and Pattie's narrative, in the years since its original publication, has been revived five separate times, as early as 1847 and as late as 1962. Few, if any, minor works of history have this kind of staying power, and what has kept the narrative alive is not the minor facts it adds to history but the compelling—and universal—story of a young man's initiation into a new and puzzling way of life. The question, however, that has long plagued those fascinated by Pattie's story is how much of it did he live, how much of it did he imagine?

IT IS A long road from an actual event to the written re-creation of it, and no man has successfully written a narrative of his life exactly as he lived it. At the event itself,

•

each man sees what his previous experience and his bias allow him to see. As the event recedes those who carry it only in their memory slowly alter it, sometimes to make a better story, sometimes because they honestly confuse it with another event from another time. Those who keep a written record, even the most dedicated and careful diarists, filter events through their minds, record those they think important, and ignore the rest. When such material, written or remembered, is worked into a narrative an additional burden is added, for not only must the events be interesting, but they also must be connected into a smoothly flowing account. It demands suppression, or sometimes manipulation, of events that are interesting themselves but do not fit into the flow of the narrative. A writer who uses an editor, as did James Pattie, further complicates the issue, for the editor's judgment is based not on whether the events are important to the author but on whether they are understandable and interesting to the reader. Some writers and some editors are more honest than others, but they all finish not with a true life but with a literary creation based on that life. The exact steps in the creation of Pattie's narrative are unrecoverable. There is, however, enough evidence, external and internal, to re-create the way in which it was done.

It was almost two years after Pattie's first meeting with Flint that a Cincinnati magazine editor mentioned he had recently seen a copy of the new book. During that time Pattie may have worked in Bracken County, but it is more likely that he worked in Cincinnati, where he could have the help and advice of Timothy Flint. There are those who claim that the association was more than just help and advice, more than just editing. W. J. Ghent, in his brief article in the *Dictionary of American Biography*, published in 1934, suggested that the book was written by Flint rather than Pattie. Others have converted that suggestion into established fact and have stated baldly that James Pattie was an illiterate trapper for whom Flint had to write the narrative.

Ranged against them is the testimony of the men who

•

were involved. Pattie, with his name on the title page and the story told in the first person, clearly intended the reader to assume he was the author. Timothy Flint specifically denied he did more than edit the work and asked—with little success—that the reader "award me the confidence of acting in good faith, in regard to drawing nothing from my own thoughts." Their claims are not automatically acceptable, but neither can they be dismissed without evidence, and those who accuse offer none. And there is considerable evidence to show that although Flint did some manipulating, the basic responsibility for the book lies with James Pattie.

Pattie could not only read and write, he could do so better than most. Only two documents from his hand survive, one a promissory note written in California, the other a letter written in Mexico City. The promissory note proves little, for it is written according to a set formula and may even have been copied from another note. The letter from Mexico, however, is clearly a Pattie creation, It apparently was written in a hurry, for letters are transposed and words sometimes left unfinished. Pattie also occasionally had trouble spelling, and "colonel" becomes "kernal" and "impossible" becomes "imposable." As always he had difficulty with Spanish, and the best he could do with "Vera Cruz" was "barrer cruss." Still, the letter is more easily read than many contemporary letters filled with wild misspellings.

This, of course, is only one letter, but on a broader scale Pattie's entire background shows a strong emphasis on literacy. His grandfather was a schoolteacher and a judge; his father, while in the Missouri militia, was the man chosen to write letters to the newspapers. James himself, before he went west, was attending school at the age of twenty-one, long after most people of that time had finished their education.

There is also strong evidence that Pattie kept a written journal during his years in the West. The narrative is filled with too many minor details, events, and descriptions to have been based entirely on memory. Many of the details

•

can be verified, and once Pattie mentioned a rainstorm on exactly the same day as travelers north and south of him. Certainly, no man, without some written record, can remember the exact day it rained six years before.

There is psychological evidence as well to indicate a journal behind the narrative. A book written from memory should have a certain evenness, reflecting the author's state of mind as he looks back over his experiences. There is none of this in the *Personal Narrative*. Instead, the changes in James Pattie's state of mind come through clearly. Sometimes there are calm periods in the narrative filled with reasonably accurate details, acceptable chronology, and plausible stories. Other times the narrative becomes almost frantically confused, and twice this confusion reaches the point of making the narrative almost undecipherable. The narrative is also frequently melodramatic, but often there is true emotion behind the melodrama, and it is doubtful that Pattie, an inexperienced writer, had the skill to re-create true feelings long after they passed away. Even Timothy Flint, a professional writer, shows no real ability in his novels to create such emotions.

There is also evidence of more than one journal behind the narrative. Pattie often has been accused of hazy geography, but again the charge is true only in certain sections. And often the problem is not inaccuracy as much as a lack of any significant detail. In other parts, places are described so vividly and accurately that they can be easily identified. The difference is that in the most accurate sections Sylvester Pattie was a member of the expedition, in the others James was traveling without his father. Possibly it was Sylvester who had the eye for the key details of an area, and James later used this to fill out his own account.

Pattie, when he returned to the East, certainly had his own journal and possibly that of his father as well. A perceptive twentieth-century editor would have recognized the value of these and published them verbatim with as little editorial intrusion as possible. Occasionally, what sounds like a first-

·

hand journal momentarily pushes its way through and tantalizes the reader with what might have been. It was not the twentieth century, however, it was 1831, and the publication of such raw material was unheard of. Instead, it had to be reworked into something acceptable, and Timothy Flint went to work.

Flint specifically admitted he was responsible for correcting the spelling and punctuation. He was a brave man to admit responsibility for the punctuation, for it consists mostly of a profuse and indiscriminate use of commas. Many are unnecessary and some either obscure or completely change the meaning of a sentence. His correction of the spelling is less obvious but more unfortunate, for much of Pattie's personality—his background, his education, his dialect—would have come through more clearly had his own words in his own spelling been allowed to stand.

Flint created a more serious distortion with the background information in the introduction and his comments in the preface. In both, the facts are reasonably accurate, but in both they are handled in such a way as to give an inaccurate picture. The brief biography of James's grandfather, John Pattie, contains mostly stories of moving west to Kentucky and fighting Indians. The facts are correct, but the emphasis is not, for John Pattie came not with the earliest wave of pioneers but ten years later. His Indian fighting was not a constant involvement in the long wars of Kentucky, but rather a brief action with the relief party to Blue Licks and as a member of a short, ineffectual invasion of Ohio. It came at the very end of the wars and was only a matter of a few months out of John Pattie's long life.

The same is true of Flint's handling of Sylvester Pattie. Again, much space is devoted to his move to Missouri and his involvement in the Indian wars there. Again, Sylvester was ten years behind the first wave of pioneers and, again, he was involved briefly in the last days of Indian fighting. Both John and Sylvester, each in his own time, did have their moments on the frontier, but both were part of a group of

·

pioneers dedicated not to hunting in the wilderness, but to conquering it with sawmills, gristmills, and farms.

In the introduction Flint created his illusion of the frontiering Pattie family by a bare recitation of very select facts. In the preface, however, he was free to add his own comments and thus gave a clearer idea of what he was about. The Patties, to him, were descendants of that group of western pioneers known as "the hunters of Kentucky." Flint had known such men when he lived in Missouri, which was filled with transplanted Kentuckians. During this time Flint was in poor health, almost destitute, and without hope of doing anything for himself. He apparently looked on the Kentuckians with admiration mixed with envy, for in the preface to the *Personal Narrative* he wrote, "To me, there is a kind of moral sublimity in the contemplation of the adventures and daring of such men. They read a lesson to shrinking and effeminate spirits, the men of soft hands and fashionable life, whose frames the winds of heaven are not allowed to visit too roughly. They tend to re-inspire something of the simplicity of manners, manly hardihood, and Spartan energy and force of character, which formed so conspicuous a part of the nature of settlers of the western wilderness."

Timothy Flint had his own dream of what a hunter of Kentucky should be and distorted the Patties until they fit that image. Out of this came the idea that they were simple frontier hunters and ultimately that James was an illiterate trapper, unable to write his own book.

Flint also admitted to occasionally inserting a "topographical illustration," based on his knowledge of other travelers in New Mexico. He does not, however, define "topographical illustrations," nor say whether they are a few sentences long or something much longer. Probably they are the latter, for there are two long sections that because of difficult chronology, rough transitions, or differences from the rest of the narrative do not seem to fit. One is a long account of a traveler, supposedly James Pattie, who made a trip from New

•

Mexico to Guaymas and back. It is introduced with a jarring transition and creates an impossible chronology. Without it, the narrative makes more sense. The same is true of Pattie's description of a long trip up the Platte and across to the Yellowstone and eventually the Columbia. The time allowed is impossibly short, the transition is again rough, and the story is entirely lacking in detail. Both of these almost certainly are "topographical illustrations."

The last influence Flint admitted was that he sometimes suppressed, or at least softened, material that was too strong for the readers' taste. Yet, the narrative contains stories of men eating horse meat or dog meat, of killing and devouring a raven or a buzzard, and of drinking blood or urine to ease their thirst. In the course of the narrative a trapper with fair skin and blond hair strips naked to allow giggling Indian women to compare their bodies with his, and Pattie, after attending a fandango, joins the rest of the trappers in escorting a lady home "in whose company we passed the night, and we none of us brought charges of severity against our fair companions." It was all rather explicit for a book written in 1831, and it raises the question as to what was suppressed. Probably very little, for Flint was shrewd enough to know that the claim of suppression was often enough to make shocking things seem less so.

There is one other influence, unadmitted by Flint but too obvious to be ignored. About the time James Pattie first reached New Mexico in the fall of 1825, Timothy Flint began work on his first novel, *Francis Berrian*. In it he included a story in which his hero, while in New Mexico, rescued a governor's daughter from Indians. Later, when James Pattie wrote the *Personal Narrative*, he included a story in which, while he was in New Mexico, he too rescued a governor's daughter from Indians.

The whole incident is puzzling, for the stories are too similar to be simple coincidence, too different to be simple plagiarism. Flint, in his novel, made no pretense of describing an actual event, but simply adapted a true story for his

•

own purposes. His version was based on a true incident involving the daughter of the governor of Chihuahua. It was a well-known story in Louisiana at the time Flint was absorbing background material for his book. Pattie, although he claimed to be writing his own experiences, also borrowed a story. His version, however, owes nothing to Flint's story, but instead is similar to several New Mexican legends of Indian abduction. Flint, either directly or through encouraging Pattie to read *Francis Berrian*, probably gave him the idea of including such a story. When he wrote it, however, Pattie did not simply lift Flint's story, but rather turned to the legends he had collected during his trip and worked out his own version.

Despite this obvious similarity *Francis Berrian* does much to disprove the contention that Flint wrote the *Personal Narrative*. It is the best of Flint's many works to compare with the narrative, for the story concerns a young American in Mexico; much of it is told in the first person; and it is based on stories told Flint by Judge Henry Bullard, who had spent much time in Mexico as a soldier of fortune. As such it demonstrates what Flint might have done had he decided to write rather than edit *The Personal Narrative of James O. Pattie*.

Even the most casual perusal of *Francis Berrian* demonstrates its essential difference. The language of the hero, as he tells his own story, is flowery, stilted, and filled with literary allusions. The plot, which centers around the hero's love for the governor's daughter despite their religious differences—he a Protestant, she a Catholic—becomes ever more complex. Finally, the story becomes so complicated that the author breaks in and, mercifully, asks Berrian to summarize the rest of it. He does so by explaining how he and the heroine have worked out their differences so they could marry. They have agreed to tolerate each other's religion, raise their sons as Protestants, their daughters as Catholics, and to spend six months of each year in Protestant New England and six months in Catholic Mexico.

•

There is none of this in the *Personal Narrative*. The language, although the spelling and punctuation have been worked over by Flint, is comparatively simple, and there are few direct literary allusions. The story line moves forward without all the major complications of *Francis Berrian*, which is particularly evident in Pattie's handling of the governor's daughter. She becomes not the great love of his life, not a major complication, but rather a pleasant interlude in his long trip. When he happens to pass by her home, there is a brief dalliance, but when the time comes to move on, he leaves and never mentions her again. Nor is there any improbable twist to assure a happy ending for the *Personal Narrative*. Instead, Pattie admits he is broke and depressed, and ends by giving advice not to follow his example of seeking wealth in a foreign country.

The books are by two different hands and reflect two different ways of thinking. Flint, through his corrections of spelling and punctuation, his preface and introduction, and his novel *Francis Berrian*, has clearly marked and sometimes even distorted the *Personal Narrative*. Nonetheless, the basic attitudes, thoughts, and stories, as well as the credit or blame and ultimately the responsibility for the narrative, rest solely with James Pattie.

What Pattie did with that responsibility is caught up in a simple historical contradiction. Based on the exploits in the narrative and his role in them, Pattie was one of the most memorable of men. Based on contemporary evidence, he was one of the least. Some men—Peg-Leg Smith was one, Bill Williams was another—made indelible impressions on those whom they met. George Yount trapped with all three and later vividly remembered Smith and Williams. Pattie, however, was only an anonymous member of a group of men who became insubordinate and deserted Yount. Peg-Leg Smith also remembered not Pattie but his horse. It was, he said, "a fine American horse," but of its owner he recalled nothing. Nathaniel Pryor, who came to California with Pattie and spent time with him there, remembered him not for

•

anything he did then but only for the book he later wrote. Even Governor Echeandia of California, whom Pattie claims to have constantly bothered, paid little attention to him. Echeandia mentioned him occasionally in the records, as he did many other Americans, but he left no indication that he took any special notice. James Pattie simply did not make much impression on those he met.

Another trait is clearly evident throughout the narrative: the great respect, almost worship, that Pattie had for his father. Later the same kind of respect is bestowed on others —among them, Juan Onis, Ewing Young, Captain John Bradshaw, and Senator Josiah Johnston. All were older than Pattie, in positions of authority, and respectable. All the others —the rank-and-file fur trappers—are almost always anonymous.

The contrast with Peg-Leg Smith is again pointed. Smith later remembered his fellow trappers Stone and Branch, Hooper and Marlow, Maurice LeDuc and Dick Campbell. Smith also remembered how, in his younger days, his father beat him, how he fought with his schoolteacher, and after he became a trapper how he hated Ewing Young. Smith had none of Pattie's deference toward authority and respectability, and it was one reason why Smith always stayed in the West while Pattie soon returned to Kentucky. It was also why no one ever forgot Peg-Leg Smith and why no one ever remembered James Pattie.

The portrait of Pattie that emerges is that of a young man who has been trained to respect his elders, to accept those who claimed authority, and in their presence to retire quietly into the background. Yet, when Pattie tells his own story in the *Personal Narrative,* another man emerges, a man who in times of action is always in the forefront, a man who when treated unjustly, even by someone as powerful as the governor of California, immediately stands up for his rights no matter what the consequences. It was out of this conflict between the man he was and the man he wished to be that the *Personal Narrative* came. He had traveled for five years

•

17

in the West and had gained nothing, had suffered innumerable indignities, and had made no particular impression on anyone. When he relived those five years in the pages of the *Personal Narrative*, he did so not as the man he was but as the man he wished he had been.

For all that, the *Personal Narrative* is not a pack of lies, for Pattie, either from a sense of basic honesty or a lack of inventive powers, did not manufacture material. He watched, he listened, he recorded, and later he adapted, but he did not invent. Much of what he did, too, was entirely human, the kind of thing most men do when they convert their lives into literary experience. The barrier between truth and lies, between fact and fiction, is not a thick, impenetrable wall but a fine line between what happened and what could have happened, between events experienced personally and events experienced no less vividly through the tales of an accomplished storyteller. Writers trying to convey experience constantly approach the line, sifting through material, reordering it, and adapting it. Some are more honest than others when they reach that line, but only the most plodding narrator refuses to approach it at all.

Pattie is often near the line and frequently crosses it. Sometimes he is only mildly deceptive; when, for example, he makes himself the sole participant in a conversation or event that more plausibly involved a large group. Other times he crosses the line and takes someone else's story for his own, and several times in the narrative he uses well-known stories but tells them with himself or his father in the hero's role. Although the stories have been changed, sometimes radically, they are all based on events Pattie witnessed or on stories he heard. They all describe not what he did, but what he wished he had done.

Sometimes he drops the mask and tells stories that sound like the true experiences of a young man on his first trip into the West. Once, he saw a buffalo calf and decided to single-handedly capture it and drag it into camp. Instead, he was butted and badly bruised, and when he returned to camp he

•

told no one for fear they would laugh at his foolishness. Another time, while camped alone, he awakened to see what he thought was a mountain lion staring at him. He leaped to his feet and ran wildly through the night until he found another trapper. These stories, told with a wry sense of humor aimed at his own foolishness, portray a much more human James Pattie who rarely is allowed to appear in the narrative.

In one instance Pattie may have reversed the order and put someone else in his own place. The clue comes from the fact that after the narrative was written, Flint decided to add pictures, which would be done by William Woodruff, an experienced Cincinnati engraver. The engravings as pictures of the West or of fur trappers are ludicrous, but there is one face—that of James Pattie—that carries over from picture to picture. Since Woodruff had enough artistic ability to portray a man accurately—he once sold portraits of Benjamin Franklin in Philadelphia—and since he had personal access to James Pattie in Cincinnati, these faces undoubtedly look like Pattie. The most distinguishing feature in the portrait is his blond, curly hair.

Against that background is the story Pattie told of a trapper with fair skin and blue eyes in an Indian camp. The Indian women insisted he strip to show he was white all over, and after much begging by the women and a great deal of banter from his fellow trappers, he complied and stood naked, comparing his skin with the Indians'. The story, as related in the *Personal Narrative,* is about a companion of Pattie's. In reality it may well have been Pattie himself.

James Pattie has often been harshly judged by those who have seen the errors and the impossibilities of some of his stories. Given the way he borrowed other men's material and used it as his own, some criticism is warranted, but he was no liar in the sense that he simply invented material to fill a book. His stories are of things he had seen and heard, usually at the time and place he claims. Many of them can be checked, and they are surprisingly accurate, with the sole

•

exception that Pattie often places himself in the midst of the story.

These stories, too, are only the visible part of the narrative. Underlying them, and holding the narrative together, is a foundation of detail that is not easily dismissed. There are descriptions of country, easily verified, that are detailed and accurate and which at the time could only have been obtained by personal observation. There are descriptions of Indian villages, customs, and behavior that can be checked against accounts of contemporary travelers, archaeologists, and anthropologists. Woven through this are legends and tales that would have to have been heard in the western country, for they would not be committed to books for years to come.

The *Personal Narrative*, then, is not a literal step-by-step account in which James Pattie, for the benefit of historians a century later, scrupulously described events in the Southwest and in California. Instead, it is truly a *personal* narrative. It is the narrative of the education of a young man; the things he heard and saw, the strange, sometimes funny, sometimes frightening things that happened to him, the disappointments he encountered, the lessons he learned, and most of all the discovery of the man he was as well as the man he wished he was.

Approached as that—and taking care to separate the legends from the events and Pattie's heroic dreams from reality —the narrative opens the road into an almost unknown world of the early West and shows insight into the mind of a man who traveled that road.

CHAPTER

─────────◆─────────

O·N·E

ATER, WHEN THE LONG TRIP INTO THE WEST was over and he came home to write his *Personal Narrative*, James Pattie would trace the dramatic change in his fortunes, and those of his father, Sylvester, to the day that his mother died. Until then the Patties—Sylvester, his wife, Polly, and their eight children—had lived contentedly in the Ozark Mountains of southern Missouri. There, on the Big Piney River, Sylvester owned and ran a combination sawmill and gristmill and nearby had a home that James later remembered with considerable nostalgia. By then he was an adult looking back, and he remembered mostly the small things— the trees that shaded the lawn in front of the house, the paths over which he ran as a child. Beyond that he recalled only that life was happy and prosperous, that his home was quiet and cheerful. Then his mother fell ill with consumption, died, and everything changed.

The biggest change, according to James, was in his father. Almost overnight Sylvester Pattie went from a successful mill owner, known for the "buoyancy of his gay spirit," to a man who was "silent, dejected, and even inattentive to business." Clearly, he had been deeply shocked by the death of his wife and the sudden disruption of the comfortable, settled way of life the two of them had created since their marriage twenty years before.

Sylvester Pattie and Polly Hubbard were married on Au-

•

gust 7, 1802. The wedding was held in Mason County, Kentucky, where for the past decade Polly's father, Thomas Hubbard, had been an important and influential man. He had come to Kentucky from his native Virginia, had spent some time in the settled area around Lexington, then moved north to Mason County, where he was one of the founders of Germantown. In the years since then he had done extremely well, and by the time his daughter married Sylvester Pattie, he was a wealthy man who owned twenty-two slaves and 320 acres of prime farmland.

Over in nearby Bracken County Sylvester's father, John Pattie, was just as prominent. He owned nine slaves and 450 acres of land, and in recent years had been chosen to serve as a justice of the court of quarter sessions and also as a member of the board of trustees of Bracken Academy. Like Hubbard, he was a Virginian who had come to Kentucky soon after it was opened to settlement. He, too, had lived near Lexington, where he worked as a schoolteacher and carpenter and also had considerable success as a land speculator. Then, during the big rush to settle along the Ohio River, he had also moved north. He arrived with his family in 1794, purchased a large farm right on the river, and built a gristmill on Bracken Creek just above the point where it entered the Ohio.

At the time Sylvester was twelve years old, an age at which he would have been expected to help his father in some capacity, although the hardest work of plowing and hoeing in the hot summer sun was done by the slaves. His father, however, was more than just a farmer. In his younger days he had been a skilled carpenter, and now he owned and operated a gristmill where he ground much of the neighborhood's grain. Undoubtedly it was from him that Sylvester learned both the basic carpentry and the skills of a miller that later allowed him to construct and run his own mill in Missouri.

Although he grew up on a farm and around a mill, Sylvester Pattie, by the time he married Polly Hubbard, was no

•

23

bumpkin from the backcountry. The land immediately west of his father's farm had been granted to Philip Buckner, who had divided it into lots and founded the town of Augusta, which soon became the county seat of Bracken County and a stopping place for travelers bound up and down the river. It was also the home of Bracken Academy, established by the Methodist Church in 1798. It was within walking distance of the Pattie home and although there is no conclusive proof, Sylvester probably attended. His father, who was one of the school's original trustees, would have been expected to support the school, not only through use of his name, but by enrolling his children as well. And when the academy was founded in 1798. Sylvester was sixteen years old, just the right age to attend such a school. Also, a letter written by Sylvester later in his life shows that he had something more than the usual education of the time. Although he occasionally misspells a word or uses the wrong tense, the mistakes are minor when compared with the wild misuses of the English language by such contemporaries as Jacob Fowler and William Clark.

If Sylvester attended Bracken Academy, he received some elocution, grammar, and penmanship; some arithmetic, algebra, and geography; but most of all he learned Latin and Greek. Notably missing from the curriculum of early-day academies was any kind of American history, particularly as it concerned the movement west. Yet, if it was lacking from academies, such history was still very much alive in Kentucky. The old-timers were great storytellers, and Bracken County was filled with those who had lived part of the history and remembered the rest through stories passed down from generation to generation.

One man who remembered the early days of Kentucky was Sylvester's own father. In 1781, before Sylvester was born, John Pattie had come overland from Virginia with his wife, Ann, and his three small daughters. It took four long months, but beyond the ordinary difficulties of frontier travel—a man getting lost overnight, the frequent rumors of

•

24

Indian trouble, the rain that later turned to snow—there was little to talk about. Instead, John Pattie's best story concerned something that happened the following summer while he and his family were living at Craig's Station.

One day in August 1782, word reached Craig's that those at Bryant's Station, thirty miles to the north, had been attacked and surrounded by Indians. John Pattie was among the volunteers who hurried to their relief only to find when they arrived that the siege had already been lifted by militia from Lincoln and Fayette counties. These same militia, too excited to wait for reinforcements, had gone in pursuit of the Indians, and while crossing the Licking River at Blue Licks, they had been ambushed. In the first assault many were killed, the rest were routed and fled from the battlefield, leaving the dead where they had fallen. Hearing of this, the volunteers, with John Pattie in the ranks, marched north, and on the morning of August 25 began the descent into the valley of the Licking River. Long before they reached it they could identify the battlefield by the large numbers of vultures wheeling overhead. At the river itself they found mutilated bodies that had been lying in the summer sun for a week. It was too messy for individual burials, and all forty-three dead men were pushed into a common grave. The volunteers were then sent home, for the Indians had long since gone north and crossed the river into Ohio. It was a story that would have particularly appealed to Sylvester, for the day on which his father helped bury the dead at Blue Licks —August 25, 1782—was the day on which he had been born at Craig's Station.

The stories John Pattie could tell of his own involvement in famous battles, however, were limited. Beyond helping to bury the dead at Blue Licks, and a few weeks' service in the militia during an ineffectual campaign in Ohio, he had no experience as an Indian fighter. But, like any other Kentuckian, he could tell thrilling stories of the explorations, captures, and narrow escapes of Daniel Boone and Simon Kenton. Both became legendary symbols of the conquest of

•

Kentucky, but when Sylvester was young they were both men who lived only a few miles from his home. Whenever the Patties traveled the road from Augusta to Lexington or Frankfort, they passed the home of Daniel Boone; whenever they traveled the twenty miles to visit one of Sylvester's married sisters, in Washington, Kentucky, they saw the large home and store owned by Simon Kenton.

Boone and Kenton were living representatives of the westward movement that had so rapidly changed Kentucky from a wilderness into a land full of farms and small towns. The same movement had continued, had grown enormously, and by the 1790s the Ohio River had become a major highway to and from the country farther west. And since the Patties' farm was right on the river, Sylvester, as he grew up, could watch the westward movement—literally—as it passed his front door.

Whatever Sylvester saw or heard of the westward movement, past or present, however, did little to lure him away from home. Instead, in 1802, when he was just two weeks short of his twentieth birthday, he married Polly Hubbard, and a few months later paid his own father $492 for eighty-two acres of land at the junction of Bracken Creek and the Ohio River. Here he and his new wife settled, surrounded by both their families. The land on one side was owned by Sylvester's father, on another by his sister Sally Howard. Farther up Bracken Creek, above the Mason County line, were the farms of Thomas Hubbard and William Harle, who was married to Polly Pattie's sister. Not all of Sylvester's friends and relatives, however, were farmers. Both Richard Thomas, a brother-in-law, and Jesse B. Thomas, who had been best man at Sylvester's wedding, were lawyers. Although, like everyone, they dabbled in farming, their main interest was politics, and by 1802 Richard was sheriff of Bracken County and Jesse, his younger brother, was county clerk. Jesse was also a captain in the Twenty-eighth Regiment of Kentucky militia, the same regiment in which Sylvester served as lieutenant.

•

By the time Sylvester reached his twenty-first birthday, in August 1803, he was a solidly established citizen of Bracken County. He was an officer in the county militia, the son of a local judge, and tied by marriage or friendship to the county sheriff, the county clerk, and to several prominent families. It was in this same year of 1803 that he first appeared on the county tax list as a landowner and also as the owner of four slaves. Three of the slaves were children; the fourth—an adult woman—was probably their mother. In later years two more children were added to the list, again probably borne by Sylvester's one adult slave.

By 1803 Sylvester was so solidly established in Bracken County that he would have been no more than an interested spectator to an event that occurred a few miles upriver in Maysville. A keelboat, specially built in the Pittsburgh boat-yards for use in exploring the Missouri River, arrived under the command of Meriwether Lewis, who was on his way downriver to join William Clark in Louisville. Lewis, as he traveled, was looking for young men to accompany the expedition, and in Maysville he signed on John Colter as a member of the party. Not many years in the future stories would come back down the river that would make Colter a legend, but at this time he was just another young man living in Maysville. Sylvester, who lived in nearby Augusta, undoubtedly heard of the expedition and of the recruiting, but given his position as a married man, a property owner, and one of Bracken County's rising young men, his interest could only have been academic.

Soon after this—in late 1803 or early 1804—Sylvester also became a father when Polly gave birth to their first child, a son who was named James. In the years to follow, other children were born at frequent intervals. In 1805 a daughter, Julia, was born; in 1807 another son, John; in 1809 Sarah; and in 1810 Janetta, known to the family as Jennie.

Throughout the decade that the children were being born, the Patties lived in Augusta, a small, quiet town that was often admired by those traveling down the Ohio. Zadok Cra-

•

mer, the author and publisher of *The Navigator*, the guide-book and bible of early Ohio River travelers, was impressed by the village. It was, he said, a handsome town of forty houses, two stores, two taverns, and a brick schoolhouse. In front of the town was a clean gravel beach that served as a landing, and to the rear was an extensive area of rich bottom-land. The whole town had a good view of both the river and of the well-kept farms on the Ohio side.

Augusta's position on the Ohio River also gave it access to the products and ideas of a world reaching upstream to Pittsburgh and downstream as far as New Orleans. And in the fall of 1811 a whole new world of promise was opened when the first steamboat appeared on the Ohio River. The boat—the *New Orleans*—left Pittsburgh on October 20, 1811, and some time on the morning of the 27th passed by Augusta. The Patties lived right on the river, and it would have been impossible for them to have missed seeing, or at least hearing, the *New Orleans* as it thrashed its way down-river toward Cincinnati, Louisville, and eventually New Orleans.

By 1811 Sylvester Pattie, approaching the age of thirty, had been a solidly established farmer in Bracken County for a decade. And to all appearances, at least, he was contented with that life and planned to stay, for in 1810 he had added another fifty-one acres to his farm and in 1811 purchased twelve more. Then, soon after this last purchase, with star-tling suddenness, he sold everything he owned in Bracken County. In December he sold the original eighty-two acres to his neighbor Abraham Sallee, and a week later sold the remaining sixty-three acres to another neighbor. Four months later, in March 1812, he took his family and left for Missouri.

It would be easy enough to attribute the decision to a sudden, virulent case of westward fever. In Sylvester's case, however, that seems unlikely, at least at first glance, for by now he should have built up considerable immunity. He had lived on the Ohio for twenty years, during which the westward movement passed right by his door. Even as early as 1799 the Boone family had gone down the Ohio to Missouri, and after 1803, when the Louisiana Purchase brought the country west of the Mississippi into the United States, the Ohio had been flooded with Kentuckians going west. Even Sylvester's brother-in-law, Richard Thomas, had long since moved to Missouri, while his friend Jesse Thomas had moved to Indiana. The temptation to go west had been there for years, and Sylvester had successfully resisted it until 1811.

But by then there was a difference. Over in Mason County Pattie's brother-in-law, William Harle, and his father-in-law, Thomas Hubbard, were making plans to move west, and in March 1811 they had begun selling all their land. At first Sylvester apparently was not involved, for while they were selling he was buying additional land. Then, just before they left, Pattie sold all his property. Quite likely the enthusiasm of Hubbard and Harle was infectious, and at the last moment Sylvester decided to join the move to Missouri.

However the decision was reached, in March 1812 Sylvester and his wife, his five children, and his slaves set out for Missouri. By now the Patties were years behind the earliest pioneers, and they traveled west with the flood rather than the vanguard of emigration. Still, they were leaving a safe, secure part of Kentucky to go into country that by 1812 had become increasingly dangerous.

The westward movement that had grown enormously and finally lured Sylvester to Missouri had also alarmed western Indians. In an attempt to stop the settlers, Tecumseh, a Shawnee chief, had formed an Indian confederacy, but before it was fully organized, it had come into conflict with the white soldiers. The confederacy had been jolted but not destroyed at the Battle of Tippecanoe in November 1811. General William Henry Harrison had proclaimed it a great victory over the Indians, but in reality it did little to remove the danger. Instead, it sent Indians seeking revenge out to attack isolated settlers and travelers, and through the spring

.

of 1812—while the Patties were on their way to Missouri—there were frequent reports of raids on the roads leading west.

In Missouri the situation was further complicated by a recent treaty in which the United States had agreed to protect the Osage Indians from attack by other tribes. This brought on conflict with some of the northern Indians—traditional enemies of the Osage—and not long before the Patties arrived, a raiding party had fallen on an isolated farm near St. Charles and killed nine members of the same family. Clearly, it was too dangerous to continue on into the interior as he had originally intended, and Sylvester decided to settle his family, at least temporarily, in St. Charles.

The town sat on the very edge of the settlements, and by the summer of 1812 its citizens were almost frantic, worrying about the threat of Indian attack. Then, in July, the United States officially declared war on Great Britain and the town was swept by ominous rumors that thousands of Indians, backed by British troops, would descend the river and destroy Missouri. Those in St. Charles, like those in settlements all over Missouri, held citizens' meetings and drafted resolutions deploring their defenseless position and begging the government in Washington for troops. Faced with this barrage of resolutions, Congress, in early 1813, passed a bill authorizing the territory of Missouri to raise and equip several companies of militia.

Among those mustered in on March 21, 1813, was Sylvester Pattie, who was commissioned a lieutenant in Captain David Musick's company of mounted rangers. Years later, when Timothy Flint wrote his introduction to the *Personal Narrative,* he included a story of how Lieutenant Pattie, in command of a small fort that was under siege, won fame when he donned the uniform of a slain English officer, slipped through enemy lines, and brought relief to the fort. It is an exciting tale and Flint, who lived in St. Charles just after the war, claimed he heard it firsthand from some of Pattie's fellow soldiers. If so, it seems to have grown with

•

the telling, for it does not at all agree with the portrait of Lieutenant Sylvester Pattie as drawn by contemporary records.

The records do verify that in the fall of 1813, while most of the Missouri militia invaded Illinois, Sylvester Pattie was left in command of a small detachment at Fort Cap au Gris. There is no mention of any attack or siege, however, although while in command Pattie did receive a message telling him that forty miles to the north, on the Salt River, there were four horses that had been lost by some rangers during a fight with the Indians. The man who brought the message was prepared to guide Pattie up the Mississippi immediately, but rather than rushing north Pattie wrote a letter to General William Clark in St. Louis. He explained the situation, added, "I have but ten men that are mounted fit for the trip," then finally came to the point, telling Clark, "I wish you to instruct me whether to go forward or not." Pattie's reluctance to ride forty miles for four horses is understandable, even intelligent. Still, this is not the same man Timothy Flint portrays as given to sudden decisions and mad dashes through enemy lines.

The same courier who took the letter to Clark probably also carried a letter that Pattie wrote about the same time to a St. Louis newspaper. On October 2, 1813, it appeared over his name in the *Missouri Gazette* and informed the public that William Steward, an eighteen-year-old private, had deserted Musick's company on the lower Cuivre and was thought to be headed for the White River settlement. Pattie also said that one John Loyd, also eighteen years old, had deserted Captain Ramsey's company and was probably making for Spring River. Anyone who delivered either of these men to any fort in St. Charles County, he said, could claim a reward. The fact that Pattie was chosen to write public letters, and the fact that he was left behind during the invasion of Illinois, indicate that after a year in the militia he was respected more for his ability with pen and ink than for his skills as a dashing combat officer.

•

Like most other rangers Pattie was mustered out at the end of 1813 on the assumption that the war was over. But when renewed Indian attacks in the spring and early summer of 1814 made it clear that the war's end was a false hope, he again joined the militia. He did not rejoin Musick's company of mounted rangers, but rather a company commanded by Captain Henry Hight. Hight was a St. Charles lawyer, as well as the county recorder, notary public, and probate judge, and his assignment in the militia was that of judge advocate. His second in command was Sylvester Pattie, who was more literate than the average officer, and who, since his father was a judge in Kentucky, had at least a passing knowledge of the law. Again, Pattie's militia duties probably involved clerical and legal matters more than actual fighting.

Yet, if Pattie won no great fame as an Indian fighter, neither did anyone else. Throughout 1814 two separate bands of Missouri militia were in the field, one marching west to the Boonslick country, the other ascending the Missouri. Neither accomplished anything, however, and in the spring of 1815 the war simply faded away in Missouri with no clearcut results. Still, Sylvester Pattie profited enormously from his service in the militia during the war. When it began he was a newcomer, a stranger to those in Missouri. But the close quarters, the camaraderie, the shared experience of wartime, introduced him to a group of men who, now that the war was over, could help him in his desire to settle in the interior of Missouri.

Pattie had come from a well-settled area in Kentucky, and although he undoubtedly had some outdoor skills, he was not a seasoned frontiersman. The year he spent in the St. Charles rangers, however, had brought him into contact with a group of men whom the *Louisiana Gazette* called "as fine a body of hardy woodsmen as ever took the field." Some of these men—William Ashley, John Baldridge, Hiram Scott, and several members of the McDonald family—had been in the backcountry before 1812 and knew it well. None, how-

•

ever, had the knowledge of the interior possessed by Pattie's regimental commander, Daniel Morgan Boone.

Morgan Boone, of all Daniel's children, had the most trouble with the shadow of fame cast by his father. He looked like a younger version of the old man, with the same small build and fair complexion, and he spoke in the same high-pitched voice. He also had the same first name, and to avoid confusion his family and friends called him Morgan rather than Daniel. Later writers were not always so careful and some of the exploits that are rightfully his have been attributed to his father instead.

Yet, when Pattie met him during the War of 1812, he was more than just an indistinct copy of his father. It was Morgan rather than Daniel Boone who came west in 1795 to obtain land from the Spanish government. Four years later he returned to Kentucky and brought his father and several other members of the family to land he had already settled on the Missouri River above St. Charles. During these years he roamed both west and south, hunting, trapping, and later surveying land. When the war ended in 1815 he had been living in Missouri longer than any other American and knew it as well as any man.

By that time Sylvester Pattie was preparing to make another move. He had settled his family in St. Charles in 1812 because it was well populated and offered safety during the war. When the war was over, that same population made the St. Charles district a poor place to settle. The Spanish government had already granted the good land to those who had reached Missouri before the Louisiana Purchase. Nor was there land available in nearby areas, for after the United States took over, settlers had continued to push west. In 1803 Lewis and Clark found a few settlers as far up the Missouri as La Charette, forty miles above St. Charles. Three years later, when they came back down the river, they saw their first signs of civilization at the mouth of the Gasconade, another forty miles above La Charette. By the time Pat-

•

tie arrived much of the land along the Missouri and even some of the tributaries had been taken.

It was Morgan Boone who first led Pattie into an area that was still unsettled. In 1816 he organized a hunting party and asked Sylvester to join it. Boone led the party far to the south, where the Gasconade River and its tributaries rose along the northern slopes of the Ozark Mountains. No settlers had yet reached the area, but it was far from unexplored. Frenchmen had been hunting and trapping there for more than a century, and by 1800 hunters from the east had crossed the Mississippi and entered the mountains.

These early hunters were few in number and came long distances to hunt. After the Louisiana Purchase, however, they reached Missouri in large numbers, and a few years later they were living in small cabins all along the edges of the Ozarks. They moved frequently and consequently had few possessions to tie them to any one place. Beyond putting in a patch of corn, they seldom bothered with agriculture, and their food consisted wholly of corn and wild game, mostly bear meat. They had no schools, but they did not notice the lack, for they took care of their own education. Each girl was trained from her earliest days to run a home; each boy was trained in frontier skills. By the time a boy was fourteen, he was thoroughly familiar with the use of the rifle, the killing of game, the trapping of beaver and otter, and knew how to dress skins and make clothes. To some, these hunters were free men, unencumbered by useless possessions and able to follow game into the remotest parts of the country. To others, they were shiftless and unambitious and rapidly degenerating into savagery. Such moralizing, however, was left to outside observers, for the hunters themselves were interested only in the single-minded pursuit of game.

As the hunter passed through the Ozarks, he saw the country from only one point of view. The large number of caves were good places to seek shelter on a rainy night and possibly a place to flush out a bear or panther. The vast stands of pine forests were made up of individual trees that

•

might contain squirrels, possums, and coons. The springs that abounded in the Ozarks were watering places for deer and elk. The hunter accepted these things as they were and instinctively knew that change would almost instantly destroy the game and with it the hunters' livelihood.

By 1815, however, there were men entering the Ozarks who saw the country in a different way. The caves were a source of saltpeter, which could be extracted and used to make gunpowder. The pine forests were a source of lumber for which there was a lively market in St. Louis. The springs and streams were a source of power for sawmills that could turn the forests into lumber, and the rivers were a way to easily deliver the lumber to the expanding towns of Missouri. In the Ozarks the day of the hunter was already passing, the day of the enterprising settler was arriving.

It was Sylvester's destiny to be one of the enterprising settlers. The hunting trip was successful, but Pattie had seen the large stands of timber and the sources of waterpower. From the years he spent growing up around his father's mill in Kentucky, he could hardly have missed the possibilities. As a result, soon after the hunting expedition was over, he returned to the Ozarks to establish a sawmill and gristmill on the Big Piney River.

The Big Piney was a major tributary of the Gasconade, which, in turn, was a tributary of the Missouri. By 1816 the first forty miles of the Gasconade were settled, but beyond that was wilderness. Fifty miles above the last settlement was the mouth of the Big Piney. Forty miles upstream from there Pattie built his mill beneath the high limestone bluffs at a point where a small creek flowed into the river. The creek was unnamed then, but later settlers remembered the man who first lived there and named it after him. Today it is still known as Paddy Creek.

Isolated, unsettled areas such as this were the only places to find unclaimed land, but settlers often paid the price by enduring frequent Indian attacks. By the time the Patties settled on the Big Piney, however, even the Indian danger

•

35

was slight. Originally, this had been Osage country, but in 1808 the Osage had signed a treaty giving up all claim to the land. They still used it for hunting, as they had done for centuries, and new travelers were often warned that if they went through the area, they would be captured by Indians. Soon after the Patties arrived, a man named Cullen did disappear. Cullen, with two other men, had come to the area in 1816 to make gunpowder in a cave near Pattie's mill. About a year later Cullen left with a load of powder and was never seen again. Many thought he had been killed by Indians, but there was no proof. It was just as possible that he sold the gunpowder, pocketed his partners' share, and disappeared. Beyond unconfirmed and suspicious stories, and beyond the tales told to travelers, there was little serious Indian trouble in the Big Piney region.

When Sylvester established his mill, he completely changed the area in which he settled. A gristmill was always the sign along the frontier that an area was ready for permanent settlement by farmers. Hunters and squatters who eked out a bare existence beyond the settlements ground their corn into meal at home with mortar and pestle. It was a slow, primitive method, and those who used it were unable to rise above subsistence farming. Permanent, established farmers, however, wanted some way to convert surplus grain into cash and were willing to pay the price of grinding, usually one-fourth of the wheat and one-eighth of the corn. John Bradbury, traveling in Missouri in those years, noted that once a mill was established to turn grain into a marketable crop, the change was rapid. The farmer, he said, then "boldly engages and employs hands to assist him in converting the forest into fields."

These new settlers drawn into the area by a gristmill also provided a market for the sawmill. They had come to settle and to farm, but unlike the hunters they wanted substantial homes rather than simple cabins. Again, it was Bradbury who saw the results: "Every planter in the vicinity, by the aid of a saw mill, is able to erect a handsome frame house."

·

Pattie, however, found a broader market for lumber than the farmers moving into the surrounding area. In the years after the war ended, migration into Missouri increased enormously, and sometimes as many as one hundred settlers a day passed through St. Charles on their way west. St. Louis, too, was growing rapidly. There was a great deal of building, and in those days almost everything was built of wood. As a result the price of pine lumber went as high as seventy dollars a thousand feet.

Surrounding Pattie's mill in the Ozarks were entire mountains covered with pine. The trees could be felled, dragged to the mill, rough-cut into uniform size, then hammered together into rafts. These rafts, which could also be loaded with grain from the gristmill, were then floated down the Big Piney to the Gasconade, down that river to the Missouri, then on to the Mississippi and St. Louis. Here, the lumber and grain were turned into cash or into supplies and trade goods to be taken back to the mill in the interior.

The mill Pattie established not only helped revolutionize the country along the Big Piney, but it also made him a wealthy man. Whatever financial records he kept have disappeared except for an unofficial-looking document that was once worth considerable money. The document is nothing more than a small scrap, torn from a larger piece of paper, but on it is written: "On demand we or either of us promis to pay Sylvester Pattie one hundred & twenty eight Dollars for value recvd of him this 26 of March 1817. John Baldridge. Hiram Scott."

John Baldridge would remain an obscure backwoods settler in Missouri, but Hiram Scott would win a measure of fame by later going west into Nebraska, where he would die under the bluffs that now bear his name.

By 1819 Sylvester Pattie was one of the wealthiest men in the southern part of Franklin County. On the tax list of that year there were more than one hundred men in Gasconade Township, but only six owned a slave. One was Pattie, another was William Harle, his partner and brother-in-law.

•

The two men also jointly owned property on which they paid $4.25 tax. Although it was a small-enough amount, only James and John McDonald, who ran another mill nearby, owned more taxable property.

A year later Sylvester was the largest taxpayer in Gasconade Township and the second largest in all of Franklin County. By then Harle had moved away and Pattie was sole owner of the mill. About this time Morgan Boone arrived to settle permanently on the Big Piney. Although he had led the hunting trip that first brought Pattie into the area, he had continued to live north of the Missouri River until 1820, when he built a sawmill a few miles from the Patties. Although there were two separate mills—one near the mouth of Paddy Creek, the other five miles upstream at Boone's Creek—the two men's lives were closely intertwined. Soon after William Harle left, leaving Pattie without a partner, Boone arrived, and a few years later, when Pattie left, Boone also sold out and moved away.

Owning a mill brought a man like Pattie more than wealth. It also put him at the center of community life, for a mill was not just a place to obtain lumber or to grind grain into meal or flour. Most millers added distilleries, breweries, wood-carding mills, cotton gins, or, in Pattie's case, a blacksmith shop. They also often served as middlemen, bringing in goods from the outside to be sold or traded. Sooner or later almost everyone within a radius of several miles came to the mill to do business. As a result it played a major part in the social life of early farm areas. Those who came stayed all day buying, selling, and trading, gossiping about their neighbors, and talking about the weather, crops, livestock, and hunting.

All this made mill owners—men like Boone and Pattie— leading citizens of the area in which they lived. In 1822 Gasconade County was created out of the southern part of Franklin County, and the portion where Pattie lived was designated Boone Township. The township was named after Morgan Boone, and he and Sylvester Pattie quickly dominated it in wealth and in political influence. At the time

·

there were only five slaves in the township, two owned by Pattie and two more by Boone. Also, each time the Gasconade County Court needed to fill a position in the township it turned to Boone and Pattie. In January 1822 they were appointed to evaluate county property, and five months later were given the responsibility, along with Benjamin Skaggs, of surveying a road from Skaggs's mill to Boone's mill. As the election approached in the fall of 1822, it was again Boone and Pattie who were appointed to serve as judges for the election at James and John McDonald's mill on Roubidoux Creek. Clearly, Sylvester Pattie, at the age of forty, was a prominent and highly successful man.

Sylvester's wife, Polly, left no account of these years. Like most women of the time she lived in almost total obscurity, and in the records she is mentioned only twice, once when she married, and once in Kentucky when she joined her husband in signing a deed. Beyond that there is nothing, but she, too, lived through the ten years on the farm in Kentucky, the move to Missouri, the War of 1812, and the building of a successful life on the Big Piney. During these twenty years she also gave birth to nine children, five in Kentucky, four more in Missouri. By the time she bore her ninth child, however, she was ill with consumption, which at the time was both prevalent and incurable.

She died as obscurely as she lived. There are no death records, no will, and no indication of where she was buried. Even the date is hazy, the only clue being provided by James's statement that Sylvester, upon the death of his wife, went into a deep depression. Also, after late 1822 Sylvester was never again appointed to a position by the county court. In February 1823, when the road surveyors submitted their report, only Boone and Skaggs were paid for the work. Clearly, Pattie had not finished the task he had been assigned the year before. It fits well into his son's claim that he became silent and dejected and lost interest in everything.

Sylvester's reaction is somewhat surprising, for the death of a wife was not uncommon. Women, worn out by the con-

•

stant work and frequent childbearing, often succumbed. Usually a husband mourned for a reasonable length of time then married again. It came not from any lack of feeling, but from necessity, particularly when a man like Sylvester was left with a large number of children. Nor was there any lack of candidates, for there were many women, with their own children, who had been left unprotected by the death of a husband. Sylvester, however, went into a long period of depression, and according to James, the only time he showed interest in anything was when he heard stories about the West—stories from up the Missouri and from the interior of New Mexico.

Certainly, Sylvester lived in the best place to hear such stories. His mill was on the route between the settlements and the western country and was a logical stopping place for hunters and traders on their way between markets in the East and the hunting grounds of the West. And those who stopped at the mill, if they had no interest in eastern news —politics, elections, fashions, and signs of progress—loved to display their vast knowledge of the West, of its rivers, of the best places to find game, and of the western Indian tribes. They also liked to talk about the fate of those who had gone west.

Some years earlier, the Missouri Fur Company had sent Manuel Lisa and a band of men west in an attempt to establish trade with the Indians on the upper Missouri River. About the same time James Baird, a St. Louis blacksmith, had led a packtrain southwest to open trade with New Mexico. Neither had much luck, and in the years that followed —while Pattie was establishing himself on the Big Piney— Missouri was filled with stories of their troubles. Lisa had run into an almost endless series of difficulties, and by the early 1820s his company was no farther up the Missouri River than Council Bluffs, just above the mouth of the Platte. The fate of James Baird was even worse, for when he and his men reached Santa Fe, they were arrested and sent to Chihuahua, where they were confined in an unfinished

•

church that had been converted into a prison. Even if these stories somehow failed to reach Pattie's mill in the back-country, he could hardly have missed hearing of them on his many trips to deliver lumber to St. Louis, where the papers carried frequent accounts of Lisa's troubles and, less frequently, stories of those in the Mexican jails.

News about those who had gone west was almost always bad, and in the years that Sylvester was a successful mill owner, he would have had little desire to emulate them. But then, about the time his wife died, news from the West began to change. In early 1821 the *St. Louis Enquirer* announced that the prisoners in Mexico had been released and several had already reached Missouri. About the same time William Becknell, with whom Pattie had served in the militia, went west to trade with the Indians. He and his party stumbled on a band of soldiers and were taken to Santa Fe where, instead of being jailed, they were welcomed as traders. By January 1822 Becknell was back in Franklin, Missouri, where he demonstrated his success by dumping bags of silver dollars into the street.

While trade with New Mexico was being opened, Pattie's old friend William Ashley also began his attempt to revive trade on the upper Missouri River. Twice during the war Ashley and Pattie had served together in the same small fort, and in 1816, when Pattie moved south to the Big Piney, one of his few neighbors was William Ashley, who was manufacturing gunpowder in a saltpeter cave a few miles from Pattie's mill. Since then, Ashley had become lieutenant governor of Missouri, which only increased his political ambitions as he began looking for a way to make the necessary money to finance his search for higher office. Therefore, he and another Missourian, Andrew Henry, organized a company, and in early 1822 advertised for "enterprising young men" to ascend the Missouri River. By spring their first trapping party, led by Henry, was on its way west.

Unlike the spectacular success stories of William Becknell in New Mexico, the earliest news concerning Ashley's enter-

•

prise was almost always bad. One of his keelboats, loaded with ten thousand dollars' worth of trade goods, hit a snag in the Missouri River and sank. The next summer Ashley started upriver with a second group of trappers. They had no more than left St. Louis when one of those on board the keelboat fell overboard and drowned. A few days later, as they were loading gunpowder in St. Charles, one of the kegs exploded, killing three more men.

News of the biggest disaster reached Missouri in July 1823. Ashley and his party of one hundred men had reached the Arikara villages on the upper Missouri where they were attacked by Indians. Twelve men were killed, eleven wounded, and Ashley was forced to retreat back down the river. A few weeks later Colonel Henry Leavenworth led troops from Fort Atkinson upriver to the Arikara villages, but, much to the disgust of the traders, instead of attacking the Indians, he made peace with them. The attack on Ashley, the military expedition, and the debate over Leavenworth's actions filled Missouri newspapers for the next year.

By then Sylvester Pattie's wife was dead, and about the only things he showed any interest in were stories—good or bad—coming out of the West. Noting this, his friends, in an attempt to bring him out of his depression, advised him to sell all his property, buy traps and trade goods, and go west. Finally, he took their advice, and in August 1824 sold his mill, oxen, carts, and blacksmith tools to Charles and Bazille Drolette for $375. Then he began to make preparations to go.

The first and most immediate task was to find something to do with his large family while he was gone. His wife was dead, as was the baby who had been born in the last days of her life, but there were still eight other children. The older ones were nearing adulthood, but the younger were little more than babies and needed considerable care. Finally, Sylvester solved the problem by making arrangements for them to live with relatives in Bracken County, Kentucky.

•

Apparently, he planned to leave all the children there, but at the last moment his eldest son, James, in his own words, "begged so earnestly" that he was allowed to go along.

In the spring of 1825 Sylvester, with his son James, arrived in St. Louis to make final preparations for the trip west. It was here, according to James in the *Personal Narrative*, that they were joined by three other men, and the five of them simply started up the Missouri River to trade with the Indians. At Council Bluffs, however, the commander of Fort Atkinson demanded to see their trading license. When they said they were unaware they needed one, he refused to let them go any farther. Then, in a near miraculous stroke of fate, they met S. S. Pratte and were allowed to join the large party he was taking to New Mexico.

In isolation the story may sound plausible, but looked at against the background of time, place, and the people involved, it makes little sense. It seems unlikely that a man such as Sylvester Pattie would have tried to go west with so few men. For more than a year, Missouri newspapers had been filled with accounts of how William Ashley, with a hundred men, had been turned back by Indians. These stories made it clear there was little hope that Pattie could enter Indian country with just five. A rash, young hunter might not have cared that it was foolish to try, but Sylvester was neither rash nor young. An ignorant man, or one isolated from the world, might not have known of the Indian danger, but Pattie was not ignorant, and he was making his plans in St. Louis, the center of all news from the West. A man like Pattie, inexperienced but reasonably intelligent, cautious, and informed, would have known that the only way to travel safely was to join a larger party.

It is also doubtful that a man with Pattie's background would have failed to obtain a license. He had been a successful businessman, and he had lived on the edge of the settlements, where he often would have talked with hunters and traders fresh from Indian country; he had once served as assistant to the judge advocate of Missouri militia, and he

•

was personally acquainted with William Clark, the man who issued trading licenses. It seems impossible that such a man could get all the way to Council Bluffs without ever having heard that he needed a license.

Instead of the haphazard ascent of the river and the accidental meeting with Pratte at Council Bluffs, Pattie probably made at least tentative arrangements to accompany him in the St. Louis offices of Bernard Pratte and Company. The firm was planning to send a large party of men to New Mexico, and joining such an expedition for protection in Indian country was exactly what Pattie needed. Not just any American, however, had access to the four Frenchmen who controlled the company. The partners—Bernard Pratte, Jean Pierre Cabanne, Pierre Chouteau, Jr., and Bartholomew Berthold—were a formidable group of men who, by birth and by marriage, were related to each other, to all the leaders of the French community in St. Louis, and most of all to Auguste and Pierre Chouteau, who had dominated the city since its founding. It was an exclusive club which did not easily admit newcomers to the inner circle and which often looked with contempt on the raw Americans who came after 1803.

Pattie, however, was not just an unknown American from the backwoods. He had served with Frenchmen from St. Charles during the war and many of his fellow officers—Henry Hight, William Clark, and Morgan Boone—had long associations with the French community. Another man who had great influence with those who ran the company was Jesse B. Thomas. Twenty years earlier Thomas was a friend and neighbor of Pattie's in Kentucky and had even been best man at Sylvester's wedding in 1802. He had come a long way since then, and in 1825 was the United States senator from Illinois. He was particularly popular in Missouri, for Thomas had introduced the compromise bill that allowed the territory to become a state. He also had given substantial support to Thomas Hart Benton when he arrived in Washington as the new senator from Missouri. All Benton supporters—like the four partners in Bernard Pratte and Company—owed

·

Thomas a debt of gratitude. In May 1825 those in St. Louis showed their appreciation by giving a large dinner in honor of Jesse Thomas. Pattie was in town making his final preparations, and any help he needed from the Frenchmen would have been forthcoming after a word from Thomas.

Pattie, however, did not join the expedition as a hired hand but accompanied it as an independent trader. Therefore, he still had to make his own arrangements to buy trade goods and supplies in St. Louis. It was not a particularly difficult task, for Pattie was familiar with the town. During the decade he lived on the Big Piney, he often floated lumber rafts down to St. Louis, where he sold the lumber, bought supplies, and carried them back to the mill on packhorses. He knew the town, he knew the merchants, and he knew how to go about obtaining and outfitting a packtrain. Preparing for an expedition to trade among the Indians was somewhat more complicated, but those in St. Louis were prepared to make it as easy as possible. The town had long made its living by commerce with the West, and merchants stocked their stores and warehouses with items designed for the Indian trade. They not only supplied goods, but they also understood the complexities of the trade, the quick shifts in Indian desires, and thus were able to provide advice on the kinds of goods various tribes would accept.

After Pattie purchased his trade goods he still had several other things to buy. He needed provisions and weapons, and since he planned to trap when he reached beaver country, he also needed trapping equipment. Provisions were obtained easily from the grocers, from the stalls in the market house near the river, or from one of the merchants. The merchants also could supply traps, knives, tomahawks, and guns, but those who wanted quality had them custom-made. The town was full of blacksmiths and several of them specialized in making tools and equipment to meet the demands of trappers. There were also several gunsmiths, although by 1825, Jacob Hawken, at 214 North Main Street, was already making his reputation as the best gunsmith for those going west.

•

45

Hawken's rifles were well known for their range and accuracy, but to some they had an additional advantage. Many hunters believed in witches who, by casting a spell on a rifle, could make it inaccurate. Rumor had it that Jake Hawken always treated his rifles with a counterspell that made them witchproof.

After all the provisions, equipment, and trade goods were obtained, the last step was to make arrangements to move them. Pattie planned to send the trade goods by keelboat up the river as far as Council Bluffs. Again, it was easy enough to make arrangements, as boats frequently left St. Louis for the trading posts along the Missouri. Pattie, however, did not travel by boat, but instead went overland with a packtrain loaded with trapping equipment and provisions. Obtaining and loading the packtrain was the last step before leaving St. Louis, and that, too, was not difficult. Horses were plentiful and could be purchased cheaply, several harness makers had pack equipment in stock, and Pattie himself was thoroughly experienced in packing horses.

Since Pratte was still lingering in St. Louis, and since there was no Indian danger east of Council Bluffs, Pattie and his four followers made the first part of the trip by themselves. Pattie also had some last-minute business that took him off the main route. Normally, a westward-bound party that had outfitted in St. Louis took the easy route to St. Charles, then picked up the Boonslick Trace, a well-developed road that led across Missouri. Instead, Pattie took a route south of the Missouri which was more difficult but which led him back to Gasconade County. On June 9 the deed for the sawmill, although signed a year earlier, was officially recorded with the county court. Three weeks later, on June 20, 1825, Pattie and his small band of followers crossed the Missouri River and began the trip west.

Whatever problems had haunted Sylvester over the past several years were behind him. His wife was buried, the sawmill on the Big Piney was sold, and the children had been sent to live with their relatives in Kentucky. Any unfinished

•

business would have to remain unfinished. Whoever it was that wrote to him in the summer of 1825 went without an answer, and the letter ended up in the St. Louis dead-letter office in October. By then Pattie was far to the west.

•

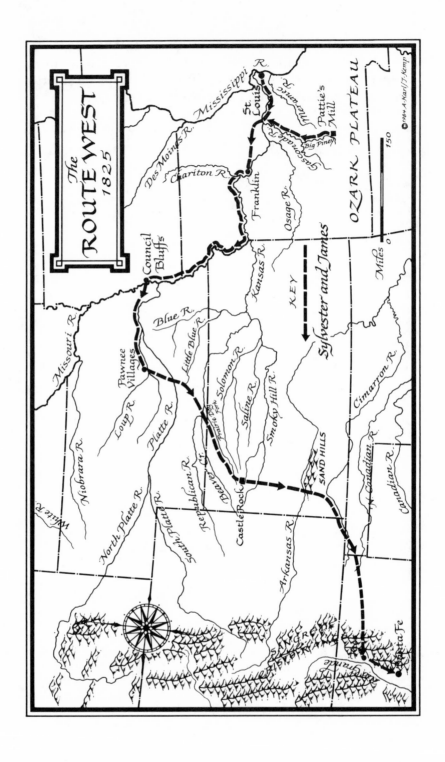

CHAPTER

T·W·O

YLVESTER PATTIE, WITH HIS SON JAMES AND the rest of his small party, crossed the Missouri on June 20, and struck north toward the Boonslick Trace.* At the point where they turned onto the trace was a tavern owned by Isaac Van Bibber, an adopted brother of Pattie's old friend Morgan Boone. West of there, between Van Bibber's tavern and the town of Franklin, farms were close enough to be reached each night and for midday dinner as well. The only problem on this stretch of road in June 1825 was the hot weather. Another party a few days behind the Patties found the heat and the swarms of flies so bad that they stayed inside during the day and traveled at night.

A few miles beyond Franklin was the village of Chariton, where the party stopped long enough to leave behind one man who was too ill to travel. Then, the small group of men, now reduced to four, left Chariton and began the trip northwest toward Council Bluffs. They were beyond the settlements now and were traveling without the benefit of towns or closely spaced taverns and farms. Roads were either bad

---

* It is essential, for all that follows, to know that Pattie in the *Personal Narrative* erroneously dated the start of the expedition as June 20, 1824. It should be June 20, 1825. See the notes for details.

•

or nonexistent, but at least the hot spell had been broken by violent thunderstorms that often rolled in from the west.

The party arrived at Council Bluffs on July 13. Since neither S. S. Pratte nor the keelboat carrying their trade goods had arrived, they settled down to wait, and for the next two weeks they made their headquarters at a trading post run by Joshua Pilcher. Two years earlier Pilcher had constructed the "handsome trading house and outbuildings" and officially named it Fort Bellevue. As usual, traders disdained the official name and called it simply Pilcher's Fort. The fort was eight miles above the mouth of the Platte and the southernmost post in the area generally known as Council Bluffs. The actual Council Bluffs, named for an Indian council held there by Lewis and Clark, was on the west bank of the Missouri some thirty miles above Pilcher's. Common usage, however, had already begun to apply the term to the whole area between the mouth of the Platte and the bluffs themselves.

The Patties were an unusual pair to appear among the traders, trappers, soldiers, Indians, and hangers-on who lived at Council Bluffs on the edge of the western country. Sylvester was not an old man—he was forty-two—but he was well beyond the age of most men venturing into the fur trade for the first time. Until a few years before he had been down on the Big Piney running his mill, serving on county commissions, and enjoying the life of a prominent and prosperous citizen. Now everything he owned was riding on the back of packhorses or loaded on a keelboat headed for Council Bluffs and beyond. Still, he had moved west once before, fought in an Indian war, hunted in the wilderness, and opened a mill on the frontier. He was as prepared as a man could be without actually having been to the mountains.

His son James, who rode with him, is much more obscure. Most of the records of the time concerned only adult males who had left the shelter of their families, and James had not yet reached that status. It was not until the departure for the West in 1825 that the *Personal Narrative*, and with it the

•

recorded life of James Pattie, actually begins. From here, until the account ends five years and several thousand miles later, the "I" or "we" of James Pattie is always present. Yet, Pattie never gives a straightforward account of his earlier years. Instead, he only drops vague, widely scattered, and often contradictory hints in the narrative. These comments, when pieced together, confuse rather than clarify and present the picture of a man at variance with his own era and his own society.

Missouri in the early 1820s was a place where a man left home and struck out on his own soon after his mid-teens. By the time a boy was fourteen or fifteen, he was thoroughly familiar with the skills of farming, of hunting, and of taking care of himself in the wilds. Many of those who had gone upriver with Ashley were such boys.

James, as he went west, however, had still not broken entirely with his family. He was traveling with his father, not by his own decision, but because he had "begged so earnestly" to be taken along. Hubert Howe Bancroft, either missing or not believing a key sentence, explained it easily by calling James "a school boy of perhaps fifteen." It is an intelligent guess, for it fits the reality of the situation and the reality of the time. The key sentence, however, cannot be ignored or dismissed. In it Pattie says that in March 1812, when his family moved to Missouri, he was eight years old. Accordingly, he was born either in 1803 or 1804, and thus in 1825 is twenty-one years old. Certainly, he may have lied to make himself appear older than he was. Still, all the other evidence—the date of his parents' marriage, the birth dates of the other children, his claim of being the eldest, the entries in the census records—points to the 1803 date as the correct one.

Thus, there is a dependence on his father at an age when most men, particularly in the fur trade, had long since gone their own way. Yet, for all this, James was forced to grow up in a hurry compared with his father. Sylvester, when he came of age, had moved easily into a position prepared by

•

his father before him, and had quietly enjoyed that life for a full decade before moving west. Once Sylvester sold the mill, however, there was no position for James to settle into, and as he came of age he was on his way into a new and unknown world. Thus, he missed the decade that had provided Sylvester with the maturity and confidence to move west and establish himself easily.

James Pattie, too, was not particularly well prepared to go west. In the introduction to the narrative Timothy Flint describes him as raised among hunters and having a love for the rifle. Pattie himself probably provided this information, but in the course of the narrative he qualifies it sharply. As he moved west his party caught a beaver, and Pattie described it as "the first I had ever seen." Later, while on the Gila River, he was left alone to hunt, and he said, flatly, "I had never before traveled alone in the woods." It is unlikely that these are lies, for Pattie usually took pains to make himself appear more, rather than less, knowledgeable.

James was also "at school" when his father made the decision to go west. At first glance it seems to mean only that he was going to a local school, but looked at against the background of pioneer Missouri it means something entirely different. At the time public schools were unheard of in Missouri, and education was provided only when the people of an area hired their own scoolteacher. Schools ran sporadically, the quality of teachers was usually low, and even good teachers could provide only the basic skills of reading, writing, and arithmetic. Those who wanted only these skills, or those who were forced to attend, were finished with school before they reached the age of fifteen. Those seeking further education went to an academy which, in turn, prepared them for college. Since James was "at school" shortly before 1825, when he was twenty-one, he must have been at either an academy or a college.

Probably he was attending school near his grandfather's home in Kentucky. By the early 1820s Bracken Academy had changed its name to Augusta College and was planning to

•

53

offer both preparatory and college work. The college program would not begin until 1825, but for several years before, the school provided preparatory work for potential students. James certainly indicates he attended school here, for at the end of the narrative he tells of arriving in Augusta and meeting his former neighbors and schoolmates. If he had not been in Augusta since his family left for Missouri, then he is offering rather detailed memories of a place he left when he was eight years old and had not seen in almost twenty years. A better conclusion is that he is remembering a place where he lived and attended school in more recent times.

If Pattie is telling the truth in these widely scattered hints, then he was quite different from most young men going west. He was no frontier boy, who knew and loved only hunting, but a young man who at the age of twenty-one had never seen a beaver, never traveled alone in the woods, and who had spent the last few years studying Greek and Latin in a preparatory school. He was prepared to observe, to listen, and to record, but he was not particularly prepared for life as a western fur trapper. Still, every man who went west, no matter what his background, had to adjust to a new life, and Pattie, during the two weeks he and his father waited for the keelboat to reach the bluffs, had plenty of time to begin that adjustment.

They stayed at Pilcher's Fort, near which there was always considerable activity, for although it sat on the edge of the wilderness, it was far from isolated. Twenty miles upriver was another trading post, that of Bernard Pratte and Company, which in 1825 was presided over by Jean Pierre Cabanne. Six miles above that, and just below the actual bluffs, was Fort Atkinson, a United States Army post.

Pilcher's and Cabanne's were well-known trading posts, but the real center of life at Council Bluffs was Fort Atkinson. In the summer of 1825 the fort was more quiet than usual, for most of the troops had ascended the Missouri to make treaties with various Indian tribes. However, the soldiers made up only half of the thousand people who perma-

•

nently lived at the fort, and all the civilian workmen, Indian traders, laundresses, and soldiers' families were still there. All the services were available, including the blacksmith shop, the bakery, the dairy, and even the library, with its copies of the *Edinburgh Review*, the *North American Review*, and Gibbon's *Decline and Fall of the Roman Empire*, So, too, was James Kennerly's general store, which provided soldiers with the extra items of clothing and food and the tobacco and whiskey that made army life bearable. Kennerly, since he had his wife and children with him, had also built a substantial two-story house in which he installed a billiard table. The home, with its billiard table, its large supply of whiskey, and a wife to do the cooking, was the social center of Council Bluffs, and Joshua Pilcher often came from his trading post thirty miles away to have dinner.

Another man doing his best to keep the wilderness away was John Dougherty, the Indian subagent at Fort Atkinson. Two years earlier he had been married in St. Louis and had brought his wife to Council Bluffs. They fit well into the fort's social life and were frequently seen at the dinners and parties given by officers. Dougherty had brought a carriage to Fort Atkinson and often used it to travel between the fort and Cabanne's, where he and his wife went to play whist. Dougherty was even seen, occasionally, along the river hunting from his carriage rather than on horseback.

It was a safe, secure, and even civilized life, but it ended just beyond Council Bluffs. Many of those who lived there permanently had, at one time or another, been west with trapping expeditions. Often their experiences were bad, and they pulled back to the quieter life of an Indian trader at the bluffs. Yet, as hard as they tried to create a cultured atmosphere, they could not completely escape the West. With each new disaster word reached Council Bluffs first, usually through a man who had been directly involved and who told his story while still in a state of excitement and shock. It was at Council Bluffs that someone like James Pattie, fresh from the East, saw the first real signs of the West and where

•

he heard the freshest and most immediate news. It was at Council Bluffs, too, where he could talk to men who could recount, firsthand, the history of the western fur trade almost from its beginning.

The place to begin was at the trading post owned by Bernard Pratte and Company. It was on the west bank of the river among the hills that sloped down to the Missouri, and although it was called a fort, the main building looked more like a house. As was usual at most trading posts, there were Indians camped nearby. A few years earlier a band of Iowa had taken up residence around the post because of their fear of the Sioux. One visitor had spent several days wandering through the village, observing the tepees, the clothing, the customs, and the Indians themselves. He found them smaller and less agile, but wilder in appearance, than the Osage and Omaha he had met coming upriver. He was particularly struck by the Iowa women and said it was rare to see one who was not attractive.

Inside the post itself lived Joseph Robidoux, a man who could give the earliest account of trading along the Missouri River. His father had come from Quebec to St. Louis in 1771 and soon began to finance trading expeditions. It made it easy for Joseph to enter the trade and in 1799, when he was sixteen, he made his first trip west to trade with the Indians. Four years later his father retired because he was going blind, and Joseph Robidoux, at the age of twenty, inherited the responsibility of running the business and bringing into it each of his younger brothers—François, Isadore, Antoine, Louis, and finally Michel.

In the years to follow he was constantly seen going up and down the river. In September 1806 Lewis and Clark met him just below the mouth of the Kansas River on his way upstream carrying trade goods for the Omaha and Pawnee. In 1812 another traveler met him coming down the Missouri in a pirogue with furs he had gathered during the winter. When the United States Army made an official report on the fur trade in 1819, it was able to pin him down long enough

•

to list him as a trader doing business at the Omaha villages. Still, he spent his time on the river, and in 1822 still another traveler met him coming downstream bound for St. Louis.

By the summer of 1825 he was still at the bluffs, but his situation had changed considerably. He had always been an independent trader, but a few years earlier he had become involved with Bernard Pratte and Company. He began to serve as their agent at Council Bluffs, but in 1823 Jean Pierre Cabanne arrived to take over. Robidoux stayed on, but it was clear that his power was gone. Those who traded at the post recognized this instantly, and what had always been known as Fort Robidoux was now called Cabanne's.

There was a great deal of tension between the two men. Unlike Robidoux, Cabanne had not been born in Missouri but was a native of France who had come to St. Louis in 1798. Within a year he had married Julia Gratiot, the oldest daughter of a prominent merchant. The marriage brought him into the inner circle of the French community of St. Louis. He had also entered the fur trade before 1800, but unlike Robidoux, he was seldom seen traveling the rivers. Instead, he spent much of his time in St. Louis as a merchant, a stockholder in the Bank of Missouri, a trustee for the town of St. Louis, and a member of the group that dominated Missouri politics in territorial days. He was a man used to giving orders, and when he arrived at the bluffs he considered Joseph Robidoux just another employee of Bernard Pratte and Company. Robidoux, however, thought he was a partner, and once, when he was reprimanded by Cabanne for doing his own business on company time, he exploded, "Employee I never wanted to be."

How the two lived and worked at the same trading post is not clear, but one visitor may have unwittingly found the answer. When he stopped at the post on his way upriver, he met Robidoux but saw nothing of Cabanne. Later, coming downriver, he stopped again, and this time met Cabanne but saw nothing of Robidoux. Those who lived at Fort Atkinson observed much the same thing. Usually, one or the other

•

arrived alone, although occasionally business forced them to visit the post together. At least once, when they came together, James Kennerly wrote in his diary, "headache this evening." Certainly, no one cared to spend much time with these two men when they were together. Either one separately, however, could give a firsthand account of early trading on the Missouri, Cabanne as a businessman, Robidoux as a trader working from village to village in Indian country. Yet, both men knew mainly the lower river and could say little about the upper reaches of the Missouri.

A few miles north, at Fort Atkinson, there was a man who could follow these accounts with the story of one of the earliest attempts to penetrate the headwaters of the Missouri. John Dougherty was now enjoying the whist parties and relaxed social life of the fort, but once he had done as much western traveling as any of those permanently living at the bluffs. He had gone to work for the Missouri Fur Company when he was eighteen and had been sent up the Missouri and Yellowstone rivers to trap. In the spring of 1810 he was a member of a party that left Fort Manuel, at the mouth of the Bighorn, bound for the place where the three forks flowed together to form the Missouri. The guide for the expedition was John Colter, already a legendary figure in the West.

When Dougherty met him, Colter had not been back to the settlements since he left Missouri with the Lewis and Clark expedition six years earlier. He had gone with the expedition to the Pacific and most of the way back. At the Mandan villages, however, he had taken his discharge so that he could accompany two trappers back to the mountains. He stayed a year, then again headed down the Missouri for home. This time he got as far as Council Bluffs, where he met Manuel Lisa going upriver. Again he agreed to turn back to the mountains, and three years later, when Dougherty met him, he was still working for Lisa. By then, he had survived the experience that made his legend.

Colter's story was well known when James Pattie was

·

growing up, and it had all the vicarious appeal to attract a boy who looked on both Kentucky and Missouri as home. Colter had signed on with Lewis and Clark at Maysville, Kentucky; Pattie knew the town from his days in Augusta, just a few miles away. Later, after he returned from the West, Colter lived at Sullen Springs, Missouri, again not far from the Patties. As things were figured at the time, he was almost a neighbor. Colter had died before Pattie was old enough to have understood the story, but it was the kind of tale that was remembered and undoubtedly it was told, more than once, around Pattie's mill on the Big Piney. John Dougherty, however, had an advantage over other storytellers. Not only had he heard the story from Colter himself, but he heard it while camped at the place where it actually happened.

In the spring of 1810 Dougherty reached the three forks with the trapping party led by Colter. While they were camped in the fork between the Madison and Jefferson rivers, Colter told them this was the place where he had escaped from the Indians. Then he told them his story.

The year before, in the fall, he and John Potts were quietly paddling their canoes down the Jefferson in search of beaver. A large band of Blackfoot appeared and ordered them to come ashore. Colter, who knew he could not escape, surrendered, as he thought he would only be robbed and released. Potts, however, resisted and shot one of the Indians. It so enraged the Blackfoot that they riddled Potts with bullets, dragged his body from the canoe, hacked it to pieces, then turned their attention to John Colter.

Colter thought he was going to be tortured and was surprised when they released him and told him to go away. He was walking away slowly when an Indian motioned for him to go faster. He was still puzzled, but when he saw Indians stripping off their blankets and leggings, he realized it was to be a race with his scalp as the trophy. The realization jarred him out of his walk, and he bolted into a run. A war whoop came from behind him as the Blackfoot began the

•

chase. He ran barefooted across the level plain covered with sage and prickly pear. The nearest place to hide was the Madison River, five miles ahead.

Halfway there blood began to gush from his nose, and with each additional step he weakened. Looking back, he saw that his only close pursuer was an Indian who had far outdistanced the rest. Colter, naked and with his face covered with blood, turned and shouted at the Indian not to kill him. The Blackfoot paid no attention; instead, he lunged at Colter with his spear. Colter grabbed the shaft near the blade, and when the exhausted Indian fell, his weight broke the shaft and left Colter with the blade. He quickly used it to pin the Indian to the ground, then, with his second wind, he ran for the Madison River. He reached it ahead of the band of Blackfoot, dove in, and hid under a driftwood pile that had built up at the head of the island. Through the rest of the day he could hear the Indians searching for him, but eventually they left and he was able to escape and return to Lisa's post.

A few months later, in the dead of winter, Colter returned to the Jefferson to retrieve his traps, which he had slipped into the river just before he was captured. He was traveling alone and not being especially careful, for he thought all the Indians were in winter camp. One evening, however, while he was cooking dinner, he heard the crackling of branches, then the sound of guns being cocked. He dived away from the fire and into the darkness just as several shots sent sparks flying. This time, under cover of darkness, it was easy to escape and return to the fort. He had made a vow, he told his listeners, that he would never return to that country; but as he told them his story, he was sitting right in the middle of Blackfoot territory.

A few days after Colter told his tale, there was another brush with the Blackfoot in which one man was killed and Colter barely escaped. Again he made a vow to leave, and this time he meant it. Within a few days he was on his way to Missouri, which he reached after one of the fastest trips

.

on record. He had finally escaped the Blackfoot, but within eighteen months he was dead from jaundice.

John Dougherty himself had some close calls with the Blackfoot. Several members of his party were killed, and eventually the Missouri Fur Company abandoned the three forks area. Between 1811 and 1819 Dougherty spent his time trading farther down the Missouri, and after 1819 he stayed mainly at Council Bluffs. By 1825 he was settled at Fort Atkinson, going hunting in a carriage, attending dinner parties at the fort, and playing whist at Cabanne's. He no longer had to continually look over his shoulder for a Blackfoot.

Colter's tale of Indian captivity and escape was a classic, but it pointed up only the most sensational danger of the West. A man who had invested heavily in a trapping and trading expedition might easily avoid Indian capture but still lose almost everything. Joshua Pilcher, the Patties' host during their two-week stay at the bluffs, spoke with feeling on this subject when recounting his experiences since 1819.

Pilcher was about the same age as Sylvester Pattie and had also spent his boyhood in Kentucky, then moved to Missouri. In St. Louis he had been in the dry goods and banking business, but in 1819 he entered the fur trade as a partner in Manuel Lisa's reorganized Missouri Fur Company. Within a year Lisa was dead and Pilcher was president of the company. He tried to penetrate the upper Missouri and Yellowstone, but in 1823 a band of traders from the company was attacked by Blackfeet. Seven men, including the leaders, Robert Jones and Michael Immel, were killed, and the fifteen thousand dollars in furs and equipment stolen. This, combined with the increasing competition from Bernard Pratte and Company, forced the Missouri Fur Company into bankruptcy. By the summer of 1825 Pilcher had formed a new company under his own name, abandoned all his posts on the upper Missouri, and was doing business from the fort at the bluffs. He had lived through the decline and eventual destruction of the Missouri Fur Company and well under-

•

stood the troubles that awaited anyone who went west to trade with the Indians.

Many of those at Council Bluffs in 1825 were like Dougherty and Pilcher. They had spent time farther west, had lost part or all of their investment, and had seen their companions killed. Now they had pulled back and were confining themselves to the easier life of trading on the lower reaches of the Missouri. Nonetheless, they were still on the edge of the frontier and were the first to see and hear the result of events happening farther west.

Three years before, those at Council Bluffs had seen the beginning of Andrew Henry and William Ashley's attempt to penetrate the upper Missouri River. In May 1822 Henry had stopped briefly on his way to build a new trading post at the mouth of the Yellowstone. A few months later Ashley passed by on his way upriver with supplies, then again on his way back to St. Louis to make plans for the following year.

Those at the bluffs heard little more of the new company until the spring of 1823, when Ashley arrived with two more keelboats and another hundred men. They stayed long enough to obtain a supply of vegetables from the post gardens at Fort Atkinson and to add two or three soldiers whose terms of enlistment had expired. At the same time they lost eight or ten of Ashley's men, who enlisted in the army. One man who was with Ashley understood exactly why they preferred army life when he said, "Here we leave the last appearance of civilization and enter [fully] Indian County."

The Patties had long known of this expedition, and it was largely responsible for their being at the bluffs. Ashley's attempt to lead "remote trapping and trading expeditions up the Missouri" was one of the few things that had interested Sylvester in the dark days after his wife died. There was much talk and several stories in Missouri newspapers, and eventually it led Pattie into his decision to go west. All these, however, were second-hand and third-hand accounts,

.

while at the bluffs there were many who had participated in one of the major events.

Two months after Ashley had stopped on his way upriver, the keelboat *Yellowstone,* which should have been far upstream by then, came back to Fort Atkinson. Ten days earlier, while trading at the Arikara villages, Ashley's party had been attacked by Indians. Twelve men were killed, another eleven wounded, and most of the rest were too panic-stricken to attempt to run the keelboats past the village. Ashley, therefore, dropped a few miles downstream and sent the *Yellowstone* with a message requesting reinforcements from the fort.

Colonel Henry Leavenworth, the commander at Fort Atkinson, agreed to reinforce Ashley with six companies of infantry and forty fur trappers led by Joshua Pilcher. For the troops at Atkinson, who spent most of their time farming and gardening, the opportunity to do some soldiering was a welcome change. The promise, however, was greater than the actual fact.

Leavenworth moved fast enough in the beginning. Four days after the news reached Council Bluffs, his troops began moving north. A month later they met Ashley and the remainder of his party somewhere near the mouth of the Teton River. Here they added several hundred Sioux warriors, who as longtime enemies of the Arikara were anxious to join in the battle. It took ten more days for the combined forces to reach the villages, and as they covered the last few miles, the Sioux raced ahead to attack on their own. The Arikara rode out to meet them, and by the time the troops arrived, the plain in front of the village was swarming with Indians. Leavenworth, unable to fire for fear of hitting the Sioux, drew his troops into a line to watch while the Arikara retreated back into their barricaded villages.

Several Arikara had been killed, and in the rush back to the village, their bodies were left behind. As the soldiers looked on, a Sioux warrior sent one of his wives to strike the

•

bodies with a club while he screamed insults at the Arikara for allowing a squaw to mutilate their dead. Another Sioux, a large middle-aged man, crawled on all fours and, growling like a grizzly bear, used his mouth to rip chunks of flesh from the bodies.

At this point Colonel Leavenworth, an officer and a gentleman, began to lose his nerve. He had little experience in Indian warfare, and he already had begun to fear that his Sioux allies were uncontrollable. He also had heard rumors that if the Arikara could defeat the soldiers, the Sioux might change sides. At the same time Leavenworth had taken the field without consulting his superiors in St. Louis, and he alone bore full responsibility for everything that happened. Thus, he refused to take any step that would commit him to an irreversible course of action.

He kept his troops in front of the village for three days. First he ordered an artillery bombardment, which had little effect, as many of the shots sailed over the village and landed in the river beyond. Then he ordered an infantry charge into the village, but on second thought he countermanded the order. Bennet Riley, a thirty-six-year-old captain in the Sixth Infantry, was to lead the charge, and when it was called off, he was furious. He complained that after all the years of growing pumpkins at Council Bluffs, he finally was given the chance for promotion only to lose it. He probably would not get another chance for ten more years. Actually, he was somewhat optimistic, for it would be not ten but fourteen years before he was promoted to the rank of major.

While Leavenworth vacillated, the Sioux scattered, first to the Arikara's cornfields, then out of the area altogether. It only heightened Leavenworth's fear that the Sioux were now waiting in the hills to see who won the battle. Therefore, he opened negotiations with the Arikara, promising to end the war if they would restore Ashley's property. The Arikara agreed, but when it came time to return the property, they produced only a few buffalo robes, three guns, and one lone horse. That, they said, was all they could do. Leavenworth's

•

choice was obvious. He could sign the treaty and forget about the rest of Ashley's property, or he could renew the attack on the village.

After a council with his officers Leavenworth ordered an attack. Then he changed his mind and decided that the treaty would be signed after all. It was all academic anyway, for during the night the Arikara slipped away and left Leavenworth's troops around an empty village. Leavenworth then announced that the Indians had been "sufficiently humbled," and led the Sixth Infantry back to its garrison at Council Bluffs. If the Patties heard Pilcher's version of the battle, it was filled with contempt for the colonel. After it was over, the trader made several bitter accusations against Leavenworth, including the fact that "you have by the imbecility of your conduct and operations, created and left impassable barriers."

Whatever the truth in Pilcher's venomous personal attacks on Leavenworth, he was accurate in his assessment that the campaign had left the river blocked. William Ashley, therefore, unable to ascend the Missouri, dropped down to Fort Kiowa, below the Arikara villages, and sent two overland expeditions from there. A party led by Andrew Henry, who had come downriver to help Ashley, went northwest toward the Yellowstone. The other, led by Jedediah Smith, headed toward the Rocky Mountains over a new route that struck almost due west from Fort Kiowa. Those at the bluffs saw neither of these parties leave, although they did briefly see Ashley as he passed by on his way back to St. Louis to handle the financial end of the business and also to run for governor of Missouri.

Some tales may have filtered down to Fort Atkinson from farther upriver, but it was not until December that those at the bluffs heard firsthand news. A week before Christmas three trappers who had been with Henry arrived at the fort. One of them, Black Harris, talked to Colonel Leavenworth and painted a dismal picture of events in the West. Not long after Henry's party left Fort Kiowa the previous summer, it

•

65

had been attacked by Indians and two men were killed. Then, when they reached Henry's Fort on the Yellowstone, they were unable to protect the horse herd from raiding Indians. Finally, Henry abandoned the old fort, moved farther up the Yellowstone, and built a new fort from which he sent trappers west to the mountains. Even this, Harris said, was not encouraging, for the Blackfeet were out hunting the trapping parties and were determined to destroy all they found. Furthermore, when Harris left the fort, the number of beaver pelts they had obtained was unimpressive.

Several months after this, William Gordon of the Missouri Fur Company arrived from the Yellowstone and reported he had been robbed of everything by a band of Crow Indians. He also reported that as he came down the Missouri he had stopped at a trading post and found it ransacked, apparently by the Arikara. The news caused Benjamin O'Fallon, the Indian agent at Fort Atkinson, to write that trappers and hunters were abandoning the mountains, "leaving the upper country stained in blood."

In August 1824, while Sylvester Pattie was selling his mill in Missouri and beginning final preparations for the trip, Andrew Henry, a partner in the company, arrived at Council Bluffs. He was on his way down the river to Missouri, where he planned to quit the fur trade for good. During his years in the West several of his men had been killed by Indians, yet he had obtained only a small amount of fur. Then, a band of Minnetaree had found his cache of supplies at the mouth of the Yellowstone and had stolen or destroyed everything. Finally, Henry had reached the conclusion that pursuing the project further was hopeless.

Ashley, however, was not entirely finished, for he still had Jedediah Smith's party of trappers in the West. And in the summer of 1824 Council Bluffs heard news of that party when first James Clyman, then, a few days later, Thomas Fitzpatrick arrived at the fort in a state of near collapse. Clyman and Fitzpatrick had been with Smith's party, which had left Fort Kiowa the previous summer and traveled west

•

until it reached the Wind River. They went into winter camp with the Crow Indians, who told them that to the west was an untouched country teeming with beaver. Smith made an attempt to reach it by crossing the Wind River Mountains in February but was driven back by deep snow. He then took his trappers south and west to skirt the mountains. On a cold, blizzardy day in March they crossed the Continental Divide by way of South Pass and found that the Crow had not lied about the wealth of beaver.

They split into two bands, with Smith taking some of the men downstream to trap, while the rest followed Fitzpatrick upstream. When they separated they agreed to meet on the Sweetwater River in six weeks or so, but when Fitzpatrick reached there Smith had not yet arrived. Rather than waste time, he took Clyman and went downstream to do some exploring. They hoped they would find a place where the Sweetwater was deep enough so that they could use boats to carry the furs east. The two men traveled a full fifteen miles but could not find enough water to float even the smallest boat. Finally, Fitzpatrick decided to go back for the rest of the party while Clyman traveled downstream to navigable water, where he would wait for them.

Fitzpatrick returned to the main camp. Smith eventually arrived and decided to keep the party in the mountains and send only Fitzpatrick and two other men downriver with the furs. While they were preparing for the trip, Smith rode down the Sweetwater to find Clyman and bring him back. He rode downstream to where Clyman had stopped to wait for the rest of the party. Smith was experienced enough to read signs, and as he looked around he saw the place where Clyman had built a shelter, a place where a band of Indians had camped, and tracks where the Indians had crossed the river. Putting it all together, he assumed the Indians had found Clyman and killed him. There was no point in looking further and he returned to the main party.

A few days later Fitzpatrick began the descent of the Sweetwater. With him were Alexander Branch, a 27-year-old

•

Virginian, and Solomon Stone, a shadowy figure who was Branch's inseparable companion during those years. The spring runoff had made the Sweetwater look navigable, and the three men built a bullboat to take their furs downriver. The river's appearance, however, was deceptive, and after dragging the heavily laden boat until it was almost worn out, they cached the furs near Independence Rock. Without the heavy load they were able to use the boat, but before they had gone very far they were upset in a series of rapids. Finally, they had no choice but to travel the rest of the way down the Platte to Fort Atkinson on foot.

When they reached the fort they found that Clyman was already there. Instead of being killed by the Indians who had camped nearby, he had successfully avoided them. He also had missed seeing Smith when he came looking for him. When none of his fellow trappers arrived, Clyman decided to head east on his own, and after a long, difficult trip finally reached Fort Atkinson. Ten days after he arrived, Fitzpatrick, Branch, and Stone also reached the fort, "in a more pitiable state if possible than myself."

Fitzpatrick, however, quickly recovered and sent word to Ashley in St. Louis, then went west with borrowed horses to retrieve the furs he had cached. By late October, when he returned with the furs, Ashley had arrived at the bluffs, and a few days later he took his party west to the Green River country.

When the Patties reached Council Bluffs that summer, no word had yet reached there of Ashley's activities. The latest news of trapping activities in the West was that brought by Fitzpatrick the previous fall, and for once it was mixed rather than entirely bad. Fitzpatrick had not only seen an untouched country full of beaver, but he also had brought the furs to prove it. Still, the difficulties he had encountered and the condition in which he reached the fort tempered the news somewhat.

So, too, did the actions of Alexander Branch and his companion, Solomon Stone. They had been with Smith since the

•

68

beginning, and they also had seen the untrapped country west of the Rockies. Apparently, they saw no great hope there, for unlike Fitzpatrick, after they survived the long walk back to Fort Atkinson, they were unwilling to accompany Ashley back to the mountains. Instead, they decided to go to New Mexico, and in the summer of 1825 they also were waiting to accompany S. S. Pratte to Santa Fe.

Several other experienced trappers from the northern Rockies also changed directions and went to New Mexico. It had only recently been opened to Americans and trapping there was not controlled by any company. In the north, however, it was clear by 1825 that those who wanted to trap could do so only by working for William Ashley. It was clear, too, at least to some trappers, that all the big profits would go to Ashley.

At the same time there was less news from New Mexico, and the sheer absence of continual disaster stories made it look more attractive. In the past few years Joseph Robidoux's brothers had led several expeditions from Council Bluffs to New Mexico, and if they had any serious trouble, no one heard of it. Those at Council Bluffs also knew that Americans would be welcome in Santa Fe. The previous summer Mexican officials had arrived at the bluffs to negotiate a treaty with the Pawnee Indians, who had been raiding into New Mexico. Benjamin O'Fallon, the Indian agent, had done everything he could to help them, and after the treaty was signed, a Mexican official wrote to William Clark to thank him profusely for O'Fallon's "efficiency in conducting the late negotiations."

All this information—both from the Rockies and from New Mexico—was available while the Patties waited at Pilcher's Fort in the summer of 1825. It was also of direct interest to Sylvester, a businessman who had invested heavily in a trading and trapping expedition. He almost certainly had a tentative agreement to join the French company's expedition; otherwise, he could not have made arrangements so quickly after Pratte arrived. Yet, there may have still been

·

a lingering thought of trying to ascend the Missouri instead. There probably was a conversation between Sylvester and the commander at Fort Atkinson, but it would have covered more than the simple matter of the license. It also would have been about conditions in the upper country and the chances of safely entering it with a party of five men. If Sylvester had not understood the dangers before leaving St. Louis, he certainly would have understood them now.

It was his son who turned the conversation into a simplified demand for a license. James, however, was no businessman, and as the narrative unfolds he often demonstrates his lack of attention to such things. At Council Bluffs, instead of saying any more about business plans, he looked over the country and said: "I have seen much that is beautiful, interesting and commanding in the wild scenery of nature, but no prospect above, around, and below more so than from this spot."

He also seems to have reached a decision here. In the *Personal Narrative* the trip up the Missouri River and the stay at Council Bluffs is given a bare summary without detail. After this, however, the detail increases significantly, and the narrative becomes a day-by-day account. Apparently, sometime during the two-week stay at Council Bluffs, James decided that what he was going to see in the future was worth recording in a journal.

•

CHAPTER

T·H·R·E·E

T HE KEELBOAT WITH THE PATTIES' SUPPLIES on board arrived at Council Bluffs on July 28. Finally, the waiting was over, and it was time to go. Two days later the Patties rode west to join Bernard Pratte and Company's main party, which was camped almost a hundred miles away on the Loup River.

Besides James and his father, there were two other men who had come up the river with them from St. Louis. These two would share all the hard travel and trouble to come, but Pattie never named them, and eventually they disappeared from the narrative without comment. One was the sick man who had been left behind temporarily in Missouri; the other was a man with no identity at all. A third man had also come from Missouri with them, but his only identifiable feature was that just before they started he became discouraged and went home.

Another man accompanying them as they left the bluffs that day was S. S. Pratte, who was to lead the expedition. He was just twenty-six, and as he rode west he carried with him a prediction of disaster. Jean Pierre Cabanne, the businessman who had so often showed contempt for the old trader Joe Robidoux, felt much the same about Pratte. He thought he was incompetent, and throughout the spring and early summer had continually railed against Pratte's ·failure to come up from Missouri and take the company hunters to

•

New Mexico. Cabanne by then was predicting disaster, and even Pratte's arrival at Council Bluffs did nothing to change his mind. The next day, in a letter to one of his partners, he asked, "How can a young man who seems to be guided by a sense of good have so little success in what he undertakes?" The only optimistic note as the party left was that Sylvester Pattie, who was older and more experienced, would be traveling with the young man.

It was a five-day ride to the camp on the Loup, and even on the first day James Pattie, from the deeply wooded country of the East, found himself in new, open country. As they crossed the divide between the Missouri and the Elkhorn, they were traveling through treeless country. That night when they camped they had trouble finding enough firewood even along the banks of the Elkhorn. The next day was more of the same, although just before nightfall, near the mouth of Maple Creek, they found a campsite in a grove of trees. It solved the problem of fuel, but since they were another day west and another day closer to Indians, a new problem arose. Any Indians, no matter how friendly, would be tempted by loosely guarded horses, and to avoid trouble they took extra precautions to secure the herd.

It was a sound idea, for the next morning, as they were breaking camp, they saw a large band of Indians riding full speed toward them. After some shouting, a flurry of signs, and the pointing of rifles, they finally forced the Indians to halt. Some conversation by a man who spoke the language finally determined that they were friendly Pawnees who, Pattie said, invited the white men to their village.

Probably there was a band of Indians, for other travelers often met roaming Pawnee in this area. The village Pattie described, however, was not here but fifty miles farther west, and he could not have visited it until several days later. By then, he had been in other villages and had other stories to tell. Thus, when he wrote the narrative he moved the village to keep from telling two Indian stories in a row.

The rest of the story, however, is accurate enough. The

•

party of white men, with a guide provided by the Indians, traveled across a valley so flat that the only distinguishable feature was the men and horses themselves. That night, camped on Shell Creek, they found no trees or even any driftwood, and for the first time they were forced to use buffalo chips to build a fire. On the advice of the Indian guide, they not only secured their horses but posted guards through the night.

The last day was the longest. They broke camp just before daylight, traveled all day, and at sundown reached Pratte's main camp on the Loup. By now July was gone and August had begun. As soon as Pratte arrived, he made plans to get the expedition started, and one of his first moves was to ask Sylvester Pattie for help. James proudly says that his father was given complete command of the party, an honor he thought came because many of the men had served with Sylvester in the rangers during the war. That much is probably true, but it is unlikely that S. S. Pratte willingly gave up his position as leader of the expedition. Most leaders, however, prefer to free themselves from minor details, and in organizing the expedition it was just these details that Sylvester handled. During the next few days in camp, according to James, his father's duties were to call the roll, divide the men into four separate messes, and assign each mess its guard duty on the trail. James, with none of his father's responsibilities, spent his time hunting deer and antelope and learning to make moccasins from the hide.

On the morning of August 6 the mules were packed and the expedition broke camp. The caravan, its progress easily traced from the dust kicked up by the long packtrain, rode up the Loup toward the three Pawnee villages. The first was the Grand Pawnee village on a high, flat bench above the river. Any time a large party of white men passed through, there was a great deal of excitement. Five years earlier Major Stephen Long's party found itself surrounded by a crowd of Indians as they entered the village. On top of the earth lodges the Pawnee had hung out all their flags, shields, quivers,

•

scalps, and any other possession that someone felt like showing off. The only people who paid no attention to the white men were women on their way to hoe the cornfields and women hard at work scraping and tanning buffalo hides.

Pratte's caravan apparently rode through this village with no more than a brief pause. Four miles upstream, however, they stopped at the Republican Pawnee village. James Pattie mistakenly places this village far to the east, but beyond that he is surprisingly accurate. The village, he said, was on an extensive plain with a thin strip of woods leading from the village up to the river. Later archaeological descriptions agree almost exactly, and place the village on the thin strip of woods along Cottonwood Creek.

It was at this point, then, rather than several days earlier, that they stopped to talk and to smoke with an Indian whom Pattie identifies as the chief of the Republican Pawnee. It may have been Fool Robe, the Republican chief who had personally welcomed Stephen Long to the village, or it may have been some other important Indian. Whoever it was, he invited them into his lodge.

James, in looking at the dome-shaped dirt lodge from outside, thought it looked like a sugar loaf. Some of the lodges, however, were as much as fifty feet in diameter, and inside they usually housed several Pawnee families. The Indians lived well enough, but most white men found the interior of a Pawnee lodge dark and smoky. The outside light was blocked off by a long hall-like entrance, and inside the only source of light was the smoke hole above the firepit in the center of the lodge. On sunny days a single shaft of sunlight slanted through the hole, making a small circle of light that further accented the smoke rising from the firepit.

By peering through the darkness and smoke, it was possible to make out the interior details. Large poles in the center and smaller poles around the edge supported a framework that in turn supported the roof of packed earth. Around the outside walls there were beds on platforms, each separated from the other by curtains woven from rushes or wil-

•

75

lows. At the back of the lodge, in the place of honor, was an earthen altar containing a buffalo skull. No Pawnee would cross from one side of the lodge to the other by passing directly in front of it. Instead, he would walk the long circle back around the lodge and cross over in front of the door.

White men were not expected to understand, nor were they given the freedom to roam through the lodge. Rather, their host brought in an interpreter, invited several important Indians and some of the white men, then posted guards to keep everyone else out. They all sat on mats around the firepit and smoked, talked, and ate fat buffalo meat. The white men were given fatherly advice about carefully watching their horses and were also given a stick that would identify them as friends to other Republican Pawnee. The stick, James said, was "curiously painted with characters, I suppose something like hieroglyphics."

The next day they moved to the Skidi, or Pawnee Loup, village. It was another three miles up the Loup River, and it was here that the expedition went into camp for several days. Pratte had come to trade for buffalo hides, and now it begins to appear that he was much more competent than Jean Pierre Cabanne thought. Each summer the Pawnee left their villages to hunt buffalo. In the days before the coming of horses, they had hunted near the villages, but by the 1820s they were roaming far to the south and west after the herds on the high plains. Had Pratte come up the river earlier, as Cabanne kept insisting, he would have reached the Pawnee villages when the Indians were scattered over hundreds of miles. As it was, they were back from the hunt, and in just a few days' trading he was able to obtain some six hundred robes.

The party also needed horses, which could be obtained from the large Pawnee herds. Besides, trading for horses was an excellent way to see the village. Since animals grazing beyond the village were easy prey for other Indians, the best stock was kept in log corrals near the lodges. These lodges

•

and corrals, however, were spread haphazardly across the village, and a trader going to look at horses could easily get lost. Most white men eventually learned to find their way by keeping track of the displays in front of the lodges. The war trophies, the captured weapons, and the small red wands with scalps on them were little help, for except to the most sophisticated eye, they all looked the same. War shields, each with its own distinctive design, were easier to follow, and white men soon learned to use them as guideposts through the village.

The horses themselves ranged from Indian ponies to horses that carried several different brands. Since the Pawnee did not brand their stock, it was clear that these animals came from somewhere else. While James was in the village he heard from someone—probably a white trader—that mounted Pawnee ranged hundreds of miles to steal horses from neighboring tribes. Sometimes they even raided into the settled areas of New Mexico, where they attacked isolated ranches and drove off large herds.

During all this trading James had an opportunity to see the village. He was somewhat confused as to where he was, for he identified the river as the main fork of the Platte rather than the Loup. Beyond that he gave a good description of the river's clean, sand bottom and the high banks lined with cottonwood and willow trees. He also noted that this village was considerably larger than that of the Republican Pawnee.

It was here that he met an Indian who claimed to have once visited Washington, D.C. James either missed the name or forgot to record it and simply called him the high chief of the village. Like most white men he used that term rather loosely, and Knife Chief, who served in that position, had never been to Washington. Instead, it was his son Petalesharo who, in 1821, had accompanied a delegation of Pawnee, Omaha, Oto, Kansas, and Missouri Indians to the East. They had arrived in November, talked briefly to President

·

77

James Monroe, then took a three-week tour of Baltimore, Philadelphia, and New York City, before returning to Washington.

Pattie, while in the Skidi village, heard Petalesharo describe the things that impressed him most. Before the trip he had always assumed that the whites were only a small tribe, and he was amazed by their numbers. Petalesharo, however, was a warrior, and he was most impressed by guns the size of logs that fired bullets as big as a man's head. James surely reported this conversation accurately, for one of the places visited by the touring Indians was a cannon foundry.

Petalesharo, the Pawnee brave, had once moved in much higher social and political circles than James Pattie. The Indian delegation had returned to Washington in time to attend the president's reception at the White House on New Year's Day, 1822. It was a major social event attended by everyone who counted—congressmen, senators, high-ranking military men, cabinet members, diplomats, and of course the president himself. The high dignitaries, however, were pushed into the shadows when the Indians arrived. They came in native dress, with the Pawnee—two from the Grand village and Petalesharo from the Skidi—wearing buffalo robes decorated with battle scenes. The other guests soon forgot the dignity of their positions and crowded around to look at the costumes and to shake hands with the Indians. Baron Hyde de Neuville, the French minister to the United States, was so impressed that he invited the Indians to his house to demonstrate their dances. It started a trend in Washington, but eventually so many embassies demanded the Indians that those in charge of the tour stopped all public appearances.

Through all this Petalesharo played only a small role. He attracted some passing notice because he was six feet tall and handsome, but he was also young, and he deferred to the older members of the delegation. In late January, however, the *National Intelligencer* published a story that suddenly centered all attention on the young Pawnee brave.

•

It concerned an event that happened at the Skidi villages in the spring of 1817. Unlike other tribes, including even the Grand and Republican Pawnee, the Skidi practiced human sacrifice. It was not an annual event, but one that demanded the right combination of circumstances—a warrior's vision, a proper captive to sacrifice, and Venus rising as the morning star in the spring of the year. Such circumstances were present after the fall of 1816 when a band of Pawnee captured a Comanche girl and brought her back to the village to await the following spring. By this time, however, opposition had begun to develop against the practice. White traders among the Pawnee spoke against it, as did William Clark when he entertained a delegation of Pawnee in St. Louis. Among those in this delegation was Knife Chief, who after his talk with Clark clearly understood that sacrifice created an impassable barrier between Pawnee and white man.

As the time for the sacrifice approached in the spring of 1817, Knife Chief argued against it. The warrior who had had the vision, who had captured the girl, and who had dedicated her to the morning star refused to listen. He had the backing of most of the tribe, who believed that sacrifice was the only way to assure a plentiful crop and to bring luck in hunting and in war. Knife Chief was ignored and ceremonies began that would culminate in the death of the victim just as the morning star rose. At the last moment, with the Comanche girl already tied to the scaffold, Petalesharo stepped forward, said his father was opposed to the sacrifice and that he had come either to free the girl or die himself. It was an awesome thing to the Pawnee, for they believed that anyone who touched the victim would soon die as a substitute demanded by the morning star. They watched in silence as Petalesharo cut down the girl, put her on a horse, and sent her off to find her own people.

When the story was published, those in Washington were equally in awe of Petalesharo, although for different reasons. In risking his life to save a maiden in distress, he had struck a sentimental strain that made him a hero. He was no longer

•

79

a retiring young brave in a crowd of Indians but rather the center of all attention. A few weeks later, when it was announced that he would be among those scheduled to dance on the White House lawn, Congress adjourned, businesses closed, and six thousand people came to see him.

Among those present were the girls from Miss White's Seminary in Washington. After seeing Petalesharo they decided to present him with a medal, particularly since Mary Rapine's wealthy father would pay for it. A few weeks later Petalesharo, somewhat confused by all the attention, was escorted to the Rapines' home near the Capitol for the presentation. The medal itself said, "The Bravest of the Brave," and when Mary Rapine slipped it over his head, she told him, "When again you have the power to save a poor woman from death and torture—think of us, and fly to her relief and rescue." Petalesharo answered, through an interpreter, "I did it in ignorance. I did not know I did good. I now know that I did good, by your giving me this medal." Colonel Thomas McKenney, the superintendent of Indian trade, was shocked by the translation and later wrote two versions of what Petalesharo meant to say, or at least what he should have meant to say. On the day of the presentation, however, what those at the Rapines' house heard was his blunt disclaimer of being a conscious hero rescuing a damsel in distress.

Not long after this Petalesharo and the other Indians left Washington. By the summer of 1825, when Pattie met him, he had just returned from the buffalo hunt and was living in one of the earth lodges in the Skidi village on the Loup. If he still had his silver medal, Pattie took no notice of it. If he still remembered the president, congressmen, diplomats, and the young ladies from Miss White's Seminary, he made no mention. Instead, what he remembered most vividly—at least what he commented on—was the overwhelming number of white people and those large guns and bullets.

While Pattie was at the Pawnee village in the summer of 1825, James Fenimore Cooper was just finishing *The Last of the Mohicans* and beginning to look ahead to his next book,

•

The Prairie. By fall he had begun the new book, and in it he created an Indian hero, a young, handsome Pawnee brave. The character's fictional name was Hard-Heart, but his real-life counterpart, by Cooper's own admission, was Petale-sharo. Cooper, who had met Petalesharo during the Indians' eastern tour, thought the young Pawnee looked like "an Apollo." He was also familiar with the famous rescue story and saw in Petalesharo the noble savage he needed for his novel.

James Pattie also had the opportunity to use Petalesharo's story, but he ignored it. Pattie, in the years to come, would spend a great deal of time among Indians, and unlike Cooper he showed no inclination to romanticize them into noble savages. Petalesharo's story was also difficult to tell without making the Indian the hero, and Pattie always reserved that role for himself or occasionally his father. Therefore, at the Pawnee villages he looked elsewhere for a story.

He found it when a war party returned to the village driving twenty stolen horses and bringing scalps they had taken from an enemy tribe. Soon after their return the party began preparing for the victory celebration. It took them a long time to paint their faces properly and to get the right effect as they donned the skins of a bear, or a wolf, or a ring-tailed panther. Then came the necklaces of bear and panther claws, followed by the proudest of all possessions, the single feather of a golden eagle. Finally, they were ready to dance.

James, young, naïve, and new to Indian dances, was both shocked and fascinated by what he saw. He was fascinated by the inventiveness of the Indians in making themselves frightening as they danced, sang, and punctuated the performance with leaps, yells, and shouts. He was shocked, too, and said it was as if the gates of hell had opened and admitted a troupe of devils into the village.

Pattie's account of the return of the war party and the victory celebration is real enough. It is followed, however, by a story in which Pattie for the first time steps out of reality and into legend.

•

81

The story, stripped of its melodramatic details and dialogue, is quite simple. The Pawnee raiders, he said, had brought in a boy who was going to be burned to satisfy the Great Spirit. The white men, led by Sylvester Pattie, were opposed and offered ten yards of red cloth in exchange for the boy. The trade goods were refused as insufficient, and the white men began to prepare for a battle. Then, "the chief," who had been insisting that the boy be killed, backed down after asking only for the face-saving addition of a package of vermilion. It was granted, the boy was freed, and the threat of a battle was ended.

Something like this happened, but not in 1825, when Pattie was there to witness it. By then the Pawnee villages were in close contact with white traders, but no one else made even the barest mention of such an event. Yet rarely did something of this magnitude escape the notice of those at the bluffs, and twice in earlier years similar events had occurred; both were recorded in several places. Later, in 1827, another attempt at a sacrifice occurred, and again it was recorded by several eyewitnesses.

Pattie's story is also too similar to another account to be simple coincidence. In 1818, a year after Petalesharo rescued the Comanche girl, another victim, this time a young boy, was brought into the village by a raiding party. He was Spanish rather than Indian, as in Pattie's account, but beyond this the circumstances are almost identical. Again, it was Knife Chief who tried to intervene, but apparently he decided that a last-minute rescue by Petalesharo would not work a second time. Instead, he tried to buy the boy with trade goods supplied by himself, by other Indians, and by Alexander Papin, a trader who was in the village at the time. Knife Chief called a council and asked the warrior who had captured the boy to accept the goods in exchange for the captive. When he refused, Knife Chief leaped at him with a war club while Petalesharo shouted for him to strike. Knife Chief, however, withheld the blow and instead offered as a face-

•

82

saving gesture a few more trade goods. The warrior accepted, and the boy was saved.

This story, like that of Petalesharo's earlier rescue, was well known, for it had been published in the *Missouri Gazette* in 1818 and again in Edwin James's *Expedition to the Rocky Mountains* in 1823. Pattie could have read both of these accounts, but usually he obtained his stories not by reading but by listening. In this case he could easily have heard it from Alexander Papin himself. When S. S. Pratte came up the river to join the Patties, he was accompanied by Papin, who, as a trader among the Pawnee, probably continued on to the villages. If so, he was there to tell the story personally, and certainly Pattie's version sounds as if it were taken directly from Papin and told with only enough changes to make Sylvester the hero.

Ironically, there was another change. By implication if not by name, "the chief" who almost stopped Sylvester in his rescue attempt was either Knife Chief or Petalesharo. Those two, rather than being the villains of the story, were in fact the heroes. It was not very generous treatment on the part of Pattie, who admitted the two Pawnee had been friendly and hospitable hosts to the traders.

Finally, the trading was over, and the expedition began to pack for the trip to New Mexico. By then, Pattie had spent four days camped near the Pawnee villages, where he had seen his first real western Indians. He saw their village, he saw them trading buffalo hides, and he saw them dancing wildly around scalps taken from their enemies. All this he duly noted with enough accuracy so that he was later able to give a reasonable description. He had also met his first western storyteller, and again he caught the story accurately enough. When he repeated it, however, he could not resist the temptation of inserting himself and his father into the midst of it. By the time he was ready to leave the Pawnee village, he had already set the tone for what was to follow.

CHAPTER

FOUR

ARLY ON THE MORNING OF AUGUST 11, with the trading for horses and buffalo robes finished, S. S. Pratte led his caravan out of the Pawnee village toward New Mexico. That first day they traveled with guides from the Skidi village, who put them on the trail south to the Platte River, thirty miles ahead.

Five years earlier Stephen Long's Pawnee guides led him over the same route and told him it was the main road south for raiders and buffalo hunters from all the Pawnee villages. For James Pattie this was borne out late in the afternoon when he heard the advance guard firing warning shots. A party of Indians was approaching, but after a few moments of tension they were identified as Republican Pawnee. They were shown the painted stick their chief had given Pratte, and after seeing it they lost interest in the caravan and continued on north toward their village. The white men traveled a few miles farther south and reached the Platte, where they went into camp.

After that first day's travel Pattie was confused as to where they were camped. Earlier, at the Skidi village, he had assumed that he was on the main Platte, and now, after a day's ride south, he thought he was on a tributary. Not only was it logical, but the river looked more like a small stream. Undoubtedly it did, for in 1825 there was no great spring runoff from the Rockies, and by mid-August it had been hot

•

and dry for almost a month. The river was low and Pattie was camped near the head of Grand Island, where it split into different channels to go around the island. It was easy, given the conditions, to mistake the Platte for a small stream, but it indicates that Pattie was not, as he implies, in constant touch with the leaders of the party. They would have known better.

The next morning, when the party broke camp on the Platte, those in charge had to make the first of several decisions on how to reach New Mexico. Five years before, Long had reached the Platte at about the same place. Accounts of his expedition had already been published, and there were also men at Council Bluffs and in St. Louis who could have provided firsthand information. Pratte, therefore, knew that by turning upstream on the Platte he could follow Long's route to the foot of the Rockies, then south to Raton Pass, one of the main entrances into New Mexico.

This route was rejected, however, and instead the caravan crossed the Platte and continued due south, still following the route of the Pawnee raiders. They were now traveling across the divide between the Platte, which they had left behind, and the Republican, which lay slightly more than fifty miles ahead.

It was dry country, compounded by a dry summer, and that afternoon they could not find a campsite with enough water for the horses. They did find water for themselves, and waited until dusk, then traveled all night to reach a place where they could water the horses. Someone was showing considerable trail sense by resting the horses during the heat of the afternoon, then pushing them through the night. It could have been Pratte who ordered it, but more likely it was simply an unspoken agreement among men who knew horses and who knew the problems of traveling in dry country.

About ten the next morning they reached a spring, probably one of those on the upper reaches of the Little Blue. There was plenty of water and grass, and they stayed in camp

•

all day to water the stock, to allow them to graze, and undoubtedly to catch up on some of the sleep they had missed. The spring was also a watering hole for antelope, and James, at least, found it a good place to hunt.

The next morning another decision had to be made about the route. Although they had rejected that of Stephen Long, they were still following another trail that led directly to New Mexico. Twenty-five miles ahead, just across the Republican River, was the old village of the Republican Pawnee. By 1825 it had been abandoned for more than a decade, but it was still a main landmark on the Pawnee road south. Twenty years before, when the Pawnee still lived there, Facundo Melgares had arrived from New Mexico, then returned home over a route that led directly south from the village to the great bend of the Arkansas. Later that summer Lieutenant Zebulon Pike had used the same road between the village and the Arkansas.

Had Pratte followed this route, his party would be well on its way to New Mexico. From where they were now camped they could reach the abandoned village in just two days. From there it was another nine days to the Arkansas River. Once they arrived there they would be on the Santa Fe Trail, already well known as the easiest way to reach New Mexico. Again, the obvious route was rejected and instead of continuing south of the Pawnee road, they began angling off toward the southwest.

The day before they had rejected Long's route on which water would have been no problem, but which was roundabout. Now they also rejected a route that, although dry, was the most direct way to reach Santa Fe. Seemingly, they ended up with the worst of both worlds—a route that was both dry and roundabout.

It would be easy to use this as evidence of Jean Pierre Cabanne's claim that Pratte was incompetent. Reading between the lines of the narrative, however, makes it clear that Pratte is doing a professional job of leading the expedition. The night drive south of the Platte had been handled well,

•

and throughout the trip to come, the party would never have serious water problems. Even on the driest stretches of the western plains, the caravan would reach water each evening, and there would be none of those frantic searches that often marked expeditions through dry country.

This same kind of competence was demonstrated on the morning that they began to angle off to the southwest. Since leaving the Platte they had been traveling across a flat plain, but they had now reached its southern edge. By turning here they could travel along the edge as the plain angled southwest toward the Republican River. If, however, they traveled any farther south before turning west, they would enter the broken country along the Republican where traveling with a packtrain was difficult.

Pratte, either personally or by listening to his guides, had knowledge of the country and enough experience to apply it. At the same time, unlike Cabanne, he did not look on this expedition solely as a Santa Fe caravan. He already had stopped among the Pawnee to trade, and he would later do the same at other villages. Quite clearly, he intended to trade with the various Plains tribes, and the place to find them was among the buffalo herds. Thus, he chose a route that would take him west until he was in the midst of the herds, where he could turn south and travel through the buffalo range almost to New Mexico. It greatly increased his chances of finding roaming bands of Plains Indians with whom he could trade.

The first day after they turned west was a long, dull ride across an empty plain until they reached an unnamed stream on which they camped. The second day started the same way, but at noon the routine as well as the long dry spell was broken when it began to rain. It was not a gentle rain, but a downpour that forced them into camp for the rest of the day. Apparently, it was no local thunderstorm, but a weather front moving across the entire plains. Travelers to the north on the Missouri, and to the south on the Arkansas, also reported heavy rains at the same time.

•

While they were in camp that afternoon, someone spotted the first buffalo. It was something that James, and all the others who were new to the plains, had been looking forward to since the trip began, and despite the rain they went buffalo hunting. They managed to kill one after a chase that James found exhilarating. He said nothing about his own involvement, however, and probably as a neophyte plainsman he watched while more experienced men did the hunting.

The next day they began moving southwest again. Already the sign of buffalo, which had been so exciting the previous afternoon, had become routine. There were buffalo in sight most of the day, but no one bothered them. The closest James came to one was that evening when he was sent to collect buffalo chips for the fire. Apparently, someone had explained both his role in the expedition and the reality of plains life, for he grumbled that he would have to do this, "not only this evening, but the whole distance . . . to the mountains."

Once the party reached buffalo country they could live well enough. Not only did it provide meat and fuel, but with enough ingenuity buffalo could be used to solve almost any problem. The Pratte caravan, for the past several days, had been having trouble with the short, tough plains grass that irritated and sometimes even cut the horses' legs. They solved this difficulty by shooting a buffalo and using its hide to make moccasins to cover tender places on the horses' legs. At the same time, however, buffalo could sometimes cause trouble, as they did a few days later by trying to crowd into the caravan's herd of horses and mules. They were stopped, but only after several bulls were shot.

Finally, the flat plain that they had been crossing for the past five days touched the Republican River at the ninety-ninth meridian, and the party went into camp for a full day. James Pattie, still somewhat confused in his geography, mistakenly identified the river as a branch of the Osage rather than the Kansas River. He should have done better in re-

•

membering the place, for a momentous event occurred in the life of a would-be fur trapper. While they were camped on the Republican, someone caught a beaver and brought it into camp. It was, Pattie said, the first he had ever seen.

After a day in camp they crossed the river and began angling southwest to pick up the Prairie Dog Fork of the Republican. Since meeting the band of Republican Pawnee north of the Platte ten days before, they had seen no Indians. On this stretch, however, as they were breaking camp, they saw buffalo running as if there was something behind them. They soon discovered that the buffalo were being chased by Indians who, intent on the hunt, were unknowingly riding directly into Pratte's camp. A shot caught their attention, and after a few minutes of looking they rode away without giving the white men a chance to identify them. Consequently, when the caravan took the trail that morning, the guards were increased, but they saw no more Indians that day.

The next day James Pattie and another man were assigned to ride guard on one of the flanks. Nothing exciting happened until late in the afternoon when they saw a herd of buffalo cows. Thus far, the expedition had seen only bulls, and when Pratte heard their story he told them they were wrong, for they were still too far east to see large numbers of cows. Pattie and the other guard went out to prove their point by shooting some buffalo. They found the herd at a water hole and killed one. The other buffalo, rather than running, crowded around the downed cow, and the two men were able to kill several more.

When Pattie's book was first published, the story of buffalo failing to run when under attack may have sounded as unlikely as any tale he told. Yet, it is real enough, for Pattie and his companion had unwittingly created a buffalo stand. Later in the century professional hunters would come to understand this characteristic of buffalo and use it to intentionally create stands in which they could kill large numbers. In Pattie's case, the two men killed eleven buffalo, all

•

of them cows. Pratte admitted his mistake and quickly sent pack mules to haul in the meat, for cows were much better eating than bulls.

Possibly it was the excitement of the hunt that caused them to relax their guard, or possibly it was the rain that started to fall about ten that night. Whatever made them careless, they paid for it when they discovered there were Indians in camp. Pattie described it as an assault on the camp, but few Indians would directly attack a large party at night. More likely, this was a raiding party trying to run off the horse herd. They were discovered and after some confusion driven off. When it was over, one of the white men had been wounded, four Indians were dead, and another was badly wounded. Before he died, he identified himself and his companions as Arikara.

The wounded white man—as usual in the Pattie narrative he is anonymous—was unable to travel, and they were forced to remain in camp for several days. It was here, on August 25, that Sylvester Pattie reached his forty-third birthday, an event that passed unnoticed as far as the narrative was concerned.

Finally, after several days, they moved west to the Prairie Dog Fork and began to ascend it. As they traveled, they were constantly in sight of herds of buffalo and wild horses that were so thick that men were sent ahead to scare them out of the caravan's path. It was along this same stretch of road that they saw their first large prairie dog village.

James gave only a quick, superficial, and not entirely accurate description of such a town. He said nothing of the burrowing owls and rattlesnakes usually seen in the towns nor does he mention eating prairie dog meat, which most other travelers tried with varying degrees of success. And there is especially no mention of shooting at the dogs for the fun of seeing if they could be hit before they darted back into their holes. Possibly, after the delay caused by the wounded man, they were in too much of a hurry to pause for the fun

·

of shooting. If they hoped to make up time, however, they were disappointed, for the next day he was unable to travel, and once again the party had to stop. In order not to waste the time completely, the rest of the caravan killed and butchered a large number of buffalo, saving only the tongues and hump ribs.

After two more days in camp they ascended the Prairie Dog Fork once more. In the afternoon they found the bodies of two men who had been shot with arrows and scalped. Wild animals had mangled the bodies so badly that it was impossible to tell more than they had been white men. They searched the area and found a place where the ground had been torn up, both by horses and by men on foot. Not far from there were the bodies of five Indians. The remains of the white men were collected and buried, and the party continued, cautiously, upstream. A few miles farther they found Indian sign that was only a few hours old, and here they stopped.

Knowing that Indians were near, they made no fire, and after dark a small party, James Pattie among them, was sent out to scout. About four miles upstream they saw twenty fires that marked an Indian camp. A moment of almost insane recklessness followed, although James treated it as completely normal. Those in the scouting party, after spotting the camp, talked among themselves about attacking the Indians. Since there were only ten of them, and since twenty fires indicated a big camp, even discussing the topic was foolish. Eventually, a sane head prevailed and the scouting party crept back downstream to the main camp.

After their return Pratte sent Sylvester Pattie with sixty men—about half the expedition—to quietly surround the Indians. They were told not to fire until the signal was given. It did not come until daylight, a long time after they were in position. James, who had never been in such an attack before, found it hard to wait, particularly when an Indian arose and, for a few minutes, stood unknowingly in his rifle sights.

•

93

Finally, at daylight, the battle began, and within fifteen minutes it was over. Thirty Indians were killed, and several more taken prisoner.

From the prisoners they found that the Indians were Crow, and that they freely admitted killing the two white men. They had run across them and had asked them to divide their powder and balls. The two men refused, and the Indians shot them and took all the supplies. The cost had been high, however, for some of the Crow's best young men had been killed. The Crow prisoners, after telling their story, were forced to bury the dead, then were allowed to go free. One of them, James said, was so delighted at being allowed to live that he gave Sylvester an eagle feather and promised to never kill another white man.

Pattie's story cannot be corroborated, but it is plausible enough. Although the Crow Indians were a long way from their home in the Wind River country of Wyoming, they often raided over long distances. Pattie's description fits such a raiding party, for there were no tents, no women, no children, only a band of Indian men sleeping around the fires. The story of two white men who accidentally met a band of warriors and were killed when they resisted was common, as was the attack on a sleeping Indian camp without prior determination of guilt. Even Pattie's description of his own impatience to shoot an Indian is realistic enough.

The only questionable part of the story—and the stories that have gone before—is the number of Indians killed. Throughout western history white men were notorious for their exaggerated claims of dead Indians, which they often counted in the hundreds. Pattie, however, if not accurate, is at least reasonable. In the first encounter, the horse raid by the Arikara, four Indians were killed. Since raiding parties rarely put themselves in a position to suffer such losses, the number seems somewhat large but not outrageously exaggerated. The same is true of the attack on the two white men in which five Crow were killed. Again, given the circum-

•

stances, it seems a large but not impossible number. The largest count of dead Indians was in the attack on the Crow camp, where thirty were killed. The circumstances of that attack, however, were much different, and historically the largest number of casualties suffered by Indians was when a sleeping village was attacked at dawn. Again, thirty dead Indians is a large number, but again, given the circumstances, it is entirely possible. If James Pattie is exaggerating, he at least has the good sense to keep his claims within the bounds of reality.

After the attack on the Crow, the caravan continued upstream, and two days later, somewhere near the hundredth meridian, they turned off Prairie Dog Fork. For the next week they traveled almost due south across the high plains of western Kansas. Usually, they were in sight of large herds of animals—deer, elk, antelope, wild horses, and buffalo trailed by the ever-present large, white wolves. There was enough meat for everyone, but James had not yet thrown off the full trappings of civilization, and he began to complain of the lack of salt, which had just run out, and the lack of bread, which he had not tasted since he left the Pawnee villages. Once, he did find an Indian pumpkin patch near a spring, and to vary his diet, he took one of the pumpkins and cooked it. Unfortunately, it was not very good.

By now they had been traveling in buffalo country for several weeks and had met only unfriendly Indians. Finally, however, on this stretch they came across a band with whom they could trade. It was not a raiding party but a village on the move with women and children. They had no interest in fighting, and the two groups camped together for the night, traded for a few furs, then went their separate ways.

As the caravan continued south, Pattie only vaguely described the high plains. It is almost featureless country, and the campsites in the narrative are no more specific than "near water" or "on a stream" or, once, "without water." His only attempt to specifically identify a camp was on a

•

spring he called Bellfontaine. The name has not survived, and later well-drilling activities have brought such changes that it is difficult to locate the camp precisely.

Two days after leaving this spring, however, Pattie arrived at a place that can be easily identified. It was a lone rock rising some eighty or ninety feet above the flat surrounding plains. They camped beneath it by a spring that they named Rock Castle Spring. The name as such did not survive, but forty years later a surveying party passed the same way and thought the rock looked like an "old English Castle." Unknowingly, they twisted Pattie's name and called it Castle Rock, and as such it still stands on the Hackberry Creek in Gove County, Kansas.

Castle Rock—or Rock Castle—provides a valuable point from which to check the route thus far. Working back from here, it is about sixty miles in a straight line to Prairie Dog Fork and somewhat farther if they were angling slightly to the west. It took them six days to cover the distance, and thus they were averaging about ten miles a day, which is reasonable. The pack mules were heavily loaded, it was late summer, and they had been traveling for a long time. George Sibley, who at the same time was crossing the plains south of them, said, "We are in no haste to move on very fast, especially as the weather is very warm, our horses tired and poor." He, too, was averaging about ten miles a day.

After a night camped under Castle Rock, the party continued up Hackberry Creek, then crossed the ridge to Plum Creek, another tributary of the Smoky Hill. It was here that James Pattie saw his first grizzly. When they came upon him, he was sitting in the middle of a circle of wolves. He had recently killed a buffalo, eaten part of it, and buried the rest. Now, he was guarding the remains against the wolves, who were waiting for him to leave.

It was too good an opportunity to pass up, and the circle of wolves was quickly replaced by a circle of men, James Pattie among them. It took an hour to kill the bear, for he continually charged at the men on one side of the circle

•

while those on the other side were afraid to fire for fear of hitting someone.

The next day they killed three more grizzlies, and that night, in camp somewhere near the Smoky Hill itself, they saw still another. Sometime after dark, with James on guard duty, the horses and mules stampeded. The first thought was that Indians had gotten into the horse herd, and several men, almost as a reflex action, took after the herd to turn it back. James, however, heard signs of a struggle and found a grizzly eating a horse that was still alive. He fired at the bear, wounded it, and brought everyone in camp to the spot. The wounded grizzly attacked the men, driving them back into the dark, then seized a man, who began to scream. Pattie said he was the one who, having reloaded his rifle, stepped forward to kill the bear and save the man.

Thus far, the story is plausible. The stampeding of the horse herd by a grizzly could easily have happened, with or without the attack on the man, with or without the personal heroics of James Pattie. But the story continues. After the bear was killed, the man who had been attacked was so badly hurt he was unable to travel. They waited for three days, during which he got no better but also did not die. Finally, two men were given a dollar a day to wait until he died, bury him, then catch up with the caravan. By now, Pattie has left the real world behind and is far into legend. The story he is telling has been told before, and Pattie is not recounting something he saw but something he heard, possibly even while camped near the Smoky Hill.

It had been a long day, full of bears, and after they made camp that night, it was bear story time. There were many such stories, but by 1825 all were insignificant compared with that of Hugh Glass. Two years earlier Glass had been a member of Andrew Henry's party, which went up the Missouri, then, to avoid the Arikara, turned west on the Grand River. While traveling on the upper reaches of that river, Glass was attacked by a grizzly and severely mauled. He was too badly hurt to be moved, and since Major Henry was in a

•

hurry, he promised a substantial reward to anyone who would stay with Glass until he was either able to travel or until he died. Two men were sufficiently tempted by the promise to volunteer. Henry moved on to the Yellowstone, and a few days later the two men arrived with the news that Glass had died. As evidence they brought Glass's rifle and the rest of his possessions. Those at Henry's post had little reason to doubt or ponder the story, for such deaths were common enough among trappers, and there was no reason to think that this was anything out of the ordinary.

The first indication that this was not an ordinary event came in October 1823, when Hugh Glass himself arrived at Fort Kiowa on the Missouri. The story he told of his survival was simple and straightforward. It was also incredible.

When he awoke and found that he had been abandoned, he managed, with a great deal of effort, to crawl to a spring a few yards away. For ten days he lay there eating the wild cherries and buffalo berries that were within reach. Eventually, he recovered enough strength to begin crawling toward Fort Kiowa, two hundred and more miles away. His progress was agonizingly slow, and he sometimes stopped to dig roots or crack buffalo bones for the marrow. Finally, he came upon a pack of wolves attacking a buffalo calf. He waited until the wolves had satisfied their hunger, then drove them off and appropriated the meat. The nourishment gave him enough strength so that he could walk rather than crawl toward the Missouri. Eventually, he met a band of Sioux who were friendly and who took him to Fort Kiowa.

Pattie certainly heard this story, for he has already used the opening scenes in the narrative. He could have read it somewhere, for several Missouri newspapers carried it before he left for the West. Pattie, however, rarely uses such material, and instead almost always produces a story at the point where he heard it. Besides, he provides details of the attack that did not appear in the newspapers, but only in another storyteller's account that was not published until years after the *Personal Narrative*.

•

The storyteller was George Yount, who later dictated his version. The man who took it down said, "Glass told to Yount all of which we have written & Allen confirmed the truth of it." When Yount described the wounds suffered by Glass, he said the bear had "torn the flesh from the lower part of the body. . . . He also had his neck shockingly torn, even to the the degree that an aperture appeared to have been made into the windpipe, and his breath to exude at the side of his neck . . ." Pattie, when he described the damage done to the man in his party, said, "The flesh on his hip was torn off, leaving the sinews bare. . . . His breath came out of both sides of his windpipe." Clearly, the two men had heard almost identical versions of the story.

Pattie could have heard the story from anyone, for he later trapped with several men—George Yount, Lewis Dutton, Hiram Allen—who knew it well. Yount, however, claimed he heard it directly from Hugh Glass himself, and there is a tantalizing possibility that Pattie heard it from the same source.

Glass, after surviving the attack by the bear, went west again, and in the spring of 1824 was in a party of five men that was attacked by Arikara. He was cut off from his companions, but again he survived and in June 1824 walked into Fort Atkinson. After this last escape those at the fort raised a purse of three hundred dollars for Glass, which he used to go to Missouri and enter into a partnership to trade with New Mexico. Given the time and the vague records, he could have gone with the regular caravan in 1825. He could also have gone with S. S. Pratte's caravan. Two years later, in New Mexico, he was definitely associated with Pratte, and he may have been with him from the beginning. All this, the time sequence, the later association with Pratte, and the presence of the bear story in words attributed to Glass, makes it possible—but not provable—that James Pattie heard the story, somewhere near the Smoky Hill, from Hugh Glass himself.

However Pattie obtained Glass's story, he planned to use

•

it to the fullest. After the wounded man was left behind, the caravan continued a few miles and came to a stream with timber on it. It was such an improvement over the spot where they had left the wounded man that they returned and had him carried on a litter to the stream. Again, this is an echo of Yount's version for he alone among those who told the story had Glass carried some distance on a stretcher. It was there, near the timbered creek, that the wounded man was left for good. A few weeks later the two men left with him caught up with the caravan, said he had died, and produced his rifle and ammunition as proof.

Pattie has clearly gone to a great deal of trouble to integrate this part of Glass's story into the narrative, apparently in preparation for the rest of it. On some future page the dead man should suddenly reappear and tell his incredible story of survival. But he never does. Pattie elaborately laid all the groundwork, but somehow forgot to tell the best part of the story.

After they left the camp where Pattie had heard the story, they followed the Smoky Hill River, then turned south to cross sixty miles of plains to the Arkansas. It was in this stretch that Pattie said, "I counted, in the course of the day, two hundred and twenty white bears." It was an improbably large number of grizzlies, although a man who had just heard Hugh Glass's story was likely to see bears almost anywhere.

Beyond that, the days were much like those that had gone before. They were still traveling among large herds of wild horses and elk, and there were still buffalo, although the herds had diminished in size. Pattie thought it was because of the great number of bears; more likely, it was because of the increasing dryness of the country. One night they camped without water, another night they camped by water that was too brackish to drink.

It was on these plains, two days north of the Arkansas, that Pattie had a hunting experience in which the high drama of Hugh Glass gave way to the low comedy of James Pattie. He had wandered off from the main column and was

•

looking for buffalo by himself. He shot two cows, one of which had a calf, and he decided to capture it alive. It was a decision made on the spur of the moment and without thought of consequence by a young and not too responsible man. No one particularly wanted or needed a live buffalo calf, but it would cause a sensation when it was brought into camp. To free himself for the chase, he laid down his rifle and pistols and began to ease toward the calf. He was ready to run after it when it bolted, but instead of running, it charged and knocked him down. Each time he tried to get up, it butted him again. Finally, he was able to grab the calf by the leg and hold on until he could stab it with his knife. After the struggle was over, he sheepishly realized he had been a fool and decided to lick his wound in private without telling anyone what he had done. He did not reach camp until after dark, and by then Sylvester had already spent part of the evening firing signal shots to guide his son into camp.

Two days later, after pushing hard all day, they reached the Arkansas River. There was no time to rest, for there was a storm coming and they had to make camp before it reached them. By the time it began to rain, they had their tents up, the fires lit, and the meat cooking. Just as they were ready to eat, however, they saw several Indians approaching. They seemed friendly, as their guns were over their shoulders and they were shouting, *"Amigo, amigo."* James did not understand the words, but someone else did and indicated that the white men too wanted to be friendly. Communications were further eased when it was found that they were Comanche and that a hunter in the caravan spoke their language.

One of the Indians—Pattie calls him a chief—asked for the leader and was directed to Sylvester Pattie, who was in charge of the camp. The Indian asked the white men, as a show of friendship, to move to the place where the Comanche were camped. Sylvester said he had no intention of changing campsites in the rain, but he did say that if it stopped raining by morning, he would be willing to move. It was an unacceptable answer, and the chief threatened to

•

have his warriors attack. Then he changed his mind and gave the white men until eight the next morning to move. If they did not, he said, the Comanche would attack.

No one slept that night. Instead, they spent their time closely guarding the horse herd and building barricades against the coming attack. The Comanche, however, did not appear until eight the next morning, when a large band arrived carrying spears, shields, and guns. All of them had their faces painted black for war.

Before they could attack, or before the white men could do more than fire a few scattered shots, another band of Indians arrived. They rode between the two groups, and when the Comanche saw these new Indians, they attacked them instead. The battle lasted about fifteen minutes, and James was so caught up in the general action that he could not describe any particular incidents. The white men wanted to help those attacking the Comanche, but in the confusion they could not tell one Indian from another. Besides, the newcomers needed no help, for they quickly defeated the Comanche.

Pattie calls this new band of Indians "Iotans," a word used mostly for the Comanche themselves. The term was used loosely, however, and in this case he is describing not a rival band of Comanche, but rather a band of southern Ute. Normally, their country was to the west, in the Rockies, but in the summer they often rode out onto the plains to hunt buffalo. Their relations with the Comanche, too, were very much as Pattie describes them.

The two tribes were related by language, and once, long before, they had been allies who often combined to attack the New Mexican settlements. After 1750, however, the Comanche began to obtain weapons from the East, and they turned on the Ute and drove them back into the mountains. By the 1820s the Ute were often referred to as a branch of the Comanche, but nonetheless they were constantly at war with them.

Such constant warfare, however, was taken far too seri-

•

ously by white men. Indian diplomacy was carried out in the field by small bands, unrestricted by tribal policy. Relations were often determined by the circumstances when they met —the numbers in each band, the possibility of surprise attack, and the emotional climate at the time. The frequent practice of taking captives from other tribes often left Indians with parents in one camp, children in another. On one occasion a captured Ute woman, whose son was fighting as a Comanche warrior, used her dual loyalties to intervene during a battle and arrange a truce. Such truces, however, were temporary and could end with the turning of the wind.

This kind of relationship comes through clearly in Pattie's account of the meeting on the Arkansas. The Ute defeated the Comanche, then made peace with them and gave them horses in payment for the Comanche warriors who had been killed. Later, the Ute chief explained his actions to the white men in a story filled with the strange, shifting relations between Ute and Comanche. Four years before, he said, his father had gone buffalo hunting with a band of Comanche. It was bad enough that the Comanche took all the best meat, but his father accepted that. On the way back, however, they met some Navaho, and the Ute instantly attacked. Instead of supporting them, the Comanche joined the Navaho and killed all the Ute. It all worked out, however, for the Comanche later paid four horses for each warrior and twenty for the Ute's father. The son, now a Ute chief himself, pointed out that in the recent battle he had killed three times as many Comanche and had paid only two horses per warrior. Thus, he said, he was well satisfied with the bargain.

The Ute denied the Comanche chief access to Pratte's party, but later he relented and allowed him to talk to them. In the conversation that followed, the subjects of war, death, and the making of peace again arose. The Comanche chief, now trying to be friendly, said he did not want war with the Americans. If any white men were accidentally killed, he said, their friends should not be too upset, for the Comanche would gladly make up for it by paying in horses and beaver

•

skins. James thought it was a shocking attitude, and said, "We did not express our natural feeling that the life of one man was worth more than all the horses or beaver skins his nation could bring forth."

Pratt's party stayed in camp several days on the Arkansas trading knives, paint, and gunpowder to the Ute for their deerskins and beaver pelts. Then, in early October, they forded the Arkansas and crossed the sand dunes south of the river. By now, they were on the Santa Fe Trail, which led to the Cimarron River, then upstream to Upper Cimarron Spring. Here they left the river and alternately crossed and followed several tributaries of the Canadian River. Eventually, the trail crossed the North Canadian itself and led the caravan to the foot of the mountains of New Mexico.

In these last days of the long trip across the plains, Pattie tired of his journal, and the style of the narrative changes abruptly. Instead of the usual day-by-day account, long periods of time are quickly summarized: "Nothing worthy of record occurred during the journey of the four succeeding days," or "From the 17th to the 20th we journied without interruption."

About the only thing he thought worth mentioning was that Pratte stopped long enough at the foot of the mountain to bury some of the trade goods. Although Pattie did not say why, he surely knew the reason. Another less reticent traveler described this as common practice and added, "Then they go into the settlements to make the necessary arrangements; after which, by means of bribes, their goods are smuggled in." After the goods were buried, Pattie handled the rest of the trip into Taos simply: "We were three days crossing this mountain."

•

CHAPTER

F·I·V·E

AMES PATTIE RODE INTO TAOS WITH
Pratte's caravan on an evening in late October
1825. They had spent the last three days traveling through the mountains that separated Taos
from the plains to the east. The trail led them over
the pass at nine thousand feet, then alongside Rio
Fernando de Taos, a mountain stream that flowed down a
long canyon with high, pine-covered walls. Eventually, the
canyon widened to reveal the broad sweep of Taos Valley
and the small village of San Fernandez, usually called
Taos.

Travelers caught their first view of the villege from a distance. From here, it looked like an Oriental town with "low,
square, mud-roofed houses and its two square church towers, also of mud." It was impressive from a distance, but up
close there were only a few dirty, irregular streets and some
adobe houses. Some of these houses, however, were quite
large, particularly that of the Taos *alcalde*. His home was
behind walls, and the entrance, through a large swinging
gate, led into an enclosed courtyard. Across the courtyard
was an overhanging roof supported by pillars of rough pine
and beyond that was a dark passageway that led to the room
in which he received visitors.

Sylvester and James Pattie called on the *alcalde* to pay
their custom duties, and James at least was irritated by the
reception. The *alcalde* was proud and haughty, and while

•

106

they were talking to him men, women, and children kept crowding up to the door to stare at them. Not only was he irritated by this, but he was shocked and disappointed by all of Taos. Naïvely, he had assumed that the only difference between Missouri and New Mexico was the language. Instead, he found that everything was alien.

The foreignness began with the very fundamentals of life. Both men and women, instead of being "clothed in our fashion," wore strange costumes. Prosperous men like the *alcalde* wore bright-colored jackets and trousers trimmed with lace, morocco leather, and an endless number of buttons. Other men, not so prosperous, wore shirts and leather trousers that came down to the knee and were held up by bright sashes. In both classes the outfit was topped by the *serape*, which James described simply as a blanket thrown over the shoulders. As might be expected from a young man of the time, he had an eye for the swords worn by the men and the knives that they had strapped to their legs. Other than that he found the weapons unimpressive, as there were few firearms and most men had to make do with bows or lances.

Like all travelers from the East he found that the women also dressed differently. The most notable difference was the absence of the bonnet, which was almost universally worn in the United States. In its place women wore the *rebozo*, a long cotton and silk shawl used to cover the head and shoulders. Beyond that they wore skirts that were short, and chemises that, according to one traveler, were "too low necked."

This same traveler, however, discovered that the best place to watch women was at the spring where they came for water. Each evening he would stroll down to the spring, station himself on the wall of a ruined adobe, and observe the women as they spent the last hours of the day gossiping. When it came time for them to go, they put the water in old earthen jars, placed the jars on their heads, and with *rebozos* gracefully draped over their shoulders, began an erect and dignified walk home. As he watched this he remembered his

•

Bible and the story of "the daughters of Jerusalem coming to the wells."

James found all of this very foreign—shockingly so in the beginning—but he was forced to admit that the people were kind, "for they brought us food, and invited us into their houses to eat." Yet this hospitality was quite new, for until a few years before it had been illegal for Americans to enter New Mexico. Those who had done so illegally always found the people friendly enough, but government policy and the attitude of officials created a barrier that kept most of the common people at a distance. In 1821, however, it became legal for Americans to enter, and New Mexicans were free to associate with them.

The first to benefit from this newfound hospitality were members of the expedition led by Hugh Glenn and Jacob Fowler. They had left Fort Smith, Arkansas, in the fall of 1821 and by February 1822 were in Taos. The people were friendly and the house in which the Americans were staying soon became the scene of a dance. The next morning the Americans received another demonstration of hospitality when an army captain's wife called on them. She had been introduced to Glenn by her husband, who had been with the troops that had led the Americans to Taos. Now, her husband was out patrolling the frontier again, and she had come for a visit. She was quite forward, and by the end of her half-hour stay, she was treating them as if she had known them all her life. Glenn's black slave, Paul, also noticed that she seemed to have more of an eye for him than for any of the white men. Since he was both shy and religious, he was thoroughly relieved when she left.

That afternoon, however, she sent a message asking that certain members of the party call on her at her home. Specifically, the invitation requested the presence of Colonel Glenn, Baptiste Roy, the interpreter, and Paul, the black slave. Paul did not want to go, but after some argument he agreed to accompany his master.

The woman and her daughters lived in a house that could

•

only be entered by an outside staircase to the roof, then through a trapdoor down into the house. Since it was built this way for protection against the Indians, there were no windows or doors and no way in or out except through the trapdoor in the roof. The three men were greeted by the women with an embrace. It thoroughly embarrassed Paul, who began to look for some way to escape only to discover he was trapped, for someone had closed the door above him. Had he been more familiar with the customs of the country, he would have known that the embrace was a simple greeting and in itself signified nothing. Yet, as it turned out, his first impulse was sound enough.

There was a huge bed in the room—big enough for all three couples if necessary—and the mother, being the oldest, had the first choice of men. She grabbed Paul, pulled him to the bed, put her arms around him, kissed him, then slipped a hand down into his pants. Paul, in an effort to escape, slid down the bed, but he finally came to the wall and could slide no more. His only other defense was to keep looking at the closed trapdoor above him in the hope it would somehow open. Then, almost as an answer to his prayers, someone opened it and Paul, seeing the light, bolted through the opening and ran back to his quarters. A few minutes after he arrived, Glenn and Roy came back to spread the story of his experiences with the captain's wife.

The Patties also found the women of Taos hospitable. Sylvester and James were taking their first walk through Taos when a woman standing in a doorway beckoned them to enter. They followed her up a flight of stairs and into a room that was neatly whitewashed and decorated with a brass crucifix and statues of saints. She served them wine and *chile colorado*, a dish James described as made of red pepper, cornmeal, fat, and water. One traveler called it a hot mess; James's only comment was "We could not eat it." Undaunted by her guests' strange tastes, the woman brought out some *tortillas* and milk, which was more successful. At least James was curious enough to find out that *tortillas*

•

were cakes made by grinding corn and wheat between two flat stones.

He was interested enough, too, to begin learning Spanish by asking the woman what the cakes were called. This first Spanish lesson, however, was none too successful, for he later wrote, "This cake is called in Spanish, *metate.*" Somewhere in the attempt to communicate, confusion arose, for *metate,* instead of being the tortilla, was the stone on which it was ground.

Neither Pattie, father or son, was in a hurry to leave, for according to James, they stayed until late evening. He offers no details, but certainly the food was not to their taste and verbal conversation was difficult because of the language barrier. Nonetheless, they stayed until church bells began to ring and the woman and her children knelt down to pray.

In his description of New Mexico James often implies that he and his father are lone travelers in a foreign land. Yet, Taos, by 1825, was not entirely isolated from the English-speaking world. George Sibley, with his road survey party, arrived a few days after the Patties. He no more than reached Taos when another party of traders came into town, and a few days later he met François Robidoux, who had recently arrived. Since Taos had only about a thousand people in the fall of 1825, it was virtually overrun by American traders.

There were also other Americans besides the itinerant traders from Missouri. Almost as soon as the country was opened to foreigners, trappers had come in, and they soon discovered that Taos was the best town in New Mexico. The village was on the edge of the frontier, and to the west and north were mountain rivers and streams filled with beaver. When the trapping season was over, fur buyers could be found among the Missouri traders and deals made without interference from Mexican officials, for they rarely came to the remote village of Taos. As early as 1821 Taos was recognized as a weak link, and the suggestion was made that a military post be established there. As late as 1839 New Mexico officials were still complaining that nothing had been

•

done to stop Americans from slipping out of Taos without paying duties.

Taos was also a good place for a trapper to live during the off-season. It provided food, supplies, fandangos, and women. Also, not long after the first trappers arrived, enterprising Americans had discovered that wheat grown in the Taos Valley could be distilled into a potent liquor. Very quickly, several stills were opened and their product, Taos Lightning, became famous all over the mountains. All this cost money, but even after a trapper was broke, it was easy to live in Taos. The mountains surrounding the valley were filled with elk, deer, bear, pheasant, and turkey. Then, when fur-trapping season came again, it was easy to reach the hunting grounds.

When the Patties arrived in Taos, the fall trapping season had begun, and most of the trappers had already left for the mountains. Since Sylvester and James also planned to go trapping, they spent only a short time in Taos, then went to Santa Fe to obtain a license. It was seventy-five miles from Taos to Santa Fe, much of it over a steep mountain trail, and normally it took three days, with most travelers stopping for the night at Empudo and again at Santa Cruz. James Pattie, however, for some reason was unable to give a clear account of the trip. The places he claims to have stayed are not on the road between Taos and Santa Fe, and in fact he is describing the approach to Santa Fe from the south. Somehow in the writing he had gotten confused and was describing another trip and another time.

Despite this, the Santa Fe of the *Personal Narrative* is real enough. The capital was impressive, particularly to those who had seen Taos first, and James was no exception. As they approached the city he guessed that it must contain four or five thousand people, and he was not far wrong. Not only was it much bigger than Taos, but it was, as well, a city that captivated even the most critical American.

One such American was Thomas James, who reached Santa Fe just a few years before Pattie. At the time he was

•

approaching the age of forty, was facing bankruptcy, and if his memoirs are any indication, he had a permanent grudge against the world. Yet, when he reached Santa Fe, he momentarily forgot his bitterness as he described the beautiful plain on which the city lay, the flat-roofed, one-story buildings that were whitewashed inside and out, and the five impressive Catholic churches filled with paintings and expensive ornaments of gold and silver.

Pattie saw it much the same way—the large plain, the "handsome" stream that ran through town, and the distant view of snowcapped mountains. He, too, found the churches beautiful, although the bells made a noise "sufficient to awaken the dead." They rang each morning, and possibly for a man just in from a hard trip across the plains they rang too early.

The Patties were in Santa Fe to plan a trapping expedition, and as usual James portrayed his father as the leader. More likely, however, it was S. S. Pratte who actually organized it, for Pattie said, "We received a license, allowing us to trap in different parts of the country. We were now divided into small parties. Mr. Pratte added three to our original number. . . ." The implication that Pratte was still in charge is clear.

Thus, James Pattie, and possibly Sylvester, too, was free to spend time seeing Santa Fe. The focus of the city was the plaza that sat in the center of a square formed by the governor's palace, the military chapel, some private residences, and several stores run by American traders. The traders' goods, all brought from Missouri, were of less interest to an American than the native products for sale in the plaza itself. Strings of red peppers and onions, as well as meat—mutton, pork, venison, wild turkey, and even bear meat—were hung on lines strung between the pillars that supported the palace portal. The other products—beans, cheese, and fruits—were spread on mats. Alongside sat the vendors, patiently waiting for a sale. Sometimes, too, it was possible to buy an Indian blanket that was superior to anything made in

•

The St. Louis Art Museum, Gift of Mrs. Chester Harding Krum

Landscape with Cattle

The Mill Boy

As a boy James Pattie lived at a mill located in country very similar to that portrayed in George C. Bingham's Landscape with Cattle. *Bingham, an almost exact contemporary of Pattie's, also painted* The Mill Boy.

The InterNorth Art Foundation, Joslyn Art Museum, Omaha, Nebraska

Bellevue Trading Post

Interior at Bellevue

The exterior and interior of John Dougherty's Bellevue trading post at Council Bluffs, where the Patties spent two weeks waiting to go west.

White House Collection

Petalesharo, Generous Chief, Pawnee Tribe

NATIONAL MUSEUM OF AMERICAN ART, Smithsonian Institution, Gift of Mrs. Joseph Harrison, Jr.

The Buffalo Bull, Grand Pawnee

The New York Public Library, Astor, Lenox, and Tilden Foundations

Grand Pawnee

Soon after leaving Council Bluffs, Pattie met Petalesharo, a Skidi Pawnee Indian whose idealized portrait was painted by Charles Bird King during Petalesharo's visit to Washington, D.C. The more realistic portrait of the Buffalo Bull and the drawing of the Grand Pawnee are by George Catlin who, like Bingham, was Pattie's contemporary.

Beaver Dens

The InterNorth Art Foundation, Joslyn Art Museum, Omaha, Nebraska

Courtesy of the Edward E. Ayer Collection, The Newberry Library, Chicago

Herd of Buffalo

*On the Great Plains west of the Pawnee villages, James
Pattie saw his first beaver as well as his first herd
of buffalo.*

NATIONAL MUSEUM OF AMERICAN ART, Smithsonian Institution, Gift of Mrs. Joseph Harrison, Jr.

The Mountain of Rocks, Comanche

NATIONAL MUSEUM OF AMERICAN ART, Smithsonian Institution, Gift of Mrs. Joseph Harrison, Jr.

The Little Spaniard, Comanche

NATIONAL MUSEUM OF AMERICAN ART, Smithsonian Institution, Gift of Mrs. Joseph Harrison, Jr.

Comanche Village

Somewhere on the far western plains, the Patties and the rest of the trading company went into camp with a band of Comanche. The paintings of the village and the warriors are by George Catlin.

A Packtrain to Santa Fe, 1820

View of Santa Fe and Vicinity

*James and Sylvester Pattie arrived in New Mexico by way
of Taos, then continued to Santa Fe, where they waited for
some time before going down the Rio Grande toward
beaver country. The painting of the packtrain to Santa Fe is
a historical re-creation by the late-nineteenth-century
artist Frederic Remington.*

Pima Indian Country

Group of Apache

On their first trapping trip in the Southwest, the Patties descended the Gila River as far as the Pima villages, then turned back. It was on the way home that they were attacked by a band of hostile Apache.

Presidio at the Copper Mines

View of the Copper Mines

Eventually, Sylvester settled down at Santa Rita, where for several years he ran the copper mines while James wandered the wild country of the Southwest as a trapper.

Santa Fe. The activity that James enjoyed the most, however, was climbing to the flat roofs of the houses each evening and looking out over the town and across the plains toward the mountains.

Pattie clearly liked Santa Fe, and unlike other Americans he did not qualify it with bitter denunciations of the people. Thomas James, although he liked the city, found the manners and morals of the New Mexicans disgusting. While he was there Santa Fe held an independence day celebration and "no Italian Carnival ever exceeded this celebration in thoughtlessness, vice, and licentiousness of every description." People caroused through the streets at all hours of the day and night, and the plaza was filled with gambling tables that were in constant use. Even upper-class women were gambling, losing their money, their jewelry, and finally even their gold-trimmed *rebozos.* The passion for gambling was an almost universal complaint of Americans in Mexico, but Pattie said nothing about it. Either he was too naïve, too disinterested, or too accepting to think it worth a comment.

The same was true of his experiences at a fandango in Santa Fe. Most Americans who came to Santa Fe in these years went to such a dance and many were disgusted by what they saw. Albert Pike, who came a few years after Pattie, said "well dressed women—(they call them ladies)—harlots, priests, thieves, half-breed Indians—all spinning round together in the waltz." He was shocked when he saw a dirty, ragged man dressed in buckskins and moccasins, "hanging and whirling round the pretty wife of Pedro Vigil." The priest was there, too, dancing with a woman who paid her husband to stay away. Josiah Gregg, another visitor who was more philosophical than most, was still disgusted by women whirling through the dance with a cigarette dangling from their lips. Even more outrageous to him was the band—violin, guitar, and Indian drum—which played at the fandango Saturday night, then played the same tunes the next morning in church. Pike and Gregg confined their disgust to their

•

journals, but other Americans often expressed it more directly. Trappers particularly were likely to sneer at everything and also to misread the line of acceptable behavior and step across it. Virtually every story of New Mexico in these days has a scene in which the dancing and drinking grow wilder and the tension greater until the fandango explodes into a violent brawl.

Pattie's experiences at a fandango were entirely different. He also noted the musicians, and the large number of women in attendance, but he was much too interested in the dancing to see anything shocking. He described one dance in which the women, bodies still and erect, moved their feet slowly while the men, bent over, hammered their feet like drumsticks. Another dance, the *valse despacio*, he described as an elegant waltz danced to a slow, mournful tune. Pattie was so enthralled he tried it himself.

The difference in Pattie's attitude is notable. There is no horror at the kind of people present, no shock at the priest's dancing, no outrage at women smoking cigarettes. Nor does the dance end with a sudden, shattering brawl. Instead, the fandango is a quiet affair at which James enjoys himself so much that he danced "until near morning, when we retired to rest."

Pattie's account of Santa Fe is a quiet and sensible description free of the moral outrage so often expressed by Americans. Yet, into the midst of it, he suddenly inserts a melodramatic story filled with contempt for New Mexicans.

The story he tells is simple enough. While he and his father were in Santa Fe, they were awakened one night by the noise of a drum, fife, and French horn. Everyone else heard it, too, and the plaza was quickly filled with "frightened women, and the still more fear stricken men, joining in a full chorus of screams and cries." The first wave of rumors was that Santa Fe was being attacked by Comanche, but eventually the crowd calmed down enough to discover the Indians were nowhere near the city. Instead, a band of Comanche had raided a settlement on the Pecos River to

•

the east, killed several people, and captured five women, including the daughter of a former governor of New Mexico.

Spanish troops, accompanied by American trappers, were dispatched, and as usual in the narrative, Sylvester Pattie was placed in command of the entire campaign. They were successful in catching the Indians, defeating them, and re-capturing a flock of sheep they had stolen. It was the Americans, Pattie said, who won the victory while the Spanish troops ran. Then, once the Comanche were defeated, the Spanish troops returned and rode over the battlefield, trampling the bodies and lancing wounded Indians. The Americans had also rescued two women, one of whom was the governor's daughter, and the Spanish commander demanded he be allowed to take them to Santa Fe. Sylvester refused to turn them over and soundly berated the Spanish troops as cowards.

The story, with its romantic rescue and its improbabilities, is suspicious enough, but the most telling flaw is the lack of any supporting evidence. The story has been repeated by many, but in each case it rests solely on the testimony of James Pattie in the *Personal Narrative*. Both Ralph Twitchell, who used it extensively in *Leading Facts of New Mexico History*, and H. H. Bancroft, who alluded to it suspiciously in the *History of Arizona and New Mexico*, had access to extensive records. Neither, however, was able to cite any other contemporary account of this event, even though it supposedly involved the daughter of a prominent citizen. In fact, the records point the opposite way. Bancroft found that records concerning Indian affairs in this period were scanty and indefinite, while another historian, Lansing Bloom, took it a step further and cited the lack of records as evidence that there was little serious trouble with the Indians.

The closest contemporary account of the rescue of a governor's daughter in New Mexico is that of Timothy Flint in his novel *Francis Berrian*. Since Flint was Pattie's editor, it has often been suggested that he added this story to the narrative. The version Flint used in his novel, however, was

•

based on an event of the 1780s that involved the capture of a governor's daughter in Chihuahua. It was a well-known story in Louisiana, where Flint obtained it, but not in New Mexico. Although Flint's novel may have given Pattie the idea, his version is based on material he gathered in New Mexico.

There was one story that was being told in Taos about the time Pattie arrived. It involved an event that occurred two years earlier, and the story was still alive as late as 1831, when Albert Pike heard it. The storyteller, an American trader, was awakened by news that Navaho were attacking Taos. He went outside, where men, women, and children were running around wildly calling on God, the Virgin of Guadalupe, and various other saints to save them. Eventually, a line of armed men was formed and the Americans drove off the Navaho while the New Mexicans stood by ineffectually. Later, the same American joined a Mexican expedition to punish the Navaho. He accompanied it west, fought a battle, and helped capture some two thousand sheep and drive them back to Santa Fe.

There are some striking similarities with Pattie's story of the rescue of the governor's daughter. Not only are the situations roughly the same, but the frightened people running through Taos are almost identical to the frightened people running through Santa Fe in Pattie's version. Pattie also claims that besides rescuing the governor's daughter, they saved a flock of sheep. Since sheep were of more interest to Navahos than to Comanche raiders, he may well have started with a Navaho story and, for dramatic impact, changed the Indians to Comanche. Pattie has already shown his willingness to borrow material, and the story of the American trader was filled with just the kind of detail he needed to flesh out the story of how they rescued the governor's daughter.

It did not, however, provide him with a woman to rescue, and he had to find her elsewhere. In the narrative her name is Jacova, and Pattie describes, in detail, a meeting with her

•

in Santa Fe after the rescue. He met her father, the former governor, in a coffeehouse. They had coffee together, then the governor took Pattie upstairs to a room where he was greeted by Jacova and her sister. The two women spent the next hour talking to each other in Spanish, which Pattie did not understand. Finally, since it was getting dark, and since he was excluded from the conversation, he decided to leave. Jacova, however, blocked the door and pointed to a bed, where he was supposed to sleep. He tried to excuse himself on the grounds that his clothes were dirty, but Jacova effectively dismissed that by providing him with clean clothes. At first, he refused to take them, but she appeared so hurt that he put them on. Finally, an interpreter was called in, and through him Pattie was told that Jacova would always treasure the hunting shirt he had used to cover her when she was naked among the Indians. She then put it on to show him she was not ashamed of it. At this point, Pattie's narrative fades out with the comment "I went to bed early, and arose, and returned to my companions before any of the family was visible."

The story has some realistic details of the kind that Pattie often modified but rarely invented. At the same time it is based on a romanticized rescue that could not have happened. Possibly, one way to understand it is to retell it, keeping the basic detail and rejecting the romantic overtones. What it becomes is this:

Pattie, in a coffeehouse, meets a man—certainly not an ex-governor—who leads him upstairs to a room containing two women. The women ignore Pattie and continue to talk in Spanish. After a time—it need not be an hour; it may only have seemed that long—Pattie attempted to leave. Possibly he misunderstood why he had been brought there, possibly he changed his mind. Whatever the case, one of the women blocked the door and pointed to the bed. An interpreter was called in and while they were talking, Pattie suddenly noticed the woman parading around the room dressed only in his hunting shirt. After this, he spent the night. Although it

•

is cynical to rearrange the romantic dreams of youth, when the story is retold this way it takes on certain obvious connotations.

Possibly it was Flint's idea to blend all this into a rescue story, but Pattie himself may have toyed with the idea even as he was recording his experiences in New Mexico. The story began with the band—drum, fife, and French horn. Such bands often did march through the plaza, not to herald an Indian attack, but to announce a fandango that night. Pattie then broke away from the band to tell the story of the rescue and its romantic aftermath. Then, when that was over he went immediately to his account of the fandango. It could have been exactly what went through his mind in the time between the band's announcement and the dance itself.

One last ingredient—a former governor—was obtained after the Patties left Santa Fe. They had spent two weeks in the city while Pratte obtained a license and divided his large expedition into small trapping parties. Sylvester, James, the two men who had come with them from Missouri, and three men added by Pratte were sent south to trap the almost untouched Gila River. They left Santa Fe and traveled eighty miles down the Rio Grande where, Pattie said, they came to the residence of the former governor and his daughter Jacova.

Actually, traveling that distance down the Rio Grande would have brought them to the ranch of Francisco Javier Chavez, who was indeed a former governor of New Mexico. He also had five daughters: Barbara, Manuela Antonia, Francisca, Mercedes, and Dolores. Not even James Pattie, with his bad ear for Spanish, could have made Jacova out of any of these. Still, he claims she was there, and each time he passes by in the future he will add another story of how much she loves him. Yet, his description of the time he spent in her bedroom, and how she washed clothes for him, precludes her being the daughter of a governor or any other *rico*. Probably, this Jacova, as separate from the Santa Fe Jacova, was a Chavez servant who did Pattie's laundry and shared his bed whenever he passed through.

•

By the time James reached the Chavez ranch, he had all the necessary ingredients for his romantic rescue, but by then the time for collecting stories and fitting them into daydreams was over. Instead, it was time to make final preparations to cross the mountains and enter trapping country.

•

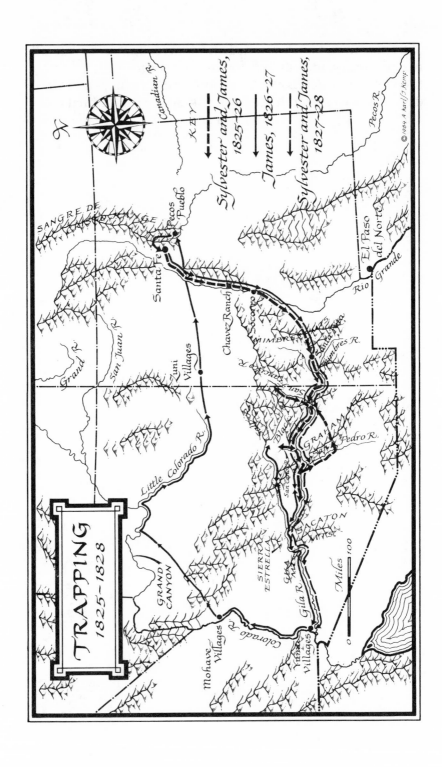

TRAPPING
1825–1828

KEY

Sylvester and James,
1825–26

James, 1826–27

Sylvester and James,
1827–28

© 1984 A.karl/J.Kemp

CHAPTER

S·I·X

YLVESTER AND HIS SMALL BAND OF TRAP-
pers spent two days making their final preparations at the Chavez ranch, which lay in the thin
green strip created by the Rio Grande as it cut
its way south across the desert. The ranch was one
of the most attractive places in New Mexico, and the
owner was always hospitable to passing trappers. Consequently, Sylvester had no trouble obtaining horses, flour,
and dried meat for the trip west. Another problem was also
solved when, just before they were ready to leave, a band of
seven trappers arrived from the north. They were also
headed for the Gila River to trap, and the two groups combined as a protection against the Indians.

One of the newcomers was almost certainly a redheaded
Missourian named Bill Williams. A month before he had
arrived in Taos with the road survey party. Soon afterward
he requested and received permission to spend the winter
trapping, and on November 14 he started down the Rio
Grande. It would have brought him to the Chavez ranch just
in time to join the Patties.

Williams was originally from North Carolina, but when
he was seven, his family moved to Missouri, where he grew
up on a farm just across the river from St. Charles. His
mother was a devout Baptist, and both Bill and his brother,
Lewis, became ministers. Lewis would eventually become a

•

famous Baptist preacher, but Bill soon left the ministry. Some stories say that he fell from grace because of a woman, others that he fell because of drink. Surely these stories are latter-day moralizing, for such sins among itinerant preachers were neither unknown nor unexpected.

Instead, he probably left the ministry because of new interests. As a preacher he had supplemented his income by hunting and trapping, and it led him to western Missouri, where he met the Osage Indians. He may have intended to become a missionary to the Indians, but if so, the idea did not survive long. He settled at the Big Osage town, learned the language, hunted with the Indians, and finally married an Osage woman in a native ceremony. His mother, the devout Baptist, later said that he had become two-thirds Osage, while the Osage, at best, had become only a very small part Christian.

Williams, in the years to come, would be fully accepted by the Osage. In the winter he lived among them in an Indian lodge at the Big Osage town. When spring came, however, the Osage were great travelers who wandered over much of the West in a search for buffalo and for adventure. Since Williams was part of the tribe, he undoubtedly accompanied them and reached the Rockies and New Mexico long before other trappers. Several men who knew him later placed his first arrival in the mountains sometime between 1807 and 1815. By 1825, however, the old free life of the Osage was ending. They signed a treaty ceding most of their land in Missouri to the United States and then moved to a reservation in Oklahoma. Shortly afterward Williams joined the road survey party and in October 1825 arrived in Taos. A month later he headed south down the Rio Grande to go trapping.

In later years, after he became a legend, he would tell listeners that he had always lived in the West and had been there since the day he rolled out of a mountain thunderstorm. He also claimed he had descended from the stars—

•

the Great Bear or some other celestial animal—and had been placed on earth for a special purpose that would someday be made clear to him.

These stories, whether he believed them or made them up to feed his own legend, came later. In 1825 he could not have told such tales, for those he joined knew him too well. The claim to have rolled out of a mountain thunderstorm would have brought only a snort of disgust, for Sylvester Pattie remembered him when he was a sergeant in the St. Charles militia. He was just a man, although at first glance he did have the look of a god, for he was tall, gaunt, tough, and muscular. Beyond the first impression, however, one could see flaws in his godlike appearance. His voice was a high-pitched whine that sometimes rose to a cackle; his long nose almost met his chin; and his face was covered with the scars left by the ravages of smallpox when he was a boy. More than that, he was no longer young, for at thirty-eight he had reached the brink of an ungodlike middle age. By then, he was already set in his ways, wearing a greasy black-felt hat and buckskin clothes and riding hunched over the saddle-horn with his rifle laid across the pommel. In later years it was enough to cause him to be singled out by newcomers to the Southwest. In 1825 he probably did not look much different from any of the others as they rode south.

The fourteen men left the Chavez ranch and slowly descended the Rio Grande. They were trappers going to the headwaters of the Gila, and thus they followed the road down the west side of the river where there were several good campsites. One was in a cottonwood grove at the foot of the sand hills just across from La Joya. The river itself was an easy place to catch soft-shelled turtles and catfish, while the marshes along the edge were filled with waterfowl—teals, plovers, and immense numbers of geese and sandhill cranes. South of here, below the village of Polvadera, the sand hills closed in and narrowed the river valley. The stands of cottonwood, however, became more abundant and made it easier to find fuel for cooking fires.

•

On the west bank of the river, sixty miles below the Chavez ranch, was the town of Socorro. The large church dominated the town, and travelers from the north could see it long before any of the other buildings. Socorro was the last settlement in this part of the country, and those going south to El Paso and Chihuahua crossed the river here to join the road down the east bank. For those going west rather than south, the next settlement was so far as to be virtually nonexistent.

Socorro, because of its position, made a small business of supplying horses and mules to travelers going west. Sylvester's party stopped to obtain a few more horses, as did other parties after them. James made no comment on the Socorro traders, either because they were lucky or because they were the first party to pass through. Later travelers, however, complained about the sharp practices, and one man, after making a deal, said, "The tricks of the horse jockeys are not confined to the Anglo Saxon race."

One advantage of being a horse trader in Socorro was that a man did not have to leave town to do business. Most New Mexicans living along the Rio Grande seldom ventured far from the settled areas for fear of Indians. Apache from the southwest and Navaho from the northwest frequently raided the ranches along the Rio Grande, driving off horses, cattle, and sheep and often taking captives. As late as 1846— twenty years after Pattie was there—a New Mexican who lived in the more settled country north of Socorro told an American he would not fish in the Rio Grande for fear the Navaho would get him.

Socorro itself was almost within sight of Apache country. Off to the west was a large range of mountains beyond which lived the Western Apache. They often crossed the mountains to raid, or simply to watch what was happening along the river. Years later a United States Army expedition was no more than a few miles out of Socorro when one of the guides pointed to something on the ridge of foothills to the west. The soldiers saw nothing except some trees, but

•

125

the guide insisted they were Apache and was later proven right when they came down from the hills to talk. James Pattie, twenty years earlier, saw no Indians along this stretch nor did he see any for a long time to come. The fourteen trappers, on the other hand, were probably seldom out of sight of the Apache.

South of Socorro the party followed the Rio Grande for four more days, then turned west and traveled another four days until they reached the Santa Rita copper mines. During the next few years the copper mines would become the closest thing to home for Sylvester and James, but at this time they were in too much of a hurry to linger. They spent only one night there, and the next morning pushed on toward the headwaters of the Gila to begin trapping.

James was now back in the wilderness, and his *Personal Narrative* once again becomes lucid. Earlier, while crossing the plains, he had given a clear and accurate account of the country. Once he reached New Mexico, however, his descriptions become vague, cryptic, and often confused. Now, with the New Mexican settlements behind him, for some reason he is able to give a detailed account. Once again, with only minor adjustments, his route is clear and his descriptions are accurate.

After a night at the copper mines, the trappers, with two men they had hired at the mines, left for the Gila. They traveled northwest through hilly country covered with pine, live oak, and piñon, and reached the Gila by way of Sapillo Creek. It was good trapping country, and the first night on the river they took thirty beaver. The next morning they decided that James and another man, once again anonymous, should ascend the river to explore while the rest of the party slowly trapped upstream.

Pattie and his companion spent the next day ascending the Gila through a wide, heavily timbered valley. James, with his eye for bears, saw several, but since they were minding their own business, he did the same. By evening the two men reached a point where the mountains closed in on

•

the river. The next day was much more difficult, for the high bluffs that closed in the river forced them to cross it thirty-six times. Several times they had to scramble on their hands and knees through heavy underbrush and grapevines, and Pattie, remembering the bears he had seen the day before, feared constantly he would meet one coming through the brush the other way. Finally, with great relief, they reached the mouth of the east fork, where the valley widened and traveling became easier.

That night they camped on the point where the middle and west forks of the Gila join. Nearby they found a hot spring next to the river, and Pattie, possibly with tongue in cheek, told a story of how he could catch a fish in the river, without moving throw it into the spring, and six minutes later extract a thoroughly cooked fish. The springs are hot, but not that hot, and Pattie's story is possible only if he liked his fish very rare.

The next morning the two separated, each to explore a different fork of the Gila and to meet back at the junction in four days. Pattie went upstream through the heavy brush of the west fork and, as usual, saw several bears. Bears and bear stories were fine when he was traveling with other people, but now, traveling alone, he admitted he was scared. Being alone in the daytime was bad enough. It was worse when it started to get dark. Finally, he found a large pile of driftwood, and set it on fire to frighten off any animals—particularly bears. If his pile of driftwood was anywhere near the size of those that still pile up along the west fork, he must have lit up the early December darkness for a considerable distance up and down the canyon. Once he had his fire going, he shot a turkey, roasted it, had dinner, and then went to bed. For the first time in his life he was trying to sleep alone in the wilderness. His only comment was "I did not fall asleep for some time."

Eventually, he dozed off, and possibly he slept long enough for the fire to die down. Or he may have known enough to move away from the fire before going to sleep, for

•

it could be seen by every Apache within miles. Whatever the case, when he awakened there was no fire, and lying on a log within six feet of him was a mountain lion. Admirably, he did not bolt, but brought his gun up slowly and fired at the lion's head. Then he bolted. He ran several yards, not knowing whether he had hit the lion. He stopped to reload, but then he heard shots from across the ridge that separated him from where his companion was camped. He forgot about the lion and never made it clear if he hit it, or if it had run in the opposite direction.

Possibly he never knew, for the shots from across the ridge made him think his companion had been attacked by Indians, and thus he had something else to worry about. He immediately set off downstream and by daylight was back at the hot spring. He said nothing about how fast he went, but what had taken all day to travel, he now covered, in reverse, in the few remaining hours of darkness. However fast he came down the canyon, it was not fast enough to beat his companion, who was already waiting for him at the hot spring. He, too, had been sleeping, but was awakened by Pattie's shot. He saw not a lion, but a huge bear standing over him. He fired two shots, one from his rifle, the other from his pistol, then descended his canyon even faster. It was a remarkable coincidence that two men could awaken at precisely the same moment to find wild animals standing over them. Possibly there were very distinct lions and bears. Possibly, too, there were just dark, moving shadows of things that looked like lions and bears.

After this the two decided to stay together, first going up one fork of the river, then crossing the ridge and coming down the other. After they finished exploring, they returned to the Gila and somewhere below the forks met the main body of trappers. It was a severely diminished group, for the seven men who had joined them at the Chavez ranch had broken away and headed down the Gila. Those left behind were angry, and James Pattie charged the men who had gone with "desertion."

•

"Desertion" is a strong word, for it implies there was some kind of formal agreement when these seven joined Sylvester's party. Given the chance meeting on the Rio Grande, it is more likely that they simply agreed to travel together. When the others wanted to go on down the Gila, Sylvester had to wait for the two men sent to explore the river. The seven who were ready to leave did not feel bound to wait, for it was not their men who were delaying the departure.

Again, it sounds very much like Bill Williams. In later years he would gain a reputation, even among trappers, as a thorough individualist who felt no binding tie to any group. When he made up his mind to leave an expedition, he would pack his horse and go, "stoically deaf to all remonstrances." Since he was thirty-eight years old by now, surely that personality trait was already well developed.

Still, those left behind were angry, not so much at the desertion, but because the others were trapping out the river as they went. At first they tried to catch up, but their horses were tired and tender-footed. Finally, they gave up and slowed down to take what beaver they could. They had no luck, for those ahead of them had either caught or alarmed beaver all along the Gila.

Sylvester's band was now below the mouth of Sapillo Creek, and once again they reached a place where the mountains closed in upon the river and made it impassable. They retreated some distance upstream, then left the river to climb into the mountains to the south. They had great trouble pushing their tired horses and, because of the season, were unable to find any game in the mountains. After three days of traveling cross-country, they returned to the Gila, near where it turns west after flowing through the Big Burro Mountains. Each evening they put their traps in the water; each morning they found them empty.

By now, they were hungry, for they still were unable to find any game. One of James's dogs, which had been with him all the way from Missouri, ran down a rabbit, but di-

·

vided among seven men it provided each with only a few mouthfuls of meat. The lack of food had its effect on the party. There was complaining, no one saw any hope of ever catching another beaver, and some wanted to return to civilization. It was late December—Christmastime—and not too far away New Mexicans were celebrating with their annual round of feasts, festivals, and fandangos.

Finally—James makes it the day after Christmas—they decided to kill one of the horses for food. The horse herd by now was a nondescript bunch. Sylvester was still riding a "fine American horse" he had brought from Missouri, but the rest of the herd was filled with animals from St. Louis, the Pawnee villages, the Chavez ranch, and Socorro. One of them, probably one of the weaker scrubs, was killed and eaten, although not much enjoyed. James thought it would have been better if it had been served with bread and salt. Still, the horsemeat, bad as it was, restored some strength and some confidence, and there was new hope of finding some untrapped streams.

On New Year's Day, 1826, they finally had some success. They reached the mouth of the San Francisco River, where they could see from the signs that the other party had gone on down the Gila and left the San Francisco untrapped. Thus, Sylvester led his small party up the river, and almost immediately their situation improved. Four miles upstream they camped, put their traps in the water, then shot two fat turkeys to roast for dinner. It was an omen of things to come, for the next morning they took up their traps and found thirty-seven beaver. It instantly restored their spirits, and James said, "Exhilarating prospects now opened before us, and we pushed on with animation." They went almost to the headwaters, found a new source of food in the Rocky Mountain sheep, which when cooked tasted like mutton, and, more important, took 250 beaver.

Later, in the *Personal Narrative,* James claimed he was among the first white men to explore the Gila and also took credit for naming the San Francisco River. Neither claim is

•

accurate, for the Gila had been known since early times, while the San Francisco had been named in 1747 by a Spanish military expedition. Unwittingly, Pattie denied his own claim by his accurate knowledge of how the San Francisco related to the surrounding country. The right-hand fork of the river, he said, headed in the same mountains as the left or west fork of the Gila. In the same area was the source of the Red River, a reference not to the Colorado, but to the Little Colorado, which rises just over the divide from the San Francisco. Since Pattie did not cross over to the headwaters of either the Gila or Little Colorado, his only way of knowing this was from someone who had. Quite likely the information came from the two men Sylvester had hired at Santa Rita. Although James insisted on calling them servants, they were probably hired as guides instead.

By late January the seven trappers were back on the Gila, where they dug a deep pit and cached the furs they had taken during the past weeks. Once again, they began to descend the Gila, but trapping was still hopeless because of those who had gone before. A few days later, however, while they were in camp, four half-starved survivors of the other party arrived. They had been attacked by Indians, who had stolen their horses and furs and in the process killed one of the trappers. The next day two more survivors arrived, one of them with a severe head wound caused by an arrow. Despite their anger, Sylvester's party treated the survivors well. They fed them, then offered to accompany them downriver to attack the Indians and recover the horses and furs. The six survivors, however, were adamantly opposed to going back into Indian country even with reinforcements. Instead, they took some horses and some dried meat and left for the settlements along the Rio Grande.

Again, it fits Bill Williams's known activities. All this happened, according to Pattie, in late January 1826. A month later, on February 24, Williams, after coming up the Rio Grande from the south, arrived in Santa Fe. His return was a surprise, for when he left in November he said he planned to

•

be gone until June. Since he had come back several months early, something had happened to change his plans. Yet, if Williams was a member of the party Pattie described, he said nothing about an attack, but rather said he had considerable success in trapping. Certainly he had enough money for a stake, for two weeks later his old boss George Sibley reported that Williams had been gambling steadily since his return. Possibly Pattie's story was overdramatized and Williams left the mountains under better circumstances. Possibly, too, he raised a stake by selling Pattie's horse.

On the Gila Sylvester went ahead with his plans to descend the river. After the others left, even though it was evening and a storm threatened, they packed up and moved downriver. It began to snow soon after they made camp in a large cavern on the south side of the river. By morning there were almost five inches of snow on the ground. The horses, without shelter from the wind-driven snow, had broken their ropes and disappeared. James Pattie and another man were sent to find them, and after some searching they found the place where they had crossed the Gila.

James was not the best man to send, for he was easily distracted, at least when there was a bear around. He and his companion crossed the river and began to follow a creek that came into the Gila from the north. A short distance upstream they saw a cave and around the mouth were signs that there was a bear inside. Pattie immediately forgot about the missing horses and suggested they crawl into the cave and shoot the bear.

James's friend, as usual, was anonymous, but at least he was sensible, for he flatly refused to enter the cave. They spent some time arguing, and James said, "I reminded him, that I had, more than once, stood by him in a similar adventure." When that didn't work, Pattie switched to the argument that a bear was much less formidable in a cave than he was out in the open. Apparently, that was even less convincing, for his companion still refused.

Finally, Pattie decided to enter the cave alone. He made a

•

torch out of a pine knot, attached it to a long stick, and with it lined up alongside his gun so he could see down the sights, he entered the cave. For about twenty yards he saw nothing, then, rising in the light of his torch, he saw a bear growling and gnashing its teeth. Pattie aimed between the eyes, fired, and began his retreat. He moved too fast, for he stumbled accidentally, put out the light, and found himself in complete darkness with the bear growling behind him. He moved even faster, falling and dropping his gun, rising and falling several more times. When he emerged, his companion told him he was "as pale as a corpse."

James admitted that "it was some time, before I could summon sufficient courage to re-enter the cavern for my gun." Eventually, he made another torch, borrowed his friend's gun, and crawled back into the cave. It was quiet inside, and after Pattie found his gun he moved a few steps farther and saw that the bear was dead. He went out again and successfully enticed the other man into the cave. They tried to drag the bear out, but it was too large. Therefore, they left the cave, found the horses—which was what they had been sent to do—then returned to camp for help. Sylvester, when he heard the story, severely reprimanded James for the foolishness of his actions. Nonetheless, the bear was a welcome addition to the food supply. They dried the meat, extracted the oil, and stored much of it in the cavern to use when they returned.

When they finished butchering the bear and storing the dried meat and bear oil, they again started down the Gila. For the first time there was hope of finding untrapped country beyond the point where the others had been turned back by Indians. They found that point two days after they left the cave and recognized it instantly from the remains of the trapper who had been killed a week before. James, in the narrative, handled it bluntly: "We gathered up the parts of the body, and buried them. At this point we commenced setting our traps."

Once they reached untrapped waters they moved slowly

•

down the Gila between high mountains, the Graham and Santa Teresa off to the south, the Gila Mountains to the north. They had been fortunate thus far, for they had moved through the heart of Apache country without seeing any Indians. It was not until they reached the mouth of the San Carlos River that they saw their first Apache. Even then, it was not a band of warriors, but a small group of Indians who were so startled that they ran, leaving behind some rabbit-skin robes, some bread made from mesquite beans, and a small child. Pattie, who had earlier complained of not having bread to eat with his horsemeat, tried some and found it delicious. The child, however, caused a problem, for although it was just a baby, it was old enough to scream and try to run from the white men. Finally, they tied it so it could not wander off, then left, assuming the Indians would return after they were gone. The next day James and another man slipped back to check and found the Indians had returned for the child. They had also taken everything of value from their own camp, and left, by way of gratitude, a large, dressed buckskin. Pattie took it, and in its place left a red handkerchief. Later, when the trappers passed by again, the handkerchief was gone, but nothing else had been left.

The trappers, after they left the Indian camp, turned up the San Carlos, but after four days of finding no beaver they turned back. Once again, they descended the Gila, and as they traveled they frequently saw fresh Indian sign. They penned the horses each night, feeding them bark stripped from cottonwood trees rather than allowing them to graze. It was a wise precaution, but still they saw no Indians.

Finally, they reached a point where the trail along the river was blocked by high mountains. They turned to the north and followed a small stream until they reached its source in a large snowbank near the summit. They climbed the mountain hoping to see, off to the west, the Gila emerging into flat country. Instead, from the top of the mountain it looked hopeless. The country below was filled with dark

•

134

storm clouds, and all they could see to the west were mountains rising through the clouds.

It was too cold to stand still. They started down the west side of the mountain and descended into the heavy mist and clouds. The country was cold and wet, the ground was slick, and in the steep descent the horses and mules frequently fell. Eventually, they reached a stream that was flowing in the right direction and which provided a somewhat level trail. It was a false hope, for before long this stream also dropped into a deep canyon. Again, they climbed out of the stream bed and onto the cliffs, where the passage sometimes became so difficult they had to unload the pack animals and carry the goods themselves. Finally, with their provisions gone and their animals worn out, they were forced to stop.

They stayed in camp for two days, and eventually the weather cleared enough so that to the west they could see the Gila winding across flat country. They could also see smoke rising from Indian villages, and since they were hungry, the danger was less important than the food they might find. This encouragement, small as it was, was enough to get them moving again. Three days later they reached the Gila and stumbled on a small village. The Indians fled, but left behind some mush made from grass seed that the trappers devoured "without scruple." That night they put their traps in the water and the next morning they had ten beaver. Although eventually the furs would be valuable, for the moment the tails, roasted over a fire, were more important.

That morning James was one of two men sent ahead to clear a trail for the packhorses. For once, he lifted the veil of anonymity enough to identify the other man as a trapper named Allen. The two of them, as they rode ahead of the party, saw several Indian camps, but they were all deserted. Once, however, they came close to a village without seeing it and without being seen by the Indians. The first sign that there was anyone around came when Pattie fired at a goose in the river and suddenly heard screams. He rode toward the

•

135

sound and saw the entire populace of an Indian village fleeing toward the mountains that bordered the river. He and Allen followed, trying to convince the Indians that they wanted to be friends. The Indians, however, were not assured by two mounted white man bearing down on them. They fired arrows, and according to Pattie, Allen lost his temper, began cursing the Indians, and finally raised his rifle to fire at them. Pattie said he grabbed the rifle and was successful in convincing Allen it would be madness to kill an Indian.

Some of the story is real enough, but not all of it. Pattie's companion was almost certainly Hiram Allen, an experienced fur trapper. He had been one of Ashley's lieutenants at the Arikara villages; he had been one of those who pulled the bear off Hugh Glass; and later, in a difficult situation, George Yount would surrender command to him because he considered him more fit to lead. He was exactly the kind of man to be chosen to go ahead of the main party to clear the trail and scout for Indians. Since only one experienced man could reasonably be spared, the likeliest companion would be a young man, like James Pattie, who could learn something from the experienced old hunter.

Probably the basic story is true enough. The two men, Allen and Pattie, pushed ahead of the main group, took some Indians by surprise, and in the aftermath one man stayed calm, the other panicked. Hiram Allen, given the things he had done in the past and would do in the future, was clearly a cool, capable, and experienced man. James Pattie, however, was the man who on the spur of the moment foolishly tried to capture a buffalo calf alive, and who rashly entered a bear's den alone. Given this, Pattie's story probably is twisted. Everything may well have happened as he described it, except that it was Allen who stopped Pattie from shooting an Indian. In writing it, Pattie, since it put him in a bad light, simply reversed the roles. It is a type of literary license often used by writers.

Whoever panicked was stopped from shooting an Indian

•

and setting off a major battle. Instead, the two white men went back to the village to look for food. They found a pit covered with a mound of fresh dirt on top of which was a fire. They opened the pit and found what Pattie thought was a large vegetable that the Indians had been baking. It was the root of the maguey, which was baked in pits, then sometimes eaten, but more frequently fermented into a liquor called mescal. This one, however, was still in the first stage of baking, and thus was for eating rather than for drinking.

Soon afterward the rest of the trappers caught up, and the next day they reached the San Pedro River, which flowed into the Gila from the south. It was a promising source of beaver, and they turned upstream to trap. The trapping was so good they named it Beaver River, and within a few days they had another two hundred pelts. They brought the fur back to the Gila, where they again dug a large pit and cached the fur. Then, once more, they followed the Gila to the west. After ten days slowly trapping along the river, they turned back.

At that point, somewhere near the Sacaton Mountains in Arizona, they had penetrated the Southwest as far as any American. By now, it had been almost five months since they had left the Rio Grande and turned into the mountains. They had traveled several hundred miles through Indian country, first the territory of the Chiricahua Apache, then the White Mountain Apache, and then the various bands of the San Carlos Apache. Finally, in the desert stretches of the Gila, they had entered the eastern fringes of Pima country. Through all this they had little trouble with the Indians, and the few small bands they met had always fled at the sight of white men.

Their luck had been remarkably good. Not only had they avoided serious Indian trouble, but despite the earlier desertion, the rough country, and several days of hunger, the trapping had also gone well. When they turned back, they had the furs they had taken during the ten days on the lower Gila. Farther east, at the mouths of the San Carlos and San

•

Francisco River, they had cached several hundred more. By the time they collected them all, they would have as much as they could carry.

Their worst problem had been the high mountains north of the Gila, and on the way home they decided to avoid them. At the mouth of the San Pedro, they dug up their furs; then, instead of following the Gila, they turned up the San Pedro to look for a new way to the east. Six miles up the river they went into camp to make final preparations for the trip home. While some of the men were in camp drying beaver skins and Sylvester was building a horse pen, James was given the task of taking the horses out to graze and watching them until the pen was finished.

As usual, his attention wandered. He was sitting on a hill watching the horses grazing below, when he heard the sound of geese and ducks. Looking down the hill in the other direction, he saw a lake and in it three beaver lodges. He immediately forgot about the horses and rushed off to tell the others. Although they had as much fur as they could carry, they could not resist taking just a few more pelts, and they dropped what they were doing and hurried to the lake with their traps. On the way they noticed that the horses and mules were bunched up, but they assumed it was because they had finished grazing. Just as James stepped into the water to place a trap, however, there were shots, yells, and the sound of stampeding horses.

Arrows began to splash into the lake; the trappers all ran for camp, but even after they reached it, they were under heavy fire. The Indians were now on top of the hill, out of range of rifle fire, but able to shoot arrows down on the white men. The trappers retreated into a grove of cottonwoods to wait for the Indians to come down the hill into rifle range. Instead, they stayed there, yelling insults and occasionally firing a random arrow into the grove. The trappers were able to regroup and found that no one had been hurt, but that they had lost all the horses, including the fine American horse Sylvester had ridden all the way from Missouri.

•

Eventually, the noise on the hill died down, and the Indians disappeared. The trappers came out of the cottonwoods and began to fortify their camp in case there was another attack. The Indians, however, were apparently satisfied with their loot, for they could be seen riding away on the stolen horses. It had been a tense several minutes, and after it was over, James "retired a little distance from camp," and stumbled directly into an ambush. He let out a surprised yell, which brought first his father, then the rest of the trappers, and for a few minutes there was a small but intense battle. Then the Indians fled, leaving behind four of their horses. It was all over, at least for the day, and during the night there was no sign of Indians.

The next morning, while the trappers were rather complacently eating breakfast, they saw several Indians trying to sneak into camp. A few shots sent them back to the top of the hill, where they paraded the stolen horses and shouted insults in Spanish. One of the trappers spoke Spanish, and he found that the Indians were, as Pattie heard it, Eiotaro. His ear for Spanish was still bad, although improving, for the actual word was "Coyotero," a term often used to describe any of the various bands of Western Apache. Given the location, these probably were part of the Aravaipa band of San Carlos Apache.

The same conversation established that the white men were not, as the Apache thought, Spaniards, but rather Americans. When they heard this, the Indians appeared to be astounded, then apologetic, and finally said they were now ready to be friends. To demonstrate this, they proposed that the white men bring the four Apache horses to the top of the hill where they would be exchanged for those taken from the trappers. The white men countered with what they thought was a more reasonable offer. The Apache would bring the American horses down and put them in the pen, then the white men would turn the Apache horses loose. The Indians dismissed this with derisive laughter, which convinced the trappers they had no real desire to be friends.

•

Therefore, they fired several shots to scatter the Indians, then began to make preparations to leave.

The loss of the pack animals made it impossible to carry both furs and provisions. Thus, they reburied the furs they had recently uncovered, loaded the provisions on the four horses they had taken from the Apache, and left the place where they had been attacked. The next three days they followed the San Pedro thirty-five or forty miles upstream, then left the river and turned into the Galiuro Mountains to the east. The last night on the river they caught two beaver, dried the meat for later use, and made the skins into make-shift canteens. To make matters worse, however, they found that their other provisions had spoiled and were unusable. They were also on foot, wearing moccasins that were not meant for long hikes in rocky country.

The first day they made the steep climb to the top of the mountains. It was late March, and although temperatures were warm in the San Pedro Valley, it was "icy" in the mountains, where some of the peaks reached almost eight thousand feet. The game was still in the lower country, and after the first day the meat of the two beaver was gone. It was on this day, as they climbed the mountain, that James's attitude toward his father began to change. He had always described him as capable of handling anything but during the climb he saw him "sinking with fatigue and weakness." James, who was twenty-one, was quick enough to blame it on age, for his father, he said, "had already passed the meridian of his days." Sylvester, at the age of forty-three, might have disagreed.

They descended the mountains into the Aravaipa Valley, where again the temperature was surprisingly warm after the cold mountains. There was game at this level, and they were able to shoot an antelope. After two days without food they did not wait to butcher it and cook the meat, but drained the blood and drank it. James thought it tasted like fresh milk. At least it restored them and also gave them meat for the next few meals.

•

The meat, however, did not last long divided among the entire party, and by the time they crossed the valley and began to climb the Graham Mountains, James was again complaining of hunger. An even more pressing problem was the lack of water. They had been successful in finding a small amount that allowed the men to drink, but there was not enough for the horses.

Early one morning, however, they saw the smoke of an Indian camp. They crept up to it, found it contained only women and children, but most importantly, they discovered, there was food and water. They fired over the heads of the Indians, scattering them into the forest, then rushed in to grab all the food they could find. Pattie justified it simply by saying, "Hunger knows no laws." The food was maguey and some seeds, which had been made into mush. There was not much of it, but again it gave them enough strength to keep going.

By now, their moccasins were worn out and most of the men were barefoot; they moved slowly and painfully down the east side of the mountain toward the Gila. Again, James Pattie prided himself on his youth and ability to bear hardships, but he worried about his "poor father who was reduced to a mere skeleton." By the time they reached the Gila, Sylvester was too weak to travel farther. The other hunters tried to shoot some game, but all they found was a raven, a buzzard, and an otter caught in one of the beaver traps. All three were small, and the raven and buzzard, at best, were sickening.

Sylvester was still too weak to travel farther without food, and he began to eye his son's dogs, which had been with them since the beginning. Finally, Sylvester prepared lots to be drawn, the loser to kill a dog. James refused, for fear he would be the one chosen. Were it his own life, he said, he would rather starve than kill one of his dogs. It was his father, however, and he said, "I was aware that it was a duty to allow it to be done." The dog was killed, and Sylvester found the flesh "sweet, nutritive and strengthening." It

•

141

would have made more sense to have killed one of the horses, but apparently Sylvester wanted to save them to pack the bear oil and furs they had left on their way down-river.

The dog meat revived Sylvester, and within a few days he was ready to travel again. Two days later they reached the cave where they had stored the bear oil. They shot some turkeys, which solved the immediate food problem, and some deer, which, when jerked, provided food for the rest of the trip. The deer hide also solved a problem for James, who had traveled a long distance barefoot. He was able to make some moccasins to cushion his feet, which by now were so painful he was unable to sleep at night. They lay in camp here for two days, then moved down to the mouth of the San Francisco, where they dug up the furs they had cached. From here, they headed directly east, and four days later emerged from the wilderness at the Santa Rita copper mines.

CHAPTER

S·E·V·E·N

I T WAS LATE APRIL 1826 WHEN SYLVESTER, James, and the rest of the party arrived at the copper mines. Five months earlier they had stopped here briefly on their way west. At that time they still had a long string of horses and hopes of finding a fortune in beaver fur. Now, the horses were gone, run off by Apache, and most of the fur was still buried in a pit somewhere on the San Pedro River, three hundred miles to the west. All they had when they returned to the mines were the four horses taken from the Apache, some bear oil, and whatever furs they had dug up at the mouth of the San Francisco River. Not only were they discouraged, but if the suffering portrayed by James in the narrative is anywhere near correct, they were also exhausted physically, mentally, and emotionally.

Fortunately, there was help available at the mines. Juan Onis, the superintendent, was friendly, and willing to do as much as he could for the Americans. James, usually ready to take offense at the least sign of mistreatment, thought Onis behaved like "a gentleman of the highest order." Later the two became friends, and it was Onis who taught him to speak Spanish. For all this, James was still unable to get his name right and always referred to him as "Don Juan Unis."

Although Onis was able to supply the Americans' immediate needs, he could not provide any further help, for he had problems of his own. Santa Rita was in a virtual state of

•

siege, and the Apache were keeping a close watch on those at the mines. Each time a party went out to make charcoal, they were attacked, and as a result the smelter had almost ceased operating. A band of Apache had also recently run off most of the horses, and Onis did not have any to lend to the Americans. The only way to retrieve the furs left on the San Pedro was for someone to go to Santa Fe and obtain more horses and more supplies for the trip.

After a few days' rest some of the trappers were ready to go. Sylvester, apparently still weak from his collapse on the Gila, did not accompany them. James, however, went along, riding one of the Apache horses, now equipped with new copper shoes. The trip east to the Rio Grande was routine until they reached the Chavez ranch. Jacova was there, according to Pattie, and he still insists she was the governor's daughter. Whoever she was—governor's daughter, servant girl, or figment of James's imagination—she was shocked when she saw him, and James's description of what he looked like after five months in the wilderness is realistic enough.

Whatever food Onis had supplied had not yet taken effect, for he was gaunt, reduced to "skin and bone" by the starvation and fatigue of the last part of the trip. His clothes, buckskin pants and hunting shirt, were still covered with five months' dirt, and his hair was long, matted, and uncombed. Part of it, however, was at least hidden from view by the old straw hat he was wearing. Strange as he looked—tired, thin, and dirty—he did not stand out, for his companions looked as bad as he did.

He later remembered those days at the ranch as an idyllic interlude. He had left some clothes there on his way downriver and, for the first time in months, he was able to put on clean clothes. He got a haircut, borrowed a better horse, and although he doesn't specifically mention it, he was undoubtedly able to obtain several decent meals.

He stayed three days at the ranch, then left for Santa Fe. In the capital he met several men who had come across the

·

plains with him the previous summer. Most of them were chance meetings between men who had once traveled together, but he must have specifically sought out S. S. Pratte, for he found him ill in bed. Not only was Pratte sick, but he complained to Pattie that he had lost several men he had sent out on trapping expeditions. He also had despaired of ever seeing the Patties again and badly wanted to talk to Sylvester. James, throughout the narrative, always maintained that he and his father were independent operators in the fur trade. The fact that he sought out Pratte, and the conversation that they had, indicate that Pratte had sent them out and had been waiting for a report.

Pattie finished whatever business he had with Pratte, obtained horses, and loaded the trade goods that he and his father had earlier stored in Santa Fe. None of those who had come with him from the copper mines were willing to return, and Pattie hired a man to help him. They traveled back to the mines, again stopping briefly at the Chavez ranch. Pattie again persists in his claim that the governor and his daughter could not resist him. This time the old man made him a present of a gold chain, while Jacova insisted she would always remember him. A week after leaving here, he was once again at the copper mines.

An expedition was immediately outfitted to go to the San Pedro River and retrieve the furs. According to James, who said he went with it, the expedition left on June 7 and returned a month later. Yet, on June 14 James served as a witness to a promissory note signed at the copper mines. It said, "Copper mines, June the 14 1826. Due Sylvester Pattie two hundred and fourty dollars it being the value received of him, witness my hand and seal. William Weir. Atest James Pattie."

Possibly only his dates are confused, but his one-sentence summary of the trip to the San Pedro and back adds weight to the argument that he did not go along. Instead, he probably waited with his father at the copper mines. When the expedition returned, they learned that the Indians had bro-

•

ken into the cache and the furs were gone. James said, "The whole fruit of our long, toilsome and dangerous expedition was lost, and all my golden hopes of prosperity and comfort vanished like a dream."

Things were not quite that bad. When the furs disappeared, the Patties had lost a considerable amount of money, but after June 14 they also had a promissory note for $240. That, too, was a considerable sum at the time, and although it was only a promise to pay, it could easily be discounted for cash by an American merchant in Santa Fe. Eventually, Sylvester would do just that, but not until September 1827. The fact that he held the note for fifteen months is clear evidence that during this time he was not severely pressed for money.

They also had found a decent place to temporarily settle in New Mexico. By July 1826 they were through with all the problems caused by the spring hunt, and the fall trapping season was still several months away. Thus, they prepared to leave for Santa Fe, probably intending, like other trappers, to spend the summer either there or in Taos. Just before they left, however, Juan Onis offered them a job at the mines.

The Apache had become so menacing that Onis needed guards to protect the charcoal makers when they went into the woods. He offered them a dollar a day, but because of his earlier help, they would not accept it. Besides, the Patties were at loose ends until the next trapping season, and the copper mines were a pleasant place to spend a summer.

The job was easy enough. All they had to do was accompany the charcoal makers into the woods, check the area, then sit back and watch them work. There was plenty of extra time to hunt deer and bear, which were plentiful. Yet, not all of this could have been done in lazy comfort, for in the summer the rainy season comes to Santa Rita. It usually begins in July, with heavy thunderstorms accompanied by spectacular displays of lightning, and continues on through August and September. Not only did the rain bring wetness and discomfort, but it often made traveling dangerous. John

•

Bartlett, who was there a few years after Pattie, saw the first rain of the year turn an almost dry arroyo into a rapidly flowing stream that was difficult to cross. A mile or so below Santa Rita, after several more streams flowed into the arroyo, it was impossible to cross even with mules.

It was during this summer that James found the time to learn Spanish from Onis. He claimed he learned it quickly and fluently, and probably he did. Although, as the narrative shows, he never quite learned to spell, his spoken Spanish was fluent enough so that he could later serve as an interpreter. Sylvester, however, never bothered to learn, and two years later in California he still could not understand Spanish.

The free and easy life of hunting and learning Spanish was in direct contrast to the life of those who worked in the mine. Most of them were not skilled miners, but convicts who had been shipped north from Chihuahua. Don Francisco Elguea, who had first opened the mines twenty years before, was a wealthy Chihuahua merchant with the necessary contacts to obtain prisoners. Elguea had since died, but his heirs owned the mine and used Onis as their superintendent. They were still receiving convicts, either because of their political connections or because Santa Rita's isolation in the midst of hostile Indian country made it an ideal escape-proof prison.

The mine itself was a dark labyrinth of underground passages. Vertical shafts reached down from the surface, and from these shafts narrow tunnels, shored up with juniper logs, radiated in all directions to reach the pockets of copper. Miners, stripped to loincloths, went down into the mine using ladders made of logs with notches cut for hand- and footholds. They crawled on hands and knees into the dark passageways and broke off chunks of rock with picks. These chunks were loaded into ore bags made of buffalo and deer skin, and dragged to a place where they could be dumped into large packs. When these packs were full, with as much as two hundred pounds of ore, carriers began to make the

•

long climb up the ladders to the surface. As they climbed, and again as they came back down, they chanted in rhythm.

All this took place underground, and it is doubtful if either Pattie ever went into the mine. It was dark, it was dangerous, it was full of convicts, and they had no reason to go there. Instead, they were familiar with the aboveground works, which at the time were extensive.

The biggest and most obvious building was the fort. When Elguea first arrived in 1804 he had the double problem of keeping the convicts in and the Indians out. His solution was to build a large, triangular fort with round Martello towers at each of the corners. The walls, made of four-foot-thick blocks of adobe, were two hundred feet long and enclosed a sizable area that could be used for prisoners when they were not in the mine. The building also commanded the approach up the canyon to the mines, and both the walls and towers were loopholed for guns, thus serving the second purpose of protection from Indians.

Outside the walls there were fifty or more adobe buildings, most of them houses for those, like the Patties and Onis, who were not convicts. One of them, however, was the smelter, where the copper was extracted. Smelting at Santa Rita was crude, but it did reduce the irregular slabs and sheets into uniform-sized ingots that could be packed on mules for shipment. The mule trains left the mines, going down Santa Rita and Whitewater creeks, then followed the trail across the desert to the south until they reached Chihuahua, where the copper was unloaded. Eventually, months later, the packtrains came back over the same route, bringing supplies to the mines.

Elguea, the original owner, and Juan Onis, the present superintendent, had worked out a routine that allowed them to work the mines. It was often interrupted, however, by Indians, who did not attack the fort, but instead ran off horses and mules and attacked the charcoal makers. It was to stop this that the Patties were hired, but for the first month they saw no Indians.

•

In early August, however, James and Sylvester, now recovered from his ailment, were out hunting when they saw six Indians near the mine. They chased them, caught two, and brought them into the settlement. Those at the mines, irritated at recent attacks, were in favor of killing both Indians, but Sylvester demanded they be spared. They were placed in the prison, then the next morning one of the two was freed and sent to tell his chief to come with his warriors and make peace. A meeting place was established, a half-mile from the mine, and a deadline of four days was set. If it was not met, the other captive would be killed. The Indian left and Sylvester began to prepare for the meeting that might or might not take place. Near the site he had chosen, workmen dug a long trench and in it, on the day of the meeting, he put thirty armed men. He also built a council fire, laid out a pipe and tobacco, spread a blanket, and sat back to wait.

The Indians, about eighty in number, came in on the appointed day. Pattie gave no description, but a few years later another traveler met the Mimbres Apache at the copper mines. The men were wearing helmetlike headdresses of black feathers, short shirts, and high buckskin moccasins. They looked, he thought, like Greek warriors. Yet, interspersed through the band were those with Mexican clothing and saddles, and almost all the men wore Mexican cartridge belts, evidence of raids into Mexico.

At the head of the band of Apache met by those later travelers was Mangas Coloradas. When the Patties met them, however, he was just another warrior, for his rise to leadership did not come until several years later. Still, he was a giant of a man who could not blend entirely into a band of warriors. Other well-known leaders of the future—Delgadito, Cuchillo Negro, Coleto Amarillo, Ponce—were also young warriors at the time. These warriors stayed back, and it was just four chiefs who came forward to talk. James identified only one—Mocho Mano—whose name had been given him because one of his hands had been torn off by a

•

bear. Whoever he was, he appears in no other account, and at the same time Pattie does not mention the recorded leader of the Mimbres in these years, Juan José.

The Apache insisted their quarrel was with the Spaniards rather than the Americans, and Pattie capitalized on this claim. Although he was nothing more than a hired guard, he let the Apache think that the Americans had taken over the mines. In a not very subtle threat, he also told them that there were many Americans, they were not cowards, they knew how to travel in the woods, and they were excellent shots. In future raids, he said, the Indians would not be safe once they were away from the mines, but would be pursued into their own country and attacked.

The Apache, with one of their warriors still captive, were willing to listen. They said that if the Americans were now running the mines, they were ready to make peace. The warriors were called in to the council, and each of the four chiefs made a long speech. It was all incomprehensible to James except for the words "American" and "Española," which were frequently interspersed throughout the speech. The Indians, however, followed it intently, often nodding their heads in agreement. Finally, the speeches ended, the pipe was passed around, and the Apache painted themselves red and began to dance. They dug a hole, and as they danced they spit into the hole to demonstrate their willingness to make peace by spitting out their past spite and bitterness.

It was then, with peace made, that Sylvester showed the Indians the trench in which he had hidden armed men. The Apache, made sensitive from years of ambush, were very excited when they saw them, but Pattie calmed them down by explaining the armed Spaniards were there only in case of trouble. Since peace had just been made, they would not be needed. The Apache accepted this, laughingly claiming it was a demonstration of the Americans' shrewdness. Yet, one chief took the opportunity to express his contempt, for he told Sylvester that if Americans came to fight Apache, they should leave the Spaniards behind. When the fight started,

•

he said, all the Spaniards would run. Apparently, not all the spite went into the hole.

The entire party—Indians, Americans, Spaniards—went to the mines where three cows were killed to feed the Indians. After the feast one of the chiefs, in an expansive mood, gave Pattie a large tract of land along the Mimbres River, a few miles east of the mines. It was good country, and years later John Bartlett, while leading a government expedition, stopped long enough to look over the valley and predict that it would produce substantial crops. Another member of the party looked more closely and found that someone had already farmed the country in the earlier days, when the mines were still working.

The tract of land showed promise, for Onis had long been aware of the possibilities of growing grain rather than importing it from two hundred miles away. On several occasions he had tried to cultivate the land, but each time the Apache had come, killed those in the fields, and destroyed the grain. Sylvester, therefore, accepted the gift, but only after he made it clear to the Indians that he intended to use Spanish labor and did not want them attacked. The chief who had given the land, insulted by the implications, drew himself up and said he had promised not to bother anything belonging to the mines and he was a man of his word. He also added that he was now convinced that Americans never killed except in battle and that they had no desire to injure those who did not bother them. If he said that, and if he believed it, he was in for some disappointments in the future.

In the days just after peace was made, the Indians kept their word and the situation at the mines changed greatly. It was possible now to grow grain and run cattle along the Mimbres, and the Apache, instead of running off stock, often brought in stray animals. They also brought venison and turkey to supply the mines, and Onis, even when he was overstocked, kept buying game to preserve the peace. Apache came to the mines almost every day to go hunting

•

with the Americans, to be impressed by the shooting of the hunters, and to hope that someday the Americans would live up to their promise to teach the Indians how to shoot.

Yet, for all the outward signs of lasting peace, at the mines there was great cynicism. James Pattie himself, at odds with his own description, termed the whole peace-making episode a "farce." Juan Onis, who had lived in the Apache country for many years, was convinced that peace would last only as long as the Americans were there. The same prediction was made by an old priest who was responsible for those at Santa Rita. Before the peace he had fled, according to Pattie, "out of reverend regard to his own person." Now, he was back to release the souls of the dead, baptize those who had been born, and possibly do some missionary work among the Indians. Before long, however, he was predicting that the peace would not last. Possibly it was more hope than prophecy, for the priest had been insulted by an Indian in front of the Americans.

The Indian was Mocho Mano, the chief whose hand had been severed by a grizzly. Mocho, as Pattie calls him, was invited to come forward for baptism, but after some thought he refused. His reason, he said, was that he was a "big rogue" now and being sprinkled with the holy water would either do him no good or make him a bigger rogue. After all, the biggest rogue of all was the priest who made the water holy, then went around sprinkling it on people for money. The Americans burst out laughing, the priest was angry, and soon after this he left, issuing his prediction that the peace would not last long.

Later, Mocho asked James how the Americans baptized people. James said there were two ways, one being to sprinkle, the other to plunge the person entirely under water. Mocho thought the latter made some sense, for when a great amount of rain fell, the grass grew. There seemed to be little point in sprinkling, however, for he could not see that a few drops of water mattered much one way or another.

Despite the cynicism and the belief that peace could end

•

at any moment, the Americans still trusted the Apache enough to accompany them on a long trip to obtain salt. James was among those who left the mines, went through the Mogollon Mountains to the north, and after traveling about one hundred miles reached the salt deposits. Again, he is accurate enough, for the distance and direction they traveled, through the type of country he describes, would have brought them to the salt lake two days south of the Zuñi villages. It was the place where not only the Zuñi, but the Hopi, Navaho, and Apache as well, obtained salt. While the Indians were gathering their supply, James kept busy with his rifle killing deer that came to lick salt. He discovered the value of traveling with Indians, for after he shot the deer the women did all the work of dressing the skins. Finally, after two days, they loaded their mules and returned to the copper mines with a large supply of salt.

When they reached the mines again, the summer of 1826 was over. It had been a good season for the Patties, even though when it began they were still suffering from the last effects of the disaster on the Gila. By now, however, Sylvester had recovered his health, had brought about a temporary truce with the Apache, and had obtained the right to farm and run cattle on the fertile land along the Mimbres. James, during that same summer, had spent his time learning Spanish, and later learning that Apache, besides being evil forces that ran off horses and stole furs, could also be friendly people and good traveling companions.

It had been a pleasant interlude, free of worries about deserters, starvation, Indian attacks, or any of the countless things that could destroy a whole year's work. As long as summer lasted, they were also free of any real necessity to make a decision about trapping again in the fall. Then summer was over, the new trapping season was about to begin, and both Sylvester and James had to make their decisions about the future. For the first time they disagreed, and this disagreement would have its effect on Sylvester, on James, and on the *Personal Narrative* itself.

•

CHAPTER

———◆———

E·I·G·H·T

NTIL NOW, THE *PERSONAL NARRATIVE* OF James O. Pattie has held up surprisingly well. Admittedly, there is a major mistake on the first page, for according to Pattie the trip began on "June 20, 1824," rather than on June 20, 1825.

Once the necessary correction is made, however, the account fits easily into known events of the time. The trip across the plains in the summer of 1825, the hunt on the Gila in the spring of 1826, and Sylvester and James's presence at Santa Rita the following summer are all established by independent sources. Sometimes the specific dates are suspect, but the general pattern is accurate.

Much the same is true of Pattie's geography. After a few corrections, and after careful study of other travelers' accounts and of detailed maps, it is not too difficult to follow his route across the plains, then up and down the Gila River. There is sometimes momentary confusion, but again the general pattern is clear.

Even Pattie's stories add a certain weight to the narrative. Many of the things that happened to him are plausible experiences for a young man on his first trip into the West. Other less plausible things occur, but in these Pattie clearly borrowed someone else's story. Usually, the probable source of the story can be placed near Pattie at the time he tells it. Again, it adds credibility, for if Pattie did not participate in

•

the event, he at least participated in a storyteller's re-creation of it.

Yet now—in the fall of 1826—all that is about to end. In the pages to come the accuracy of the *Personal Narrative* will begin to disintegrate, slowly at first, then with increasing speed, until it reaches temporary but total chaos.

Pattie's story is reasonably accurate when it begins at the Santa Rita copper mines in the fall of 1826. Several months before, Sylvester's small party had returned from trapping the Gila with stories of large numbers of beaver. James had gone on to Santa Fe, where he talked to several people, including S. S. Pratte, and the story rapidly spread through the various bands of trappers. The fact that Sylvester's party had trouble with Indians and had lost most of their fur did not diminish the hope of finding beaver. It only determined that future parties should be large enough to protect themselves.

Even before the summer had ended large numbers of trappers were on their way to the Gila River. In late August Governor Antonio Narbona of New Mexico noted that four different bands, either organized or led by Bill Williams, Ceran St. Vrain, Michel Robidoux, S. S. Pratte, John Rowland, and Ewing Young, had left Santa Fe. Narbona estimated the number of trappers in the various groups and found they totaled almost one hundred.

About the same time James Baird, who lived in El Paso, heard of all the trappers going to the Gila. Baird, who had once lived in Missouri, was one of those who had come to New Mexico in 1812, been arrested, and held captive for ten years. Later, he used that time to satisfy the residency requirement so he could become a citizen of Mexico and trap legally in that country. Now, a large number of Americans had invaded the area, and Baird wrote a letter of complaint. He said, "I have learned that with scandal and contempt for the Mexican nation a hundred-odd Anglo-Americans have introduced themselves in a body to hunt beaver in the possessions of this state and that of Sonora to which the Rio

•

Gila belongs." Baird begged officials to stop the invasion so "we Mexicans may peacefully profit by the goods with which the merciful God has been pleased to enrich our soil."

His letter was sent to Alexander Ramirez, president of the El Paso district, who did his own checking among some of those who lived at the copper mines. He found that Baird's report was indeed true, and that about seventy American trappers had passed through Santa Rita. He did little about it, however, for James Baird, who had made the complaint, died just a few days after he wrote the letter. Still, Ramirez's report confirmed the rumor that Santa Rita, once one of the most isolated places in Mexico, was now being used as a major staging area for American trappers going to the Gila.

In the midst of this were James and Sylvester Pattie. They had been at the copper mines all summer, and they were still there when the various bands of trappers began to arrive. Given their experience in trapping on the Gila, they should have been a welcome addition to any of the parties going west. Possibly they would have been had Sylvester not refused to go trapping again.

James had thought that their plan was to wait out the summer at Santa Rita and then join the fall hunt. Sylvester had said nothing to indicate there had been any change, but at the last moment he said he was going to stay at the mines. Juan Onis, the superintendent, was convinced that as soon as the Americans left, the Apache would resume their raids. Thus, he offered Sylvester the chance to lease the mines for five years at a thousand dollars a year. To make the offer more attractive he said he would pay for all provisions during the first year and for any improvements that were made on the property. Almost immediately, Sylvester accepted the offer.

There was more to Sylvester's refusal to go trapping than the sudden appearance of a new opportunity. He had assumed that James would also stay at the mines, and when Sylvester discovered he was going trapping anyway, he protested vigorously. In his arguments to his son he may well

•

have given his own reasons for staying behind. There was the danger, he said, and he spent some time picturing the difficulties of traveling on the Gila. It was a subject on which Sylvester could speak with some feeling, for he had collapsed and almost died on that same river the previous year.

Sylvester's argument, according to James, "was unavailing to change my fixed purpose." Although he too understood the dangers, he said, "I . . . felt within me an irresistible propensity to resume the employment of trapping. I had a desire, which I can hardly describe, to see more of this strange and new country." In his stubbornness he rejected Sylvester's advice, even though his father "suffered greatly in the view of my parting with him." Apparently, there were some hard feelings when they parted. At least in the next part of the narrative, James sometimes refers unhappily to the fact that he rejected his father's advice. He is also thoroughly relieved when he meets his father again and finds him "apparently with nowise abated affection for me, though I had rejected his counsels."

It may have been the tension of parting with his father that caused James to have trouble when he joined the trapping party led by Michel Robidoux. Robidoux was the youngest of six sons, all of whom had followed their father into the fur-trading business. Michel, however, was only five when his father retired, and thus the responsibility of bringing him into the business and training him had fallen to his older brothers. Now, at the age of twenty-eight, just a few years older than James Pattie, he was free from the dominance of his brothers and leading his own fur-trapping party. James, at the same time, was traveling without his father, and since he had been down the Gila before, he considered himself an experienced hand. Also, before he left the mines, his father had told him that he would find traveling with Frenchmen much different from traveling with his own kind of people. It was not long before James began to show his contempt for Frenchmen in general, and for Michel Robidoux in particular.

•

159

The first part of the trip, however, went well enough. They left the mines, reached the Gila, and began to descend it. They were traveling through Apache country, and there was frequent Indian sign, but they saw no Indians until two weeks later, when they reached the mouth of the San Pedro. Here they met a small band of Apache and stopped to trade with them.

While they were trading, James let his eyes wander over the Indians, and he noticed that some of them were wearing articles of white men's clothing. He looked closer and saw that some of the clothes were things his father had left behind in the cache on the San Pedro. The Apache were also offering to trade robes that Pattie thought had been made from beaver skin taken from the same cache.

It was the horse, however, that caused the trouble. While the Frenchmen and Indians were haggling over robes, Pattie saw an Apache on a horse that had been stolen from his party the previous year. Had it been just another horse—a pack-horse picked up along the way—he might have ignored it. This horse, however, belonged to Sylvester and was the one he had ridden all the way from Missouri. Pattie, whose "blood instantly boiled," leveled his rifle at the Indian and ordered him to get off.

The Indian, facing a loaded rifle, immediately dismounted. The other Apache and the Frenchmen, until a few minutes before drawn together to trade, now broke into separate, hostile groups, each waiting to see what was going to happen. They were too close in number for either to react immediately. The Indians had a slight edge—twenty men to the Frenchmen's thirteen—but they were hampered by the women and children in camp. The Frenchmen, although outnumbered and in the heart of Apache country, were well armed and one of their party had a rifle aimed directly at an Indian.

It was an Apache who finally broke the stalemate. He approached Pattie and asked if he recognized the horse. Pat-

•

tie said he not only recognized it, he claimed it as his own. Finally, the Indian was able to make some sense out of Pattie's anger, for he asked if he had been one of those whose horses and furs had been taken the previous year. Pattie said he was, and that if his furs and horses were not immediately returned, he and his party would kill all the Indians. The Apache quickly produced 150 furs and three horses. The rest of the horses, he said, had already been eaten, and there was nothing that could be done about it. After some more discussion as to who was to blame for the attack, the issue was settled. The Apache produced a pipe, they smoked to friendship, Pattie gave them some red cloth, and the Indians responded by providing information on the route and the tribes that lay ahead.

There were four different tribes, but Pattie did not quite catch the names. He did hear an Apache say, however, that they were all "bad, treacherous, and quarrelsome." Despite this, the trappers had little trouble as they continued down the Gila. They passed through the area of the first two tribes without seeing any Indians. The Pima were the third tribe, and when they reached the village, they found only peaceful farmers who spoke a little Spanish and who were friendly.

Three days below the Pima village they reached another village, where the Indians came rushing out to meet them. The trappers, looking at the painted faces and the bows and arrows, decided they were hostile. They did not enter the village but instead stopped to face the Indians. Once the situation cooled enough for talk, they announced they had come as friends; at this the Indians threw down their weapons and invited them into the village.

The Frenchmen accepted this as a sincere show of friendship and entered the village to trade. Once they were in the village, however, James found he was not at all comfortable. The Frenchmen, instead of staying together, began to wander off in all directions to see the village. At the same time Pattie saw several bands of Indians with their heads together

•

in serious discussion. He began to fear that the friendship was all pretense and that the Indians planned "to cut us all up."

It was this situation that finally brought the tension between Pattie and Robidoux to a head. Pattie went to Robidoux with his suspicions, and the Frenchman laughed at him and called him a coward. He persisted, saying it was not cowardly to be on guard, and he insisted that they leave the village immediately. Robidoux exploded, saying that he would not go until he was ready, and if Pattie did not like it, he could leave on his own.

Pattie was not entirely alone among the Frenchmen, for one of them was a man he had known in Missouri. He was more willing to listen to Pattie's fears and finally agreed to leave the village with him. The two, pretending they were going out to feed their horses, left and found a place to camp about a quarter-mile from the village.

Just before sunset Robidoux also led his party out of the village and established camp about one hundred yards from the two men. He brought with him a large number of Indians, who, as Pattie watched, unloaded the mules and turned them into the Indian horse herd. They also offered to stand guard for the Frenchmen during the night. Pattie, who thought the Frenchmen were lazy, said they were delighted at not having to face the drudgery of unloading the pack mules or the monotony of standing night guard. Since they would not be standing guard, they stacked their arms against a tree, and one of the Indians looped a rope around the guns and tied them securely to the tree. It was to protect them from theft, he said.

Pattie went to the Frenchmen's camp and again tried to reason with Robidoux. He pointed out the danger of allowing his men to stay among armed Indians without their own guns. Again, Robidoux slashed out at Pattie, calling him a coward, and this time adding a curse. Pattie in turn attacked Robidoux as a liar, as well as a fool for disarming his men and allowing them to go to sleep among armed Indians. Tol-

•

erance and patience, Pattie admitted, had never been his strong point and "I gave him as good as he sent."

The story of the argument is Pattie's, and in it Robidoux continually reacts violently and foolishly to Pattie's sensible advice. Yet, there is more to it than that. Robidoux may well have been the proud, headstrong man portrayed in the narrative, but he also had his reasons for disliking James Pattie. Pattie himself quotes Robidoux as saying he wished "to God that he had never taken me with him, to dishearten his men, and render them insubordinate." It is a fair-enough claim, for Pattie not only had been told by his father that Frenchmen were different, but he himself found them lazy and led by a fool. Quite likely he had been undermining Robidoux since the beginning, and by now Robidoux's temper had reached the point at which anything Pattie said was wrong. The argument ended when Robidoux said he would no longer allow Pattie to travel with him. Pattie agreed, for he felt safer traveling alone than in the company of a man who had only enough sense to lead his men into destruction.

Pattie went back to his own camp, where he and his lone companion fixed their meal and ate it. They had just finished when the village chief came to invite them to supper. It was a meal they would enjoy, he said, for the Indians had prepared some fine pumpkins especially for the white men. Pattie said no, they had already eaten. Then, the Indian asked, could some of his warriors sleep with them that night? They were too poor to own blankets and the nights were cold. Pattie said no. He was poor, too, and he and his companion had only enough blankets for themselves. The Indian went back to the French camp, "evidently sulky and in a bad temper," and told Robidoux it was dangerous for the two men to sleep alone, for they might be attacked by Indians.

Now it was Robidoux's turn. He came to Pattie's camp and, holding his temper in check, explained that refusing to eat or sleep with the Indians was making them angry and would cause trouble. Robidoux had calmed down and was trying to be conciliatory, but Pattie was still angry. He told

•

163

Robidoux to eat and sleep with as many Indians as he wanted, but not in his camp, because neither the Indians nor Robidoux himself were welcome. Robidoux again lost his temper, shouted curses at Pattie, and finally returned to his own camp.

Pattie and his companion saddled their horses, packed their mules, and staked them nearby so that when the other camp quieted down they could slip off into the dark. Around midnight, just about the time the other camp was quiet, they heard a whistle and instantly knew it was the signal to attack. Within minutes they heard clubs thudding against heads, the groans and shrieks of dying Frenchmen, and the yelling of Indians. Through all the noise they could also hear a group of Indians coming toward them. It was too dark to see, but they fired anyway to show that they were not asleep. The Indians turned back, Pattie and his companion mounted, and they pushed their horses hard for the Sierra Estrella Mountains south of the Gila.

By daylight they had reached the mountains and began to ascend a stream that flowed out of a canyon. Three miles upstream they stopped, convinced that the Indians would not follow them into the canyon. While the horses rested and grazed, Pattie's companion climbed the ridge to watch for Indians. After an hour he came back and said something was coming. Pattie climbed to the ridge and saw something black moving across the desert. He looked at it for a long time and finally decided it was a bear. He was even more convinced that it was a bear hunting food when it reached a tree and climbed it.

Having solved that problem, Pattie allowed his eye to wander farther over the desert. Off in the distance he could see smoke rising from the village. Although he could hear nothing and see nothing more specific than a few clouds of smoke, he allowed his imagination to work. At this moment, he thought, the Indians were celebrating, dancing through the village with the scalps of Frenchmen. It was their own fault, of course, brought on by their laziness and

•

foolish trust of the Indians. Yesterday he had been angry with them for all those faults. Today he remembered that despite everything, they had been a cheerful group of companions. Now they were all dead.

It was the bear that brought Pattie's attention back to his immediate problems. It climbed down from the tree and began to move toward the mountains. As it crossed the small green oasis at the mouth of the canyon, Pattie caught the glint of sun on metal buttons. So it wasn't a bear. It was an Indian dressed up in a Frenchman's coat. As he began to ascend the stream, the two men lay quietly on the ridge waiting for him to come within easy rifle range. When he was close enough to be recognized, the bear who had become an Indian now became Michel Robidoux. He was near collapse from fatigue, thirst, and wounds that had already begun to swell and fester. They gave him food and water, and Pattie dressed the wounds. Apparently, it was exhaustion and thirst rather than the wounds that had worn him down, for by evening he was recovered enough to travel.

There was still some unfinished business between James Pattie and Michel Robidoux. Pattie smugly congratulated himself on being too humane to bring up their bitter arguments of the previous day. Instead, it was Robidoux who raised the subject and said he should have listened to Pattie. Obliquely, he admitted that his temper had gotten in the way of his good judgment. Pattie said only that it was too late to do anything about it and besides, "the will of God had been done."

The air had been cleared, and after a long silence Robidoux began his account of what had happened that night in the Indian village. The rest of the party had stacked their arms, but he had hidden a small pistol in his pocket. When the Indians attacked, he shot the one coming at him, and this gave him the slight edge he needed to run. He was still hit several times with clubs but was able to escape. As far as he knew, the rest of the Frenchmen had been beaten to death.

Pattie, Robidoux, and the other man left the mountains

•

and began to move, apparently headed east toward the safety of the copper mines. By sunset they could see the Gila a few miles away. After dark they reached a place on the river where they could see three fires burning close together. It was clearly someone's camp, presumably that of the Indians who had recently attacked and who were now searching for survivors.

Until now the story of the trip down the Gila and the massacre of the Frenchmen has been among Pattie's best. The scenes are vivid and realistic, the people involved are plausible and consistent. The account of Michel Robidoux catches the real tension of an argument between two arrogant and headstrong young men traveling together for the first time. The sudden shock in the Apache camp when Pattie aims his rifle at an Indian rings true, as does the later attempt by Indians to lull the Frenchmen into a false sense of security. There is hardly an artificial note anywhere until the very end when, suddenly, everything goes wrong.

Pattie, when he saw the Indian camp, left Robidoux in charge of the horses, and with the other man crept close to estimate its size. They reached a point where they could clearly see into the camp. There were only two men. The rest, they assumed, must be sleeping where they couldn't be seen. Pattie decided they should shoot the two men as soon as they were silhouetted against the fire. While waiting for a clear shot, however, Pattie heard one of the men tell the other, in perfect English, to wake up the relief guards. Hearing the English words, Pattie leaped to his feet and unthinkingly rushed into the camp. Just as one of the guards was about to shoot, he shouted, "A friend, a friend." Pattie and his two companions had accidentally stumbled on a band of American trappers led by Ewing Young. The trappers were startled by the sudden appearance of the three men, and one of them asked, "Where in God's name did you spring from? You seem to have come out of the earth."

Suddenly, in ending his story, Pattie destroyed the reality he had so carefully created. Yet, it is not the obvious errors

•

that cause the problem, for they can be explained away. The illogical decision of three men, recent survivors of a massacre, to attack rather than avoid an Indian camp could be accepted as foolishness rather than inaccuracy. The sudden appearance of a band of trappers in an almost unexplored wilderness in time to rescue Pattie is not as contrived as it seems. Other documents place Ewing Young on this part of the Gila in the days just after the attack on the Frenchmen. However, one of Young's men, George Yount, left his account of this episode, and it cannot be reconciled with James Pattie's story.

Yount's story of the slain Frenchmen is much less dramatic. Young's party reached the Pima villages, he said, and broke into small parties to trap. The Pima did not try to prevent their trapping, but did order them to confine their operations to certain areas. When they approached the forbidden places, the Indians became very uneasy. On the second day a small band of trappers discovered why when they stumbled onto the scene of the massacre. The Frenchmen's traps were still in the river, their possessions were strewn across the field, and there were eight bodies "much disfigured, and rent by birds and beasts of prey." The small group that discovered them buried the bodies and waited for the rest of Young's party to gather. Then they divided the property of the slain Frenchmen among themselves, and in retaliation attacked the Indians and killed several.

In Yount's version there are no survivors from the French camp, and he says nothing about three men suddenly appearing in the middle of the night as if they had come "out of the earth." Such an appearance would have been a dramatic, even sensational, way of hearing the news, and one that a man was not likely to forget. Yet, Yount does not mention Pattie or any other survivor, and his only comment about Michel Robidoux is a clear indication that he thought Robidoux had been killed. Obviously, as far as George Yount was concerned, Michel Robidoux never joined Young's band of trappers.

•

167

All this creates one of the most haunting problems in the *Personal Narrative*. The dramatic midnight meeting cannot have occurred, and it is doubtful that there was any meeting at all. Yet, Pattie in later pages will demonstrate conclusively that he was with Young's party. If he was with Young, but did not join him on the Gila, he can only have been with him from the beginning. How, then, was he able to create the vivid, realistic account of his travels down the Gila with the Frenchmen? Possibly the answer lies in the fact that after the spell of those stories is broken, one can hear the faint echoes of the same stories as Ewing Young travels down the Gila.

First there was the tension, not between Robidoux and Pattie, but between Ewing Young and Tom Smith. Young, who was in his mid-thirties, had been born in Tennessee but had moved to Missouri in the early 1820s. He briefly speculated in farmland, then joined an expedition to New Mexico, where he planned to manufacture gunpowder. He discovered, however, that the necessary ingredients were unavailable and went trapping to build a stake. After that he made several trading trips between Missouri and New Mexico, and in the fall of 1826 organized the expedition that brought him down the Gila. Like the Patties, he was interested in trapping for the wealth it could bring, and when the opportunity later came he left the mountains for good. James was impressed by him and called him "a genuine American leader."

Tom Smith, who was about the same age as James Pattie, was a man who liked the excitement of trapping more than the wealth it could bring him. He had not yet lost his leg and won his famous nickname of Peg-Leg, nor had he yet started spinning tales of a lost mine. Still, even without the things that made his legend, he stood out in a crowd of trappers. He was famous for his daring in taking scalps and for the earsplitting war whoops he learned from the Indians. George Yount later said there was something about him—something hard to describe—"before which the most daring savage will recoil."

•

168

Smith had come up the hard way. He was born in Kentucky and grew up with a father who believed in giving his children frequent beatings. Once he flogged his son so severely that he laid him up for a week. It was the schoolmaster, however, who finally drove Smith from home. The teacher, enraged at one of Smith's pranks, demanded that he remove his coat to receive a beating. Instead, Smith grabbed a dogwood poker and "gave him a tremendous poke, 'below the belt,' which sent the school-master reeling to the other side of the room." Smith ran away from home and drifted through several jobs before he arrived in the Southwest to become a trapper. Unlike Young, Smith had little ambition to make his fortune and retire from the mountains. He lived the life as long as he could, then, when it was over, he moved on to San Francisco, where he spent his last days standing on the sunny side of Montgomery Street telling stories of the early days and sometimes startling the city with his war whoops.

Young and Smith had little in common, but circumstance forced them together in the fall of 1826. Smith, with a party of men, had gone hunting on the Gila, but they had been driven out by Apache. The party returned to the Chavez ranch on the Rio Grande, where they met another group led by Ewing Young. Smith, who claimed that Young had once tried to kill him, thought he was "an ugly customer in more respects than one." Smith's desire for revenge against the Apache, however, was so strong that he agreed to join Young after he obtained a promise that the Indians would be attacked without quarter.

Clearly, there was tension between the two from the beginning. Then, when they reached the Apache, Young refused to attack "not from fear, but a dogged purpose of thwarting any suggestion of young Smith." Smith, however, was no James Pattie, who moved to a separate camp to sulk. Instead, he agreed to Young's friendly approach of inviting the Indians into camp. The Apache came in led by a man wearing a broadbrimmed palmetto hat and a white shirt

·

with bright red sleeves. He was standing in the middle of camp holding out a blanket into which Young was scooping double handfuls of flour when Smith shot him. The Indian went down and the flour flew up in a huge white cloud that covered Young. He was too startled to move, and Smith, for the rest of his life, remembered him looking "as rigid and erect as a colossal statue in a snow storm."

In the battle that followed, Smith killed an Indian with his knife and shot another. Then, while he was reloading, he saw an Apache trying to force a horse over the edge of a cliff. According to Smith it was "a fine American horse which he had stolen the year before from Patty." Smith fired, knocked the Indian off the horse, and the battle was over.

The appearance of the horse in the midst of battle is surprising. Supposedly, Pattie had already rescued it by facing down a band of Apache. Now it reappears ridden by an Apache in the midst of battle. And although the Indians had stolen several horses from the Patties, it is unlikely that these were two separate animals. James described it as his father's own personal horse, Smith as "a fine American horse." Surely, any man who owned a fine American horse used it as his own personal mount.

The tension between leader and follower is there, as is a story of the rescue of Pattie's horse. George Yount, who was with Young, also described an experience with Indians on the Gila. He and some others were trapping when they met a small band of Apache. The Indians were friendly and wanted the white men to camp with them. Yount said, "At first they were affectionate, then importune, at last insolent and abusive." As a result the white men quickly left. Yount's story is vague and cryptic, but he clearly had the experience of meeting Indians who seemed to be friendly but who soon turned hostile.

Finally, Young's party reached the place where the Frenchmen had been attacked. They found no survivors, but they saw the results, they buried the dead, and they divided the Frenchmen's possessions among themselves. Any man with

•

a strong imagination and a willingness to feel other people's experiences as his own would have spent some time trying to reconstruct those last minutes in the French camp.

Pattie, then, could have been with Ewing Young from the beginning and used the things he saw and heard to create his own version of a trip with the Frenchmen. If so, he did it well. Momentarily, at least, he was not just a young man telling his own story, but a true writer who took other people's experiences, changed them, inserted himself, and wove it together into something new. The individual stories are well disguised and the whole sequence is believable. Had he not, at the last moment, added an improbable, melodramatic ending, his story would not be at all suspicious. As it is, the ending, and the echoes of Smith's and Yount's stories that are different, yet not quite different, create doubts that are not easily dismissed.

•

CHAPTER

N·I·N·E

HEN PATTIE WROTE OF HIS EXPERIENCES ON the lower, desert reaches of the Gila River, he told the story of a band of slain Frenchmen. He did it well, putting himself, and the reader, in the midst of the action. Yet, it is doubtful that he was ever in the French camp, or heard the whistle signaling the attack and the sounds of clubs thudding against the heads of Frenchmen. More likely, he used his imagination to create the story after he was with a group of trappers who stumbled on the bodies and personal effects of the dead Frenchmen.

After the Frenchmen were buried, however, Pattie again returned to events he had actually experienced. The band of trappers led by Ewing Young moved on down the Gila toward the Colorado River and an eventual confrontation with the Mohave Indians. The events they lived through in the next several weeks were the same that Pattie described in the *Personal Narrative.*

At the mouth of the Colorado they camped at the Yuma villages, where they were able to obtain some food—pumpkins, melons, squash, and dried beans—in exchange for red cloth, which the Indians tore into ribbons and tied around their arms and legs. Pattie thought the men—"well proportioned and straight as an arrow"—were the finest examples of Indians he had ever seen. The party spent little time

•

among the Yuma, however, for they were anxious to begin trapping on the Colorado.

They moved upstream, and a few days above the Yuma villages met another band of Indians. Pattie heard from someone that they were called Cocomarecopper, and he was not far wrong. Actually, they were members of the small Halchadhom tribe, but because of the close relationship and almost identical language they were often called Cocomaricopa. Since it was cold and raining, the trappers spent a day in camp near the Indian village before continuing on up the Colorado.

Three days above the Cocomaricopa village, they reached the Mohave. As they passed through the first town, women and children began screaming and rushing through the village looking for a place to hide. It was a strange reaction, for this was not the first time the Mohave had seen white men. Six months before, Jedediah Smith had passed through these same villages and had little trouble as he traded for horses and hired guides to lead him to California.

When Young's party arrived, however, the situation was much different, and both Pattie and George Yount remembered that the Mohave were hostile. Possibly it was because Mexican officials, disturbed by Smith's arrival in California the previous year, had encouraged the Mohave to block the route by attacking trappers. Smith always suspected this was the case, and certainly the frightened women and children Pattie saw scurrying into hiding indicates that someone had been spreading horror stories among the Mohave.

Whatever caused the change, it was clear that the Mohave were unfriendly. They were willing to trade baskets of vegetables for the popular strips of red cloth, but they also tried to lure individual trappers away from the main body so they could attack them. Then a "dark and sulky" Indian whom Pattie thought was a chief came into their camp. He was backed by a large number of Indians, and he demanded, in sign language, that he be given a horse. The trappers refused,

•

and the Indian, still using signs, pointed to the river, to the furs taken by the trappers, and indicated that he should be given a horse to pay for what was taken from his people's river. Again, the trappers refused. The Indian drew himself up, fired an arrow into a tree, and gave a war whoop. Ewing Young, the leader, said nothing but calmly raised his rifle, fired at the arrow in the tree, and cut it in half. Whether or not the story is true, the telling of it demonstrates Pattie's feeling for his new leader, Ewing Young. A year before he would have attributed the same cool reaction to his father.

After the Indians left, the trappers began building a fortification of logs and skins, which was not very solid but high enough to prevent arrows being fired into camp. The night passed without an attack, however, and the next morning the same "dark and sulky" Indian rode into camp. Once more he demanded a horse, and once more it was refused. Then, Pattie said, "he started off on full gallop, and as he passed one of our horses, that was tied a few yards from camp, he fired a spear through the animal."

Again, there is that echo of a Tom Smith story from another time and another place. Several months before, Smith was camped on the Salt River when a band of Apache arrived to invite the trappers to their village. When the trappers refused, the Indians left, and as they were "passing the animals picketed out upon the grass, one of them ran his spear into one." Surely, the same thing told in virtually the same words did not happen twice. Possibly Smith confused time and place; possibly Pattie heard the story from Smith, liked it, and included it at what seemed an appropriate time.

Yet, there is no doubt that Pattie was there, for he and George Yount saw much the same thing. There are some differences in specific details, and Yount says nothing of Pattie's claim that the Mohave attacked after the Indian who had run his spear through a horse was shot and killed. Still, the two men agree surprisingly well on major points. They were surrounded by Mohave, and they spent a sleepless night without fires waiting for the attack. They also agree

•

Church at El Paso del Norte

On the Gila River above the Yuma Villages

When a clerk at the mines absconded with the Patties' money, James went to El Paso to search for him. When he failed to find any trace, he and his father were forced to leave the mines and follow the Gila into the wilderness to trap.

Pima and Cocomaricopa Indians

Junction of the Gila and Colorado Rivers

Once again, the Patties trapped down the Gila, passing through Pima and Cocomaricopa Indian country, until they reached the point where it joined the Colorado. Here, with six others, they split off from the main party and headed for California.

San Diego

The Burial of Mr. Pattie

*The eight trappers, after reaching California, were imprisoned
at San Diego. It was here that Sylvester Pattie died and was buried.
The picture of the funeral—one of the original illustrations in
Pattie's book—is, of course, wildly fanciful. Still, the artist,
William Woodruff, had access to Pattie, and the young man standing
at the graveside may indeed resemble the real James Pattie.*

Mission San Luis Rey

Father Antonio Peyri

California Historical Society, San Francisco

Santa Barbara

California State Library

Two of Pattie's memorable experiences in California were at Mission San Luis Rey, where he debated religion with Father Antonio Peyri, and at Santa Barbara, where he watched whales swimming offshore. The scene of Mission San Luis Rey is by Auguste Duhaut-Cilly, the one of Santa Barbara, by Alfred Robinson; both men were in California at the same time as Pattie.

California Historical Society, San Francisco

Fort Ross

California Historical Society, San Francisco

Monterey

Pattie, after a brief visit to the Russian settlement at Fort Ross, returned to Monterey, where he boarded a ship bound for Mexico. Both drawings were made by Auguste Duhaut-Cilly within a few months of the time Pattie was at each of these places.

A Mexican *Mesón*

The Alameda, Mexico City

Jalapa

The Puente
Nacional

Vera Cruz

The Harbor at Vera Cruz

After arriving in Mexico at the Pacific port of San Blas,
Pattie went to Mexico City, stayed briefly, then continued
on to Vera Cruz, where he caught a ship for New Orleans.

Courtesy Marion Koogler McNay Art Museum, San Antonio, Texas

New Orleans

The InterNorth Art Foundation, Joslyn Art Museum, Omaha, Nebraska

Steamboat on the Ohio River

*After five years of wandering in a foreign country Pattie
arrived at the mouth of the Mississippi. When he reached
New Orleans, he was broke and unable to continue toward
home. Finally, Pattie borrowed enough money to buy a
ticket to Kentucky, and finished his long voyage in the
comfort of a steamboat bound upriver.*

that it did not come until daylight, and when it did the Indians were easily routed. Yount said, "It was richly amusing to our trappers to witness the speed which marked their flight." Pattie said, "We sallied after them, and gave them the second round which induced all . . . to fly at the top of their speed."

Pattie, however, could not resist the temptation to make changes, to improve on the stories, and to place himself in the dramatic role. During the long night of waiting for the attack, Yount said, the Indians occasionally fired arrows into camp. After one volley a trapper suddenly yelled that he had been hit. According to Yount, "An arrow had come whizzing through the darkness, and struck the individual who thus exclaimed, between his skin and the log he sat on, and pinned him fast through the seat of his Buckskin unmentionables." Pattie's version was that a few nights after the main attack, he was asleep in a camp that was fired on by Indians. "My own hunting shirt had two arrows in it, and my blanket was pinned fast to the ground by arrows." The next morning, he said, they chased the Indians, caught them, and killed several. Then they hanged the bodies from trees as a warning that they would retaliate if they were attacked.

They had no more trouble with the Mohave, but soon they began to have trouble among themselves. They had been out trapping for months, they had been attacked by Indians several times, they were all exhausted, and according to Yount, the time had come when "all romance had vanished." Tom Smith, who had never liked Young, was going among the men encouraging them to desert. Finally, he left, but took with him only three trappers and two Mexican servants.

Pattie himself stayed with the main party led by Ewing Young. He thought of Young as a genuine American leader, and a man who could coolly cut an Indian arrow in half with his rifle. He admired and trusted him, and he had no reason to desert. Besides, in the days to come, he and George Yount —who also stayed with Young—clearly lived through the same experiences. Pattie said of the trip that followed: "A

•

march more gloomy and heart-wearing, to people hungry, poorly clad, and mourning the loss of their companions cannot be imagined. . . . Our provisions were running low, and we expected every hour to see our horses entirely give out." Yount agreed, and talked of hunger and of horses that "could only stagger along a few miles, in the cool of the day—& when laid down, it was almost impossible to get them to their feet."

It is during this long, difficult trip that the *Personal Narrative* began its descent into chaos. Until now, Pattie had described the country well enough so that his route can be followed with little trouble. His Indians—the Umene, the Cocomarecoppers, and Mohawas—are easily identified as Yuma, Cocomaricopa, and Mohave. After he leaves the Mohave villages, however, his geography becomes vague, he gives almost no landmarks, and those he does give cannot be put together into any coherent pattern. His account of Indians is equally confused, and in the days to come he will meet the "Shuenas," who are unidentifiable, and, later, a woman who pounds her chest and shouts, "Cowera, Cowera." Pattie thought it was her tribe, and later writers have tried, unsuccessfully, to identify it. Identification from such a thin clue is hopeless, particularly since the woman probably yelled, not her tribe, but the first thing that came into her mind when she was startled by a band of white men.

Finally, all the confusion culminates in a story that could not have happened. After several hundred miles of hard travel, Pattie said, the party reached Navaho country. From here they crossed the Continental Divide and reached the South Platte River. In quick succession they trapped on the North Platte, the Bighorn, the Yellowstone, which they followed to its head, and Clark's Fork of the Columbia. Then they reached the headwaters of the Arkansas, crossed the mountains to the Rio Grande, and eventually reached Santa Fe.

It is an impossible story. There are no geographical details in the narrative, but only a succession of rivers that sounds

•

178

as if it is being recited from a list. Also, from the time Pattie reached the South Platte until he returned to Santa Fe, he was with a band of trappers that traveled some two thousand miles in eighty-five days. Yet, the trip seems to have begun without any intervening stop for supplies or fresh horses, just after Pattie's account of how they were hungry, poorly clad, and their horses on the verge of collapse. Pattie, instead of making such a trip, may be reciting a list of rivers he had picked up in conversation with other trappers. More likely, Timothy Flint has momentarily stepped in with one of the "topographical illustrations" he admits inserting into the narrative.

This impossible story, combined with the confused geography in this part of the narrative, makes it difficult to follow Pattie's wanderings after he left the Mohave villages. However, at least a general idea of the return trip can be obtained by ignoring that story and accepting the fact that he was with Ewing Young's party. George Yount was also with Young, and although his geography is equally confused, he does give a vague idea of how they returned to New Mexico. They left the Mohave villages on the Colorado, traveled south of the Grand Canyon, and eventually emerged at the Zuñi villages in western New Mexico. During the last days of the trip, most of the men were starving, they had eaten what horses they could spare, and they were traveling through country barren of game. It was not until they stumbled into a Zuñi village that they found help.

When they entered the village, at about ten in the evening, the Zuñi were shocked at their condition and immediately began to help them. The Indians brought food, but they knew enough about starvation to not feed the trappers a large amount of heavy food. Instead, they carefully doled out small portions of a light, nourishing bread and while the trappers ate, the chief walked among them telling them to eat slowly. Despite the warnings they were all sick that night, and George Yount, at least, was also unsatisfied, for he spent the night dreaming of food. The next morning

•

Young and Yount had breakfast with the headman. Again they ate lightly, but again they were violently ill.

Finally, they were well enough to continue on to Santa Fe, and the trip that Pattie began several months before was almost over. He had traveled a long distance, trapped through much of the Southwest, survived several Indian attacks, and lived through the long, hungry trip home. Like the rest of the party, in the last days he had almost starved but had refrained from killing the remaining horses so that they could carry the furs. It was worth it, for as they rode toward Santa Fe, they had almost twenty thousand dollars in fur.

Something, however, was bothering Ewing Young, for when they reached the village at Penablanca, twenty miles from Santa Fe, he stopped and hid all the furs in the house of Luis Cabeza de Vaca. Then they continued on to Santa Fe, where they found that Young's instinct had been sound. Somehow the rules had changed; they were all guilty of trapping without a license, and all the furs were ordered confiscated. Although Young had hidden the furs, it did him little good, for one of his Mexican servants told the governor where they were. Soldiers were sent to Cabeza de Vaca's house to seize them, but they ran into an unexpected complication when the owner fired at them. Either Young had promised him a reward if he protected the furs, or he simply did not like soldiers entering his house. Whatever the case, he resisted until the arrival of reinforcements, who attacked the house and killed him. The furs were seized and taken to Santa Fe.

Young's part in this is clearly established by Mexican records. The other two—George Yount and James Pattie—also agreed that this is how it ended. Yount said the furs "were appropriated by his Excellency to his own private benefits." Pattie said, "The Governor, on the pretext that we had trapped without a license from him, robbed us of all our furs."

Pattie's statement is a strangely accurate ending to a

•

highly confused series of events, but the most impossible moment in the narrative is yet to come. It begins with that mistake on the opening page in which Pattie starts the trip in 1824 instead of 1825. Until now, it has been easy to correct that error by simply adding a year to all of Pattie's dates. Once that is done the narrative fits well into the documented activities of the time. Halfway through the narrative, however, a shift occurs, and suddenly Pattie's dates are correct and are conclusively confirmed by a number of records.

It is easy to demonstrate that Pattie—with Young and Yount—arrived in Santa Fe in the early spring of 1827 and that he left for California in the fall of the same year. Between the two trips, then, he had just a few months in New Mexico. In the *Personal Narrative,* however, Pattie brings himself back to New Mexico in the summer of 1826 and leaves for California in the fall of 1827. Thus, he has not just a few months, but a little more than a year. He solved the problem rather easily by telling another year's worth of stories until he catches up with himself. But the net effect is that the narrative contains six years of adventures in five years' time. Living through the same year twice is a simple, even an attractive, way out of a confused chronology, but unfortunately it will not work in reality.

But Pattie—or possibly Flint, with another topographical illustration—added material so carelessly that the extra year can be located and excised. Immediately after his return to Santa Fe, according to the narrative, Pattie went on a trading expedition to Guaymas, Mexico. The story at first glance seems to hold together. The various Mexican towns are in their proper order, and the description of those towns and the country in between them is reasonable. Someone made such a trip, but not James Pattie, for although the story is real enough, the attempt to blend it into the narrative is very clumsy.

Even as it begins there is a serious slip. Pattie claims that after his long trapping trip he returned to New Mexico,

•

where he lost everything when the authorities confiscated all the furs. Then, immediately following, he said, "Here I remained until the 18th, disposing of my goods, and reserving the remainder for a trip which I contemplated to the provinces of Sonora." Surely, through all those months of trapping, he was not packing enough trade goods for a trip to Sonora, and since his furs were confiscated, he had nothing with which to buy goods. Given his situation the claim makes no sense, and the most plausible explanation is that the story belongs to another man who has just arrived in Santa Fe with goods to trade.

In the course of the trip that follows, there is one paragraph in which Pattie visits Jacova again, then continues on to the mines where he meets his father. Again, the attempt to integrate the story is clumsy and suspicious. He had been parted from Sylvester for eight months, had gone trapping against his advice, had barely survived, and had gained nothing from it. The meeting with his father, however, is casual, and Pattie says only that he "remained three days," then left for Mexico. Yet, after the trip to Mexico is over—and after the extra year has been accounted for—Pattie goes on another brief trapping trip. He is gone for only a few months, but when he starts home again he says he will tell his father "what I have suffered in body and mind, for neglecting to follow his advice." That comment, although completely out of sequence, is a more believable description of his state of mind as he came back from the long trapping trip he had taken against his father's advice. All that need be done to put it in proper sequence is to delete the trip to Guaymas and go immediately to that later trapping trip.

Given Pattie's situation after he arrived back in Santa Fe, it makes sense that he went trapping again. His furs had been confiscated, and he had lost everything that he had gained on the long trip to the Colorado. Although he says he did not reach Santa Fe until August, other records indicate he probably arrived with Young in late February or early March 1827. Thus, the trapping season was still underway, and

•

there was a chance to salvage something. The fact that he was broke was no great problem, for most trappers, even when they made money, quickly spent it and had nothing when it was time to go trapping again. As a result those who financed such expeditions were ready to provide an outfit and supplies in exchange for the promise of a larger share of the fur.

Going directly from Pattie's arrival in Santa Fe to the later trapping trip also solves one other problem that baffled two of Pattie's editors, Reuben Gold Thwaites and Milo Quaife. Pattie began his trip at the Santa Rita copper mines and said that after two days "we struck the Pacos about twenty miles from its junction with the Del Norte." It was this comment, combined with the claim that the trip began at the copper mines, that confused the two editors. The geography simply will not work, and both editors finally decided he must be referring to the Puerco River rather than the Pecos. That decision, however, was made in sheer desperation, for the Puerco does not work any better than the Pecos.

If, however, Pattie's trip began at Santa Fe, and if the confused reference to the Del Norte is ignored, then everything falls into place. After traveling twenty miles, Pattie said, they reached a place where they saw many "deserted sheep folds, and the horse pens where the Spanish vachers once kept their stock. The constant incursions of the Indians compelled this peaceful people to desert these fair plains." In fact, twenty miles from Santa Fe in the direction Pattie indicates is Pecos Pueblo, which by 1827 was almost deserted because of frequent Indian raids. Thus, by taking Pattie directly from Santa Fe to Pecos Pueblo, the confusion in the narrative ends, and the extra year is removed. Finally, Pattie is able to return to a coherent account of his activities.

When he passed Pecos, he thought the whole area was deserted. Actually, eight or ten families still lived there in 1827, but it was easy enough to miss them. In these years a traveler often saw only a lone Indian standing like a statue on the roof of a house or leaning against a fence looking at

•

those passing by. Other times no one was around, and the pueblo was silent except for an occasional bark from a dog or the clucking of a few chickens.

The whole place filled Pattie with a "melancholy feeling," but it disappeared as the trappers ascended the Pecos into its canyon. The river here was a clear, beautiful stream, and the mountains on both sides were covered with pine trees and aspen. It was good country for the trapper, good country for the hunter, but Pattie still had the eye of a midwestern farmer, for he thought it the "loveliest region for farmers that I have ever seen." The main difficulty was that no one could live and farm in this valley until the wild Indians who roamed it were subdued.

He soon found out how difficult they could be. For a week the white men slowly trapped up the river with no trouble. Then one morning, just as it was getting light, the guards gave the alarm. The trappers had just enough time to duck behind the trees before the Indians fired several arrows. Unlike Indians Pattie had seen in the past who fled after the first volley, these continued to fight even after several were hit. Finally, one of the white men fell, and the Indians rushed forward to scalp him. Pattie stepped out from behind his tree to protect the man but was hit in the hip by an arrow. Those with the scalping knives turned their attention to him, and "here I should have been instantly killed," had the other trappers not driven them off with their rifles. When the Indians were driven back there was a momentary lull in the battle, and Pattie was able to reach around and pull out the shaft of the arrow. The arrowhead, however, did not come with it, but remained embedded in his hip. Almost immediately another arrow hit him in the chest. This time the shaft would not separate from the head, and finally he broke it off so he could continue firing his rifle. After about twenty minutes the Indians were beaten off, and as they retreated they left their dead and wounded behind. According to Pattie, "truth is, we were too much exasperated to

•

184

show mercy, and we cut off the heads of all, indiscriminately."

When the battle was over, Pattie still had part of an arrow in his chest and an arrowhead buried in his hip. The pain was severe, and it got worse when one of the other trappers began cutting them out with his knife. The operation took some time, but the makeshift surgeon finally removed the arrow from Pattie's chest and part of the arrowhead from his hip. The rest of the flint arrowhead had shattered against a bone, and it was impossible to take out all the fragments.

Sometime after the battle Pattie heard that the Indians who had attacked them were "Muscallaros." It was a sensible enough identification for although the heart of Mescalero Apache country was in the Sierra Blanca Mountains to the south, they roamed from the Big Bend in Texas to the mountains of Colorado. Whoever made the identification had been in Indian country long enough to have overcome the white man's usual habit of thinking that all Indians were the same. Not only could he make the broad distinction among Apache, Comanche, Navaho, or Ute, but he could also make the finer distinction among the various bands of the Apache.

An experienced man could easily make such an identification from the weapons, the clothes, the war paint, and a myriad of small but telling details. Pattie himself saw these things and was able to give a reasonable description of the Mescalero. Their weapons were bows and arrows that were both powerful and effective. The bows were made of flexible wood and backed with buffalo sinew. The arrows, which Pattie had seen up close, consisted of a reed shaft, a piece of hardwood inserted in the end, and a sharp, pointed flint arrowhead. The Indians themselves, although small, were well built, and were dressed in buckskin loincloths, shirts, and moccasins. Their long black hair fell to their shoulders, and when they were painted for battle, they were a formidable-looking enemy.

•

185

The Mescalero's dawn attacks were a nuisance to men hunting beaver, and the trappers decided to go elsewhere. They loaded the horses, which the Indians had failed to stampede, and headed west. They traveled all day, all night, and all through the next day. Pattie's wounds were bothering him, although before they started, he had smeared them with some salve his father had given him before he left the mines. Still, it was a long, painful ride. Finally, on the evening of the second day, they ran into a band of Navaho.

In those days the Navaho were at the height of their power as warriors and raiders. The Spanish soldiers were gone and the New Mexicans, in the early days of independence, were too weak and too confused to challenge them. The Navaho raided throughout the Southwest, taking sheep, horses, and captives from the Hopi, the Zuñi, the various pueblos, and the New Mexican settlements. In all these places people had learned to dread the war cry—*Ahu! Ahu!*—as the Navaho swept in to raid.

The Navaho Pattie met, however, were friendly. They were on the trail of a band of Mescalero who had killed one of their people. When the trappers told their story of killing several Mescalero, and produced the scalps to prove it, the Navaho took the scalps and began to prepare for a dance. By now, Pattie was somewhat of a connoisseur of Indian dances, for over the past years he had seen performances among the Pawnee of Loup River, the Ute on the Arkansas, and the Cocomaricopa on the Colorado. Still, he thought the dancing of the Navaho over Mescalero scalps was the fiercest he had yet seen.

Pattie saw more than he understood. He thought the Navaho were simply dancing in celebration of the white man's victory. There was more to it than that, for according to Pattie they placed the scalps on a pole and danced for three days. It was no victory celebration, but rather the Enemy Way ceremony, which was performed in circumstances like this to protect warriors against the ghosts of slain enemies.

•

While the ceremony went on, the trappers had nothing to do but relax and sample the various dishes, made from dried berries and vegetables, that the women brought them. Some of them Pattie thought were quite good.

He also received treatment for his wounds from a Navaho medicine man. He applied a poultice of unknown ingredients to the wounds, and it immediately eased the pain. In later years Navaho medicine men admitted their treatment would not work on white men because they didn't believe. In 1827, however, the treatment Pattie received was not much different from what he might have been given at home in the backcountry of Missouri. Apparently, he believed, for the pain went away, and after a few more applications, the wounds healed nicely.

After Enemy Way was over, the trappers decided to return to the place where they were attacked, and the Navaho agreed to accompany them. When they arrived, the mutilated bodies of the Mescalero were still there, and again Pattie misunderstood the attitude of the Navaho. He thought they took much pleasure in seeing the bodies, but given their fear of death and ghosts, no Navaho took pleasure in seeing a dead man. The grave of the one trapper who had been killed was also there, and the Navaho placed gifts on it. Pattie said, "These simple people believe that the spirit of the deceased will have immediate use for them in the life to come." Again, he misunderstood, for the Navaho considered life after death a shadowy and unattractive thing. If they did offer gifts to the dead American, it was to satisfy the ghost and keep it in the grave.

Navaho ghosts come at night, and they return to the scene of their death. Therefore, the decision to move several miles upriver before camping was probably made at the insistence of the Indians. The Navaho, however, were still restless, for they spent the night chanting and dancing. The next morning, when the white men took up their traps, they found them empty and assumed that the beaver had been

•

frightened off by the continual loud noises during the night. They told the Navaho their problem, and after that the Indians politely kept quiet at night.

The party slowly trapped the river until finally they reached the New Mexican settlements again. At the first settlement the whole company was invited to a fandango, and after several weeks in the wilderness they were anxious to attend. Not only were the trappers there, but so was everyone else, including rich women and even the priest. The music was provided by a violin, a guitar, and four men singing.

Pattie was somewhat self-conscious, for he was dressed in buckskin and wearing a bright red loincloth. His clothes were dirty, but he was treated well, and the ladies, even the "handsomest and richest," were willing to dance with him. Despite his claim that he had learned Spanish, he still had trouble communicating, but managed to get his message across "by squeezes of the hand, and little signs of that sort." When the dance ended, Pattie said, "it seemed to be expected of us, that we should escort a lady home, in whose company we passed the night."

The trappers continued on toward Santa Fe. As they went, they passed through country filled with game, and as usual Pattie had an eye for bears. Some they killed for meat, others they killed, he said, "for the same reason we were often obliged to kill Indians, that is, to mend their rude manners." Finally, they reached Santa Fe, where they evaded New Mexican officials and sold their furs.

While Pattie was in Santa Fe, he met several people he knew and began to ask about all the others he had once traveled with. Many, he found, were dead, some by lingering disease, others at the hands of Indians. It put him in a morbid mood to hear of those who "in these remote and foreign deserts found not even the benefit of a grave, but left their bodies to be torn by wild beasts, or mangled by the Indians." He made a resolution—temporary, as it would turn out—that he would return to his father and not venture into the

•

wild again. A few days later he started for the copper mines to see his father and to tell him "what I had suffered in body and mind for neglecting to follow his wise and fatherly advice."

.

CHAPTER

———❖———

T·E·N

WHILE JAMES SPENT THE LONG MONTHS TRAP-
ping, his father led an easy, comfortable life at
the Santa Rita mines. Sylvester's desire, it
seems, was to be a frontier adventurer, but his
fate lay elsewhere. Once before, in 1812, he had
moved his family to an unsettled area, did some
hunting, but finally settled down to run a prosperous sawmill. In 1825 he again pulled up roots and went west to trap.
After several months on the Gila, an attack by Indians, the
loss of much of his fur, and an almost fatal illness, he had
returned to the copper mines. When a new opportunity came
to go trapping, he passed it up and accepted the settled job of
managing the mines.

Once again, it was a profitable enterprise. He had leased
the mines, and was making money from that operation as
well as from the ranch on the Mimbres River, where he
raised cattle and grew grain to supply the mine. He had also
discovered a way to make money by exploiting those working at the mine. The laborers, he claimed, preferred to be
paid with goods rather than with money. He had no objection to such a system, for in purchasing the goods and passing them on to the workers, he was able to make another
two hundred percent profit.

Even though his son was gone, he was not completely
isolated, for there were several other Americans working
with him at the mine. James, in the narrative, left the

•

impression that his father was in absolute charge, but others who knew the situation claimed that Sylvester had at least two partners.

One was James Kirker, an Irishman who had come to the United States in 1810 to avoid serving in the British Army during the Napoleonic Wars. For a time he worked in a New York City grocery store, but when the War of 1812 began he signed on as a crew member on a privateer. He was captured by the British, eventually exchanged, and finally reached New York again. He went back to the grocery store to inquire about his old job and found that the owner had died and left his young widow in possession of the property. Kirker married the widow and thus became a prosperous grocer with a wife and, later, a son. In 1817, however, he abandoned his family and went to St. Louis, where he again opened a grocery. A few years later he was listed in the St. Louis directory as "grocer, north Water, above Team Boat Ferry," and since no other address is given, he probably lived in back of his store. It was in these same years that Sylvester was floating lumber down to St. Louis and buying supplies. Probably, the two men had at least a passing acquaintance long before they both drifted west and met in New Mexico.

Another partner in running the copper mines was Nathaniel M. Pryor, who, like Sylvester, was a Kentuckian transplanted to Missouri. He was a relative—probably a nephew —of the Nathaniel Pryor who accompanied Lewis and Clark, and he was no doubt related to the large Pryor clan who had lived near the Patties in Missouri. Beyond that his early life is obscure except for the fact that he picked up enough skills to later become both a silversmith and clockmaker. He had first reached New Mexico with the Glenn-Fowler party and had spent the winter of 1821–22 trapping in the mountains north of Taos. Four years later, when he returned to New Mexico, he arrived in Taos just a few weeks before Sylvester and James. There is no indication of where he went after that, but it is conceivable that he could have gone with them to trap on the Gila. Certainly, soon after the expedition was

•

over, he was at the copper mines working with Sylvester Pattie.

None of these partners knew much about copper mining, but that was no great handicap. Their main function was to supervise and to keep the Apaches at bay. It was not even necessary to concern themselves too closely with business. Pattie had found a Spaniard who had spent some years in the United States and who, besides speaking English, French, and Spanish, also had some business skills. Pattie was impressed enough by this, and by the man's intelligence and honesty, to make him not only his clerk but superintendent of the mine as well.

Sometime in the spring of 1827 James arrived at the mines. He had taken his time coming down the river from Santa Fe, stopping for a while at the Chavez ranch, then again at several small towns to "rest and amuse myself." He appeared to be in no hurry to reach the mines, possibly because he was unsure of the reception he would receive from his father. Finally, however, he arrived and found that Sylvester was healthy and prosperous. More important, he also found that his father had "nowise abated affection for me, though I had rejected his counsels." His father was even more delighted when James announced that he was determined to stay at the mines and not go trapping anymore.

It was an easy vow to keep, for Sylvester had created an attractive place to settle. His ranch was on the Mimbres River, which, if little more than a creek by eastern standards, was a major source of water in this dry country. It was a beautiful location, with land fertile enough to grow grain and enough grass and water to support a herd of cattle. The river itself was lined with thick groves of cottonwoods interspersed with ash and oak, and there were plenty of deer and wild turkeys for the hunter. It was an ideal resting place for a man who had spent months in the wilderness alternating between starvation and Indian attack.

Sylvester's new position also showed promise of making

•

the Patties wealthy men, which, after all, was the main reason they had come west. James rather cryptically mentions thirty thousand dollars as the amount of cash his father had available in the summer of 1827. At the time thirty thousand dollars was a tremendous amount of money, particularly since a few years earlier Sylvester had sold his sawmill, equipment, tools, and oxen for $375. It is such a large amount of money that James, who often exaggerates, would be suspect if he were not backed by other testimony.

R. W. H. Hardy, an Englishman, was traveling through northern Mexico in these same years and found that "some of the largest fortunes . . . have arisen from the extraction of copper." He also heard of Pattie by reputation, although not by name. While he was in Janos, Mexico, he heard of "El Cobre" to the north, where an American had succeeded in conciliating the Indians and making considerable money from the mine.

Twenty years later Lt. Col. W. H. Emory stopped at Santa Rita on his way west. By then, the mine had been abandoned for several years, but its reputation was still very much alive. Emory heard a story, not of Pattie, but of Robert McKnight, who took over just after Pattie left and who "amassed an immense fortune." About the same time, Frederick Wislizenus, during a trip through northern Mexico, also heard that large fortunes had once been made at the copper mines. He was willing to add details, and said that Stephen Courcier, McKnight's partner at Santa Rita, "is reported and generally believed to have cleared in seven years about half a million dollars from it." In light of these statements, Pattie's thirty thousand dollars seems reasonable.

Almost by accident the Patties had found what they had searched for futilely in the beaver streams of the Southwest. They had a decent, even attractive, place to live and the promise of a fortune to come. James even had a servant, named Iago, to follow him around. The only sour note as far as he was concerned was the superintendent and clerk hired by his father. When James arrived back at the mines, Sylves-

•

ter had been lavish in his praise of the man's character and integrity. He was so impressed that he had given him total responsibility for running the mine. James was jealous, or as he put it, "I . . . had my doubts." Still, he had no solid basis for his dislike, and so he kept quiet.

James's ruffled feelings were apparently somewhat soothed when his father began to include him in the business. He was sent to El Paso del Norte to buy wine and whiskey, which could be sold profitably at the mines. When he reached El Paso with his servant and pack mules, the weather was so bad that he decided to lay over until it cleared. While he was waiting, he ran into an American who was living there with his Mexican wife. The man, who was a gunsmith, had been a trapper with Andrew Henry on the upper Missouri. Naturally, he and Pattie had much in common, and they began swapping stories. Later, Pattie mused over the combined tales they told and said such stories would seem incredible to anyone who had not trapped and hunted in the West. To those who had lived the life, however, "the incidents which we mutually related, would all seem natural."

When James returned to Santa Rita, he found that his father had even more ambitious plans for him. He was to take a large sum of money to Santa Fe and buy American goods, which could be sold at the mines for a considerable profit. If he could not find sufficient goods in Santa Fe, then he was to go to Missouri to make the purchases. James, however, refused to go, giving as his reason only the vague comment "my thoughts still detained me in that country."

Sylvester, therefore, sent the trusted Spanish clerk instead. He was given the money and the same instructions, and told to write from Santa Fe to inform those at the mines whether or not he would have to go to Missouri. He left, and after a reasonable time had passed and no letter arrived, James went to Santa Fe to check. He discovered that no one there had either seen or heard of the clerk.

The lost money was bad enough, but more serious, accord-

•

ing to James, was the lost opportunity. Not long after the clerk disappeared, the owner of the mine, facing expulsion because he was a Spaniard, decided to sell. Sylvester and his partners had been leasing the mine and now wanted to buy it. Almost all their cash, however, had been given to the clerk, and thus they had nothing left.

This, essentially, is the story as related by James Pattie. Undoubtedly some of it is true, particularly as it concerns the clerk who absconded with their money. Yet James had a naïve concept of business, and his account of how they lost the mine is oversimplified. Other sources indicate that Pattie and his partners were forced out in a successful power play by Robert McKnight and Stephen Courcier. Nathaniel Pryor, one of the partners, later gave his version of what happened. He said that he and the others had claimed the mine under Mexican law but were soon "ousted" by Robert McKnight. He offered no details, but the times and the men involved suggest how it was done.

By 1827 two things were clear in northern Mexico. There were immense fortunes to be made in copper mining, and Spaniards were being expelled from Mexico. Anyone who understood these two facts knew that it was an ideal opportunity to move in and take over Spanish-owned copper mines at bargain rates. Robert McKnight certainly understood, for he was no newcomer to northern Mexico. In 1812 he was one of those who had come from Missouri to open trade in Santa Fe. He had been arrested and held prisoner for almost ten years. He was not, however, kept in jail, but rather allowed to spend much of his time mining and trading in Sonora. He knew northern Mexico, he knew mining, and undoubtedly he knew many important people throughout the area.

When Mexico became independent, McKnight was allowed to return to Missouri, but after a short visit he decided he liked Mexico better and went back. As he crossed the plains with the Santa Fe caravan in 1825, he was accompanied by Stephen Courcier, who would become his partner

•

197

in the copper mine. If McKnight knew mining and northern Mexico, Courcier soon demonstrated he knew something about business methods. He began buying copper mines owned by Spaniards—not only Santa Rita but Galeana as well—and soon he and McKnight dominated copper mining in Chihuahua. Courcier became an enormously rich and powerful man in Chihuahua, and when he died he left a fortune to his son, who devoted himself to raising cattle on a large *rancho* south of the city of Chihuahua.

Under other circumstances it could have been Sylvester and James Pattie, but they missed the opportunity. Given Courcier's and McKnight's determination and success in taking over the copper industry, there was probably little Sylvester and the others could have done to stop them. Still, the money taken by the clerk might have made a difference at the crucial time.

James, at least, saw it that way and blamed himself for having refused to make the trip when his father asked. Had he done so, they would have been rich, but instead he "clearly foresaw poverty and misfortune opening before us." He said he was disturbed, not for himself, "for I was young and had the world before me," but for those at the mines who had worked hard to accumulate something for their families. He was particularly upset about his own father, who had left behind a large and motherless family that was depending on him. "There is no misery like self condemnation," he said, "and I suffered it in all its bitterness."

Apparently, he tried to make amends through a trading trip, for in August 1827 he obtained a permit to take trade goods to Chihuahua. The permit was issued not to James alone but jointly to Pattie and James Glenn. Since Glenn remained in Santa Fe, and since Pattie had little with which to buy trade goods, Glenn undoubtedly supplied the goods and Pattie made the trip. He says nothing about trading in the narrative, but does describe a trip to El Paso and Chi-

•

huahua, still searching for the missing clerk. That, surely, would have been the foremost thing on his mind, but the trip was still an opportunity to make at least a small profit from trading.

Any income was welcome at this time, for Sylvester was trying to organize another trapping expedition. When he and his partners lost the mine, they had only a few choices. They could find another job in New Mexico; they could go back to the United States in worse condition than when they left; or they could once again head for the beaver streams. Trapping was apparently the best of a bad lot, for it was what they decided to do. In September Sylvester went to Santa Fe and obtained a permit that allowed him to make a trading trip to Chihuahua and Sonora. It was clearly a permit to trade and not to trap, and just as clearly he was going trapping and not trading. It was, however, a permit of sorts, and it might provide some protection for the party.

While Sylvester was in Santa Fe, George Yount was also organizing an expedition to the lower Gila, and the two men decided to join forces. After they combined parties, they had almost thirty men, and for once the two Patties are not the only recognizable men among a band of anonymous hunters. Instead, almost half of those who went with this expedition are identifiable. Several were old friends from earlier days. James Kirker and Nathaniel Pryor had been partners in the copper mines, George Yount had trapped with James the year before, and Hiram Allen, two years earlier, had descended the Gila with the Patties.

Another man who joined them for this trip was Isaac Slover, a thoroughly experienced hunter who was originally from Pennsylvania. Slover, during his early years, rarely appeared in the records, but each time he did he had moved farther west. In 1800 he was living in Kentucky, and by 1819 he had a farm on the Saline River in Arkansas. During these years he developed the varied skills of a frontiersman, for he farmed, hunted, traded with the Indians, and once guided a

•

traveling missionary through the forests of western Missouri. The missionary was thoroughly impressed by his skills both as a hunter and as a woodsman.

Slover, like Nathaniel Pryor, had first come to New Mexico in 1821 with Hugh Glenn and Jacob Fowler. By the time they reached the Rockies, Slover had impressed the leaders enough with his skills that he was chosen to lead trapping parties into the mountains. He stayed with the expedition and returned east in the summer of 1822, but by early 1824 he was back in New Mexico. Over the next several years he trapped in various parts of the country, and in the fall of 1827 he was with those who started down the Gila.

The band of trappers brought together by Pattie and Yount had all the makings of an easy and well-managed expedition. In age they fell almost naturally into a chain of command. Isaac Slover, at forty-seven, and Sylvester Pattie, at forty-five, were the oldest. Then there was a considerable jump to Kirker and Yount, who were both thirty-three. The rest—James Pattie, Jesse Ferguson, Richard Laughlin, William Pope, Nathaniel Pryor, and William Workman—were all younger, ranging from Pattie and Pope in their early twenties to Pryor, who was almost thirty.

There was no need, either, to make major adjustments to strange customs, for most of the men came from similar backgrounds. Many of them had once lived in either Kentucky or Missouri and several had lived in both. Even the two foreigners, William Workman from England and James Kirker from north Ireland, had spent time in Missouri before they came west. Only the New Mexicans, Miguel Hurtado and Juan José Garcia, had no midwestern background. They, however, had been hired as servants, not as true members of the expedition.

Although it appeared to be an easy, agreeable group of men, matters soon deteriorated. Americans were notorious for their reluctance to accept authority. The militia, particularly in frontier states, was often hampered by the men's

•

insistence on electing their own officers, then ignoring them. In the fur trade this trait was even more pronounced, for those willing to accept things as they were, and those amenable to discipline, had stayed behind in the settlements. It was mainly those seeking their own personal fortune, or those seeking to escape the restrictions of society, who made their way west. As they went west, they passed beyond United States law when they crossed the Arkansas, and beyond Mexican law when they left the Rio Grande.

James Pattie had done enough fur trapping in the past few years to thoroughly understand this. He said, "Men bound only by their own will and sense of right . . . are certain to grow restless, and to form smaller clans, disposed to dislike and separate from each other, in parties of one by one to three by three."

The reluctance to accept discipline was also heightened by the specific conditions of fur trapping, and again Pattie showed keen insight into the problem. Men who were constantly hungry, tired, and in danger had short tempers, particularly when they arrived in camp after a long day of trapping. All they wanted was to be left alone to throw themselves on the ground and sleep. Someone, however, had to do the cooking, someone had to build breastworks against Indian attack, and someone had to spend part of the night standing guard. Someone, too, had to see that these things were done, and whoever took that responsibility had to face reluctant and short-tempered men.

The obvious solution was to divide the party, allowing half to trap, the other half to tend camp and stand guard. It was a reasonable solution, but according to Pattie it was also a main factor in breaking up big trapping parties. Those who did the trapping soon began to feel that they were the only ones bringing in any revenue. Then, four or five of the best trappers realized that they could catch just as many beaver themselves and not be forced to divide the profits among so

•

many men. These men, the expert trappers, Pattie said, were marked by "a perception of their own comparative importance, a keen sense of self interest, which sharpens in the desert, the mere love of roving in the wild license of the forest, and a capacity to become hardened by these scenes to a perfect callousness to all fear and sense of danger, until it actually comes." Such men were willing, with hardly a second thought, to go off on their own. James—and Sylvester as well—understood the problem, not just intellectually, but by sad experience. James said, "I have learned by wounds and sufferings, by toil and danger of every sort, by wandering about in the wild and desolate mountains, alone and half starved, merely because two or three bad men had divided our company, strong and sufficient to themselves in union, but miserable, and exposed to almost certain ruin in separation."

Understanding a problem is one thing, finding an effective solution is another, and here Sylvester failed. Soon after the party left the copper mines, he organized a meeting of the trappers and had them draw up bylaws. Each man, at Sylvester's insistence, agreed that he would obey the leader and that he would not desert the party. Yet, as they traveled down the Gila there was trouble almost from the beginning.

The first problem was leadership. The logical man to lead, in age and in experience, was Isaac Slover. Logic, experience, and ability, however, usually were less important than the question of who put up the money to organize the expedition. In this case two men, George Yount and Sylvester Pattie, had been responsible, and each thought that he was, or at least should be, the leader. Yount, in his memoirs, claimed he led the party; James, in the *Personal Narrative,* claimed his father was the leader. James's claim is probably not so much inaccurate as it is a true reflection of the conflict between the two men. Yount had originally organized the expedition, but then Pattie had joined, apparently adding enough men to tip the balance and have himself elected leader. Yount, however, still thought of it as his expedition,

•

and at least some of those whom he had recruited continued to look on him as the leader.

The trappers, with their divided loyalties, soon ran into other problems. In the past two years several bands of trappers had descended the Gila, and by now it was almost trapped out. Besides that, neither Pattie nor Yount had enough money to thoroughly equip and provision an expedition. Almost from the outset, James said, they were short of provisions and had to kill first their dogs, then some of the horses for food.

Not only was the expedition poorly planned, but Sylvester Pattie had become a tyrannical leader. When the trappers drew up the agreement concerning their behavior, Sylvester proposed that anyone who openly suggested deserting his company "should be shot dead." Clearly, even the thought of discussing desertion enraged him. He had come west to make his fortune by trapping, but had discovered it was a hard, dangerous business with no guarantee of instant wealth. The last time he trapped, in the spring of 1826, he had run into serious trouble, much of which he blamed on those who deserted the party. Since then, he had refused to do any trapping, but after he lost the copper mine he was forced to try it again. It might well be his last chance, and to prevent ruin, he proposed that all deserters be shot. The trappers, according to James, accepted the proposal, but certainly no one took it seriously.

No one took it seriously, for not long after it was signed the party divided. Sylvester reminded those who would no longer follow him of the agreement to shoot deserters, but they dismissed it with maddeningly simple logic. When it was signed, they said, the majority agreed with it. Now, the majority disagreed, and thus they were no longer bound by it. Sylvester, according to his son, was entirely guiltless, and the division was attributed to the other trappers' unwillingness to follow the plans they had agreed to. Another man who was there, however, claimed that the majority broke away because they were fed up with Pattie's leadership.

•

He also said that there was a major change in plans, which gave those who wanted to break away a perfect justification.

Somewhere on the Gila they heard of Spanish settlements that were visited frequently by American ships. The stories they heard from the Indians were somewhat confused, and James at least got the impression that the settlements could be found at the mouth of the Colorado River. Given this information—or misinformation—some of the trappers decided it would be easier to sell their furs to ship captains than to carry them all the way back to Santa Fe. It would also avoid the possibility of having them confiscated by New Mexican authorities. Thus, eight men—the two Patties, Isaac Slover, William Pope, Richard Laughlin, Jesse Ferguson, Nathaniel Pryor, and Edmund Russell—decided to go to the Spanish settlements.

The rest wanted to return to New Mexico. Possibly they put little faith in the Indian stories, or they had some pressing reason to return, but more likely it was just to get away from Sylvester Pattie and his attempt to exert life and death control over them. The two Mexican servants, Garcia and Hurtado, had agreed to follow Pattie but did not want to go to California; they asked that they be allowed to return to New Mexico. Their request was granted, but when they asked for their pay, Pattie, with no money, was forced to give them three beaver traps as payment for their services.

Once the decision was made, the separation was friendly enough. Nathaniel Pryor remembered an amiable division of the traps and furs belonging to the entire party. Those going to California, he said, had decided to use canoes to descend the Colorado and thus traded all their horses to George Yount. James Pattie, too, claimed there were no hard feelings and that they all shook hands and wished each other the best of luck. If so, George Yount apparently hid his true feelings, for years later he was still grumbling. He said, "One would surely conclude that intelligent Americans might keep peace among themselves, and live in harmony and mutual forbear-

•

ance—but, unfortunately such was not the case—Eight of Yount's party became insubordinate, and parted from the main body." Soon after, Yount led his party to the Colorado River and eventually returned to New Mexico.

•

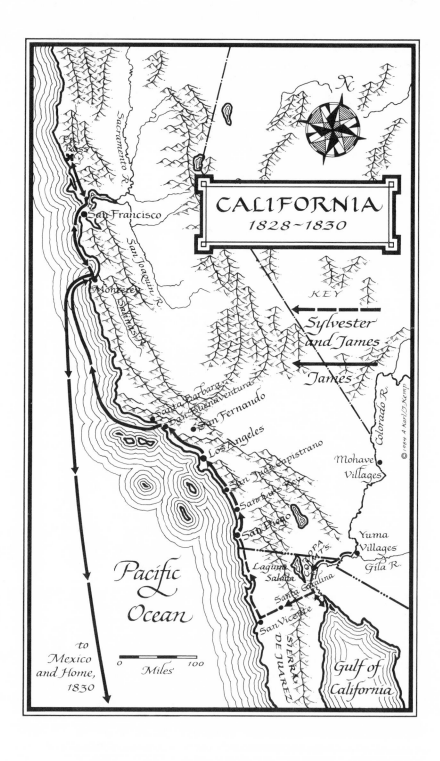

N

CALIFORNIA
1828~1830

KEY

Sylvester
and James

James

Sacramento R.

San Francisco

San Joaquin R.

Monterey
Salinas R.

Santa Barbara
San Buenaventura
San Fernando

Los Angeles

San Juan Capistrano

San Luis Rey

San Diego

Mohave
Villages

Colorado R.

Yuma
Villages

Gila R.

OPA MTS.

Laguna
Salada

Santa Catalina

San Vicente

SIERRA DE JUAREZ

Pacific
Ocean

to
Mexico
and Home,
1830

0   Miles   100

Gulf of
California

© 1984 A Karl/J.Kemp

CHAPTER

---◆---

E·L·E·V·E·N

T HE EIGHT MEN BOUND FOR CALIFORNIA DE-
scended the Gila River until they reached the
Colorado. Here they were in the heart of Yuma
country, which James had visited the year before
with Ewing Young. There had been no trouble
then, and the Yumas still seemed friendly. Some of
them could speak a little Spanish, and they were able to
provide vague information about the California settlements.
Still, the trappers were uneasy among hundreds of Indians,
and James felt that "eight of us seemed no more than a little
patch of snow on the side of the black mountains." As a
precaution they camped on the shore opposite the Yuma
village, and when the Indians swam across the river, they
allowed only a few at a time to visit the camp.

They spent almost a week here making canoes, for they
planned to travel the rest of the way on the river. They cut
down the largest cottonwood trees they could find, hollowed
them out, and made two canoes. When they tried to load
them, however, they found there was not enough room for
eight men with all their furs, traps, blankets, and supplies.
They kept cutting cottonwoods and hollowing them out
until finally they had eight canoes. These they divided into
pairs, lashed each pair together, and built a platform in the
middle. With these, they were able to easily carry everything
they owned.

The next month was an easy, relaxed period as they

•

floated down the Colorado. The first night on the river they put forty traps in the water and the next morning took out thirty-six beaver. Although they were headed for California, they were in no great hurry, and they stayed on the Colorado to take advantage of the trapping. They moved leisurely down the river, setting traps and staying in an area until it was trapped out, then moving on to another place where the trapping was just as good. Some mornings there would be as many as sixty beaver, and eventually they had so much fur they had to build another canoe to carry it.

Not only were they taking fur, but the beaver were fat and provided them with plenty of meat. It was wintertime, and the lower Colorado was filled with large numbers of waterfowl, many of them species that James had never seen before. Along the shore game was somewhat scarce, but there were some deer, panthers, and wildcats. As they neared the mouth of the river, they also killed a jaguar that came into camp while they were working on a canoe. It was the first James had ever seen, and he thought it resembled an African leopard.

As they descended the river they passed out of Yuma country into that of the Cocopa Indians. The first band they met lived on the fringe of Cocopa country, and Sylvester stopped his small party long enough to smoke and to talk with them. The trappers also gave the women some old shirts and indicated that it was proper to use them to cover their nakedness. The women either could not or would not understand, for they continued to wear nothing. Although James did his part to bring the idea of proper dress to Cocopa women, he also availed himself of the opportunity to look closely. Later he said they had "the most perfect figures I have ever seen."

The most important thing the trappers learned at this outlying village was that the California settlements were not downriver, but cross-country to the west. There was no one here, however, who spoke Spanish, and the conversation took place entirely by signs. Finally, after a great deal of

•

pantomime, Sylvester and the others were able to reconstruct the situation approximately. There were white men living to the west, although this band of Cocopa admitted they had never seen any. Still, they knew it was true because their chief, who lived farther downriver, had told them so, and he had seen white men with his own eyes.

The eight trappers descended the river to the heart of Cocopa country and found the chief already expecting them. He had prepared a feast, and after they finished eating, he delivered a long, tedious speech of which James understood not a word. Finally, they got to the main question of the California settlements. Again, it had to be done through signs, and again the message was that the settlements were to the west. James also understood, more from wishful thinking than from any real information, that they were not very far away.

Since trapping on the Colorado had been so successful, they decided to continue downriver until they reached tidewater, then strike west for California. By now, they were almost one hundred miles below the mouth of the Gila, and the surrounding country had flattened out. James, used to traveling rivers that flowed under bluffs, now felt as if the river was on the ridge and that he was looking down into the tangled mass of mesquite and scrub trees. All the country near the river was marshy and filled with waterfowl, including large flocks of swans and blue herons. It was no longer very good beaver country, however, and most of the traps now caught raccoons instead. Not only did the raccoons fill traps intended for beaver, but their constant squalling after they were caught grated on the nerves of the trappers. Finally, it appeared that the good days of trapping were over, and the party stayed close to the west bank searching for tracks that would indicate the road to California.

Before they found a trail, however, the river began to act strangely. Since they had built the canoes at the mouth of the Gila, they had traveled without effort as the current carried them downriver. Now the current died and they were forced to paddle. They spent some time discussing the odd

•

actions of the river, and finally decided that somewhere downstream another large river, swollen by melting snow, was pouring into the Colorado. Shortly after they reached this conclusion the current came alive again and soon they were moving twice as fast as before. They revised their opinion, and this time came to the right conclusion. They had reached the point near the mouth of the Colorado where a powerful incoming tide poured into the narrow river channel and brought the downstream current to a virtual standstill until the turning of the tide allowed the river to race, even faster, the last few miles to the sea.

When they had it all figured out, they relaxed and enjoyed their ride on the river. It was a beautiful evening, the tide was carrying them rapidly downstream, and they floated with it until it was time to make camp. The point of land where they camped was low, and for some unexplainable reason the ground was damp, but still it was well above the banks of the river. They had their supper and went to sleep, entirely secure in their camp.

Sometime in the night they were awakened by a rushing noise that James thought was the wind and rain of an approaching storm. He stretched his blanket over his bed to form a makeshift tent, but the water, instead of assaulting him from above, struck from below. Within a few minutes his bed was floating, and like the rest of the party he found himself waist-deep in water. Finally, they all reached the canoes, which had almost been capsized by the force of the incoming tide, and began to paddle through the flooded country retrieving their floating blankets. James admits that although they had some vague idea of the tide, they had no real knowledge of how it worked. Consequently, after collecting their blankets, they grabbed some trees, intending to hold the canoes where they were until morning. A few hours, later, however, the tide turned back and left them and the canoes on dry land far from the river.

They had spent a wet, miserable night, but the warm sun of the next day dried everything out and also renewed their

.

confidence enough so that they could make plans. They were still hoping to find a trail somewhere downstream, and when the next tide came back they jumped in the canoes and rode the outgoing tide. Finally, when they reached a place where the surf was too high for canoes, it became apparent that they had traveled as far as they could go in this direction.

It was clear, too, that they were in a trap. They had been enormously successful in taking beaver during the past month, and they had furs worth twenty-five or thirty thousand dollars. It was enough, James said, to provide "a little independence for each one of us, could we have disposed of them." The same furs that promised so much for the future, however, were a positive hindrance in the present. The bulk and weight of so many furs had been no problem as long as they traveled in the canoes. Now, further travel on the river was blocked, downstream by the high surf and at the head of the gulf, upstream by the swift, opposing current of the Colorado River. They had no horses, and they had too many furs to carry on their backs.

Faced with this they decided the only solution was to turn back up the Colorado. They rode the incoming tide as far as they could, then used oars, ropes, and poles to force the canoes against the current. Finally, they reached a point where it was impossible to move any farther upstream. They found high ground, dug a deep hole, lined it with timber, and cached their furs. Then, carrying their rifles and packs loaded with blankets and a supply of dried beaver meat, they began to walk west toward the California settlements, where they hoped to obtain horses so they could retrieve the furs.

The first day was through the heavy, almost impenetrable brush of the area east of Volcano Lake. In the past the trappers had traveled mostly by horse and later by canoe, and no one was used to so much walking. That night they collapsed and the next morning complained of the soreness and stiffness in their legs. The only good thing about that first day, James said, was that there was plenty of water to drink.

Even that changed the next day when early in the after-

•

noon they reached the edge of a salt plain. They no longer had to struggle through thick brush, but now the ground was so soft they sank ankle-deep with each step. There was no water, and the hot sun glaring off the white salt plain made it seem as if "the heavens and the earth were on fire." The only relief came when the sun went down and it cooled off. Still, they found no water.

The next morning they went on, and in the early afternoon they saw a small lake. James later said, "I have no words to express our delight at the sight of a little lake before us. We sprang greedily to it." When they tried to ease their thirst, however, they found that the water was filled with salt and undrinkable. In the distance they could see the snowcapped mountains of the Peninsular Range, but the mountains were too far away to be of any help. Just across the lake, however, were the lower ranges of the Cocopa Mountains, which, if they did not contain water, would at least provide a high place from which to look for it. They used dry reeds to build small rafts for their packs and swam the lake, pushing the rafts in front of them. On the western shore they saw some signs of Indians, and later from one of the hills they saw smoke off to the south. It appeared to be an Indian village, which almost certainly would contain water.

When they reached the village they were faced with a decision. They could approach, and despite their great thirst and with water in sight, go through the long process of making friends with the Indians. Or they could rush in, grab whatever water they saw, and worry about making friends later. They chose the latter, making sure their rifles were loaded in case the Indians "showed disposition for fight, or to keep us from the water." Instead, the Indians fled into the surrounding country and the trappers rushed for the water. Sylvester tried to warn them to take it easy, but most of them drank too much, too quickly, and were soon violently ill. After they vomited, however, they felt somewhat better and began to prepare for a counterattack from the Indians.

•

The Indians returned, armed, painted black, and yelling "like so many fiends." The trappers, barricaded behind a fallen tree and with their rifles ready, kept signaling the Indians to stop. It finally worked, for they not only halted, but quieted down enough so that the white men could make themselves heard. There was some confusion in the attempt to communicate until one of the Indians began to yell in Spanish. He was a runaway from the mission of Santa Catalina, which lay across the mountains to the west, and he provided the means of communication for the two groups.

Neither band trusted the other very much. The Indians sent forward only eight men to talk while the rest hung back and watched. After some conversation, however, they asked if the others could also come and talk to the white men. The trappers refused, saying they would allow it only if the Indians would also bring their women and children back into camp. This they refused to do, for they said they did not trust the white men far enough to risk the lives of their women and children. Even James admitted that "there seemed reason in this." Finally, the two groups reached a compromise in which the man standing in the distance would be allowed to approach, but only if they left their weapons behind. Some agreed, laid down their arms, and came in to talk. James, however, saw another group turn around and sullenly walk away from the white men.

After some more talk the white men and Indians began to relax, to be less suspicious, and finally to trust each other. The Indians allowed the women and children to return, and the trappers agreed to stay in the village for the next few days. It would be that long before the chief, who could provide information and guides to the settlements, would return to the village. Besides, after the experiences of the past few days, they needed some time to recuperate.

At first the Indians—particularly the women and children —were shy, but eventually the shyness wore off and they began to look closely at their guests. They liked the red flannel shirts the trappers wore, and when one of them took

•

off his shirt, they were excited by the whiteness of his skin. It came as a distinct surprise, for until then they had seen only the trappers' faces, which were heavily tanned. One of the trappers—and it may well have been James himself—had a particularly light complexion, soft, white skin, and blue eyes. He was the center of attention, for it seemed that the women did not believe he was that white all over. Finally, they proposed that he strip so that they could see his entire body. He refused, but after the women brought him some dried fish and the other trappers began to urge him on, he took off his clothes. It was a huge delight to the women, who laughed and chattered among themselves as they looked at his body. Then each woman, to show the contrast, walked up and stood next to him. If it was James, he provided a major service to his companions, for after this the women were continually bringing them dishes of roots, vegetables, and cooked fish.

A few days later the chief reached the village and the white men entered into negotiations for guides to take them to the California settlements. They promised to pay the chief for his services, but after looking at their conditions, he inquired as to how they planned to do that. Since the weather was mild they offered to give him their blankets, which he found satisfactory, although he indicated he would prefer red cloth instead. The trappers had none of the red ribbons used for trade, but they did have red flannel shirts, which they tore into small strips and distributed among the Indians. They also gave the chief two of their blankets and promised the rest to the guides after they reached the settlements.

The next morning they started southwest toward the snowcapped mountains, beyond which were the California settlements. The mountains were easily visible but could be reached only after a long trip across difficult country. The first barrier was the Cocopa mountain range, which they reached not long after they left the village. The mountains were small, but it was an exhausting climb, and when they

•

reached the summit there was no water. All they could see was a large salt plain that filled the twenty miles between there and the snowcapped mountains, but they refrained from asking the guides. If they didn't ask, they could at least hope that they were wrong.

They descended the mountains and started across the large salt plain of Laguna Salada. The ground was hot, and with each step they sank in up to their ankles. There was no shade, the air was dry, and by midday they had still not found any water. Their only break was when they found a lone scrub tree under which they crawled for shade. It was here that the guides, seeing them lying down to rest, urged them to get up and continue traveling. To emphasize the message they told them that there was no water until they reached the mountains. It was not welcome news, and James said, "This unseasonable and yet necessary information, extinguished the last remainder of our hope, and we openly expressed our fears that we should none of us ever reach it."

The hope that they would soon find water was gone, and they tried to ease the thirst by chewing tobacco but could raise no moisture. They put rifle balls in their mouths and shifted them around to create some saliva to ease the dryness of their throats, but it did little good. They even drank their own urine, but James found that "this hot and salt liquid seemed rather to enrage than appease the torturing appetite." Finally, two men gave out and crawled into the shade of a bush. The rest, assuming they would never see them again, tried to say good-bye, but found it difficult because of their dry mouths and thick tongues. They went on and by late afternoon were beset by still another problem. The sun glaring off the white salt flats so blinded them that they had trouble seeing the guides well enough to follow them.

When the sun went down it provided some shade and also brought a certain amount of coolness, but soon it was too dark and the trappers were too tired to keep going. They lit a fire and began shooting their rifles to guide those left behind into camp. In the distance they could hear the two

•

stragglers also firing rifles. Eventually, the two men reached camp, but were greatly disappointed, for they had assumed the shots meant that the others had found water. The belief had given them the necessary energy to travel. When they discovered there was no water, they were angry and complained that they should have been left to die. One of them reached into his pack and took out a small bottle of laudanum and drank it. The others thought he would quietly go to sleep and die, which they assumed was what he wanted. Instead, he began to act as if he were drunk, talking and laughing and saying he felt as fresh as he had when they started out that morning. If he had realized the laudanum would cure thirst and fatigue instead of letting him quietly die, he would have shared it with the others.

The next morning, as soon as it was light, they began to travel. They had been able to sleep and that, plus the coolness of the night, had somewhat revived them. But the second day soon became worst than the first. It was already hot by ten in the morning, when they reached a sand hill and began to climb. The sand was so loose and the hill so steep that with each step they slipped back almost to where they had begun. Finally, they gave up and moved along the hill looking for a place where it was not as steep.

Several hours later they found what looked like a reasonable place to make the climb. Most of them reached the top, but the two oldest men, Sylvester Pattie and Isaac Slover, gave out halfway up the hill. James thought it was because they were old and said, "Age had stiffened their joints, and laid his palsying hand upon their once active limbs and vigorous frames." Again, it only demonstrated James's youth, for Sylvester was forty-five and Isaac Slover forty-seven.

Still, they did give out, threw themselves on the ground, and refused to go any farther. James, the true romantic, insisted he should stay and die by his father's side. Sylvester, the realist, pointed out that would only guarantee James's death as well and be of no help to his father. He insisted that James go with the others until they found water, which he

•

could bring back to the two men who had collapsed. James, with the others, went on, descending the hill, then climbing another just as bad. When they reached the summit of that hill, however, they could see in the valley below them a clear, running stream. James said, "Such a blissful sight I had never seen before, and never expect to see again." They rushed down the hill, and although they knew better, began to rapidly drink. Within a few minutes nothing could be heard but the sound of groaning and vomiting men.

James and another man, after they recovered, dumped the powder from their powder horns, filled them with water, and started back to relieve the two men who had collapsed. When they reached them they were lying in the sun. Their lips were black, their mouths wide open, and they were lying so still that James thought they were dead. The water, however, revived them, and after an hour they were able to climb the hills. Later that afternoon they rejoined the rest of the party. The others had already begun to celebrate by building a large fire, roasting dried beaver meat, and drinking water at will.

After this the traveling improved greatly, for they were now following a stream and had no more worries about water. They also shot a deer and ate fresh venison rather than dried beaver meat. A few days later they reached a camp of some Indians from Santa Catalina Mission. The trappers discharged the guides who had brought them this far and accompanied the new Indians when they returned to the mission.

The final part of the trip involved a steep climb over the Sierra Juarez Mountains. During the climb James, who was wearing thin deerskin moccasins, severely bruised his heel. For a time he was able to continue, but finally his leg became so swollen that he gave up. The others encouraged him to keep on, for the Indians said it was only three miles to the mission. James, however, refused to move, and the others finally agreed to continue on to the mission and send someone back with a horse to bring him in.

•

After the rest of the party left, he built a fire, made sure his rifle and pistol were in working order, and went to sleep. Sometime in the early evening he was awakened by two Indians, who had been sent with orders to bring him to the mission. James, who had just awakened and who was "feverish, stiff, sore and withal testy," was not very civil, particularly when he found they had not brought a horse. The Indians said there were no horses at the mission, but they were willing to carry him themselves. With that, one took his legs, the other his arms, and they carried him to the mission, where he was ushered into the guardhouse to join his companions.

James, who during his days in New Mexico had been reasonably tolerant of Mexican officials, was enraged when he found himself and the rest of the party in the guardhouse. They produced the permit they had received in New Mexico, and if it did not specifically allow them to trade in Baja California, it at least proved they were not "robbers, murderers, nor spies." The corporal at the mission, who "resembled a negro, rather than a white," would say only that he had no way of knowing who they were or why they had come. Pattie was infuriated by his refusal to listen to reason and said, "The cowardly and the worthless are naturally cruel."

The problem, however, probably stemmed not so much from natural cruelty as it did from a petty official's unwillingness to make any decision until he heard from his superior. Besides, those at Santa Catalina were more than ordinarily suspicious, for it was a frontier mission subject to numerous raids by Indians who lived along the Colorado River. Even James noted that most of the livestock had been driven off by raiding Indians.

After a week at Santa Catalina a column of soldiers arrived to escort the eight men to San Vicente, which was not only a mission, but also the military center of the frontier region of Baja California. It sounded impressive, but the military center actually contained only eight or ten soldiers commanded by a lowly ensign. In the narrative James demoted

•

him even further and said it was a sergeant with whom they did all their business.

The "sergeant," however, was polite enough and promised to make arrangements for their comfort. To test him, they asked for something to eat and he promptly gave orders to feed them. A steer, which James said "reeled as it walked, and seemed sinking by natural decay," was killed and the meat—"the blue flesh"—was put in a pot. Corn was put in another pot, and when it was all cooked James thought it looked like something a farmer would feed a sick cow. While the trappers tried to eat, they were surrounded by a crowd of men, women, and children, who stared as if they were visiting a zoo. One of the trappers finally asked if they thought they were animals. After some thought a member of the crowd answered that since the visitors were not Christians, they were not much better than animals.

Nothing a Spanish-speaking Catholic could say would have outraged Missouri and Kentucky Protestants more than this. They replied, "with a suitable mixture of indignation and scorn," that they considered themselves much better Christians than the crowd around them. They also said that if they didn't get something better to eat, they would leave the mission, live where they wanted, and hunt for their food. They could easily do this, for much to their surprise, no one had yet taken their weapons. The only thing that stopped them was their belief that they were the victims of petty bureaucrats and that as soon as someone important heard of their plight they would be treated well.

Their complaints, and the message that they were thinking of leaving, reached the sergeant, who came in to investigate. He looked at the food they had been given, said it was not fit for a dog, and arranged for some decent meat and some *tortillas.* With this, the trappers calmed down, and after they ate they presented their problem to the sergeant. All they wanted, they said, was to purchase horses so they could return to the Colorado River and retrieve their furs. They

•

asked that the sergeant contact his superior, the governor of both Californias. The sergeant promised he would try.

In the meantime the eight Americans had nothing to do but wait for an answer. They were given freedom to roam the area around San Vicente, and they spent some of the time hunting deer. The rest of the time they spent looking at the curiosities of this new country. Ten miles west of the mission, the San Isidro Mesa ended in high bluffs overlooking the Pacific Ocean. The trappers—particularly James—liked to sit on the bluffs and watch the seals, sea otters, and other "sea monsters of the ocean." When the tide was out, they would scramble down to the beach and walk along looking at the many varieties of seashells.

Eventually, the governor sent word, and with it a squad of soldiers to escort the Americans to San Diego. The trappers were much relieved, for they felt they would no longer be dealing with petty frontier officials, but with an important man who would have "no difficulty in granting a request so reasonable as ours." Possibly they would have been less confident had they known the content of the letter the governor had written to his military commander in San Diego. It said, "Eight armed men have appeared at a frontier post with a *guia* of the New Mexican custom-house as a passport. Arrest them and seize their arms."

•

CHAPTER

—◆—

T·W·E·L·V·E

THE EIGHT AMERICAN TRAPPERS RODE INTO San Diego in a column surrounded, front and back, by mounted lancers. The town's only street was lined with people, for every man, woman, and child had turned out to see the strangers. From a distance the trappers had seen an American ship lying in port, and now in the crowd they could see American sailors, who looked at them with as much curiosity as the native Californians. Eventually, the eight men reached the guardhouse, where they were confined and told that the governor could not see them until the next morning. Their quarters, James said, were filled with fleas, but they were too tired to notice and slept without moving. The next morning, however, James awoke and found himself covered with red spots where the fleas had bitten during the night.

Sylvester and the rest of his party, since they had left the Colorado River six weeks before, had pinned all their hopes on reaching the California settlements. Finally, at San Diego, they had reached their goal only to find that at first glance the town was a disappointment. Thirty or forty shabby houses, some with poorly tended gardens, were strewn across the sandy plain across the bay. Beyond them, on the slopes of a barren hill, was the *presidio*, an irregular collection of dark-colored buildings. One traveler, about this time, described it as the saddest place he had seen in all of California.

•

The Americans, however, did not plan to settle here, but only to obtain horses, retrieve their furs, and bring them to the coast to sell to a ship's captain. This prospect was more promising, for they had already seen the ship *Franklin* in port and the American sailors in the crowd. It clearly confirmed the rumors that in California there were American traders who were ready to do business. Also, James at least convinced himself that all the troubles in Baja California had been caused by petty bureaucrats. Now, in San Diego, they would soon be in the presence of the governor, who would listen to their reasonable request and easily grant their wish.

James, however, knew nothing of the governor, and his hope was based entirely on the assumption that a man in such an important position would be intelligent, stable, and willing to listen to reasonable explanations. Such an assumption, as he would soon learn, was completely naïve in California in 1828.

The governor of California was José Maria Echeandia, who, until recently, had been an unknown lieutenant colonel of engineers in Mexico City. Somehow he had survived the political upheavals as Mexico broke away from Spain, and in 1825, with a new constitutional government in power in Mexico, he was plucked from the obscurity of his engineering post and appointed territorial governor of California.

He was not a robust man, however, and his apathy, lack of energy, and delicate health were well known in California. Some who met him thought he was the very essence of Spanish dignity and politeness, others thought him a raging tyrant. Surely, he was a different man from one day to the next, and many who knew him spoke of his uncertain character, his capriciousness, his self-indulgence, and his willingness to surrender to a whim no matter what the consequences.

Most of these traits became evident to Californians immediately after his arrival. In October 1825 he had reached San Diego in an exhausted condition after his trip north from Mexico. He refused to continue on to the capital at Monte-

•

rey, and insisted that Luis Arguello, the outgoing governor, come to San Diego to turn over the office. Then, after he officially took office, Echeandia announced that since he was governor of both Californias, he planned to make his headquarters at San Diego, which was more centrally located. Besides, he said, the climate in the south was better for his health than the fogs of Monterey. Many Californians thought that this overly cautious concern with his delicate health was a more important factor in the decision than all the arguments of a centrally located residence for the governor. Persistent rumors, too, claimed that he had become enamored of Josefa Carrillo, the daughter of a prominent family, and was staying in San Diego to pursue her.

After sixteen months in San Diego he was finally forced to travel north to see the rest of California and to attend the territorial deputation at Monterey. On the way north, and again on the way home, he stopped for long rests at Santa Barbara, and by the time the trip was over, he had been absent from San Diego for more than a year. He finally returned in April 1828 and was presented, almost immediately, with the problem of the eight American trappers. Quite likely his health and his nerves were in poor condition. He was not a strong traveler and had just returned from a long trip. Besides, during his absence, Josefa Carrillo had announced that she planned to marry Henry Delano Fitch, an American trader. This, too, would have done nothing to improve Echeandia's disposition especially toward other Americans.

The American trappers, who had arrived in California by land, also presented a problem that Echeandia would rather not face again. Two years earlier, in 1826, another band of foreigners had suddenly appeared in California after crossing the desert from the east. They had arrived at San Gabriel Mission, where the leader, Jedediah Smith, had written the governor asking permission to buy horses and travel through California to San Francisco Bay. Instead of granting the re-

·

quest, Echeandia ordered Smith to appear before him in San Diego.

Smith's band of trappers greatly disturbed Echeandia. Foreigners were not unusual in California, for ships from England and the United States had been trading there for years. Smith's party, however, was the first to come by land, and it had broken down the Californians' belief that they were protected from Americans by the large belt of desert to the east. Echeandia may have partially understood this, but it is unlikely that he was astute enough to fully grasp the large political implications. Instead, the major problem was that Smith's arrival created an entirely new situation. Policy toward foreign traders who came in ships had been determined before Echeandia's arrival, and he had only to follow clearly established procedure. Smith and his trappers, however, were something for which there was no precedent.

Echeandia, in his confusion, did not handle the situation well. When Smith arrived in San Diego, the governor questioned him and was so dissatisfied with the answers that he called him back twice more to cover the same ground. His suspicions came from the fact that he had never heard of the fur trade and was totally incredulous that anyone would cross the desert to hunt beaver. The whole thing seemed to him to be a not very plausible story to disguise the true military purpose of the expedition. He had no precedent, however, and he would have preferred to send Smith and all his men to Mexico, where someone else could make the decision. Finally, several ship captains whom Echeandia knew testified that Smith's business was legitimate, and the governor allowed him to leave by the same route he had entered California.

If Echeandia hoped the problem would go away that easily, he was disappointed. A few months later rumors reached him that the trappers were now camped in the San Joaquin Valley. Echeandia, who was now in Monterey, sent a message to Smith telling him to leave immediately. When the

•

soldiers who carried the message reached the American camp, they found that Smith, with two other men, had already gone east across the Sierras. Unable to inform him of the governor's orders, the soldiers allowed the rest of the trappers to stay where they were until he returned. Several months later Smith returned with another band of trappers. He had been attacked by the Mohaves on the Colorado River, had lost ten men and almost all his provisions. By the time he reached his original party on the Stanislaus River, he had no choice but to again ask the Californians for help. This time he went to the mission at San Jose, and from here he was escorted by soldiers to Monterey. A few days later he was again facing Governor Echeandia.

The governor was even more suspicious than he had been ten months earlier and said he needed some time to think about the situation. He showed no signs of making a decision, however, and again would have preferred that someone in Mexico take the responsibility. Once again, Smith went to the ship captains for support, and this time Captain John Rogers Cooper signed a bond guaranteeing Smith's behavior in California. With this in hand, Echeandia agreed to give Smith three choices. He could wait for orders from Mexico, he could go to Mexico himself, or he could leave California in the same direction he had come. Smith chose to leave, and on December 30, 1827, he led his trappers out of San Jose, thus ending the problem that had plagued Echeandia for the past year.

Three months later, in April 1828, Echeandia arrived back in San Diego and was immediately faced with the problem of another band of trappers who, like Smith, claimed they had come only to seek help. By then, Echeandia was in no mood to be the calm, sensible, and understanding leader that the trappers hoped to meet.

The conference began when the eight Americans were ushered into the governor's office, "with our hats in our hands." James refused to concede anything to Echeandia, but

•

surely he greeted them politely. All other foreigners, even Jedediah Smith during all his troubles, admitted the governor always behaved like a gentleman. Whatever politeness he allowed himself quickly passed away as he moved to the questions at hand. He wanted to know who they were, how they got to California, whether they had a passport, and most of all why they had come. The trappers poured out the story of all their difficulties during the past several months and also produced the permit they had received in Santa Fe. They were confident that it all sounded reasonable, and they had no way of knowing that Echeandia, in the past fifteen months, had heard a similar, suspicious story not once but twice.

Echeandia listened, then examined the papers of the Americans. He smiled—Pattie thought it a sinister and malicious smile—and said he believed nothing of their story. Then he gave his own version of why they had come. They were spies for the Spanish king, he said, and had come to lurk about the country spying out weak places so the Spanish could bring in troops and reconquer California. He, however, had detected their scheme and was prepared to prevent it. With this, James said, he took another look at the permit, then tore it up, saying it was a forgery they had written themselves. If they were truly what they claimed to be, they would never have left without a passport from their chief executive.

Nothing could have outraged a band of American trappers more than the accusation that they were serving the Spanish king, or any king. In response they gave Echeandia a quick lecture on their view of American history, government, and attitudes. They were all "born and bred thorough and full blooded republicans" who would rather die than be spies for the Spanish king. Some of them, not many years before, had fought against another king, who had sent savages to attack their homes. As far as passports were concerned, in the United States only slaves, to prove they had the consent of

·

229

their masters, and soldiers, to prove they were on authorized leave, needed to carry such papers. Private citizens were free to travel wherever they pleased without showing papers.

In the midst of their argument Echeandia ordered them to be quiet. James thought it was because they were beginning to reach him, and he was afraid he might give in. More likely, the reason was exactly what he said, that he "did not wish to hear any more of our long speeches." He told them he had had enough of their lies and ordered them returned to the guardhouse.

James, when he wrote the narrative, was bitter toward Echeandia. His account of the meeting is clearly prejudiced, and even the smallest action of the governor is described in the worst possible way. When he smiled, it was a "sinister and malicious" smile; when he looked at them, it was a "look of vengeance." Yet, the general conversation, as described by Pattie, is entirely plausible. Echeandia's statement that beaver trapping was only a cover for military operations was the same statement he had made to Smith. His suspicion and fear of the Spanish king were also reasonable in a man who owed his appointment to a government that had just outlawed Spaniards. It is even likely that Echeandia, faced with physical and personal problems, and just a few months removed from the long, nagging problem of Jedediah Smith, may have lost his temper in front of the Americans. Certainly, their presumption in delivering a long-winded lecture on American history and government would have exasperated a man with steadier nerves than Echeandia.

After the meeting the Americans were escorted back to the guardhouse. The day before they had seen where their arms were stacked, and as they returned they formed a plan to seize the rifles and escape. The soldiers, however, had anticipated such a move, for when the trappers reached the guardhouse, the weapons were gone. They had no choice but to allow themselves to be locked up.

The sergeant who had escorted them announced that each

•

man would be placed in a separate cell. James, in describing his reaction to this news, became thoroughly melodramatic. He threw his arms around his father's neck, burst into tears, and said he feared that the separation would be forever. Sylvester, apparently embarrassed by this show of emotion, told his son he was being weak and unmanly. The sergeant, who had been watching, asked if they were father and son. When he found they were, he said he thought it was cruel to separate "father and child," and went to ask the governor if they could be placed in the same cell. He soon came back with the governor's refusal. Apparently, Echeandia was not touched by his sergeant's description of the scene, particularly since the father and child were both grown men. Thus, James and Sylvester were separated. "When I shook hands with him, and we were torn in sunder," James said, "I will say nothing of my feelings, for words would have no power to describe them."

The melodrama and sentimentality of the scene, however, show a falseness in the writing, not in the emotion, for James had reason to be concerned for his father. Several weeks earlier Sylvester had collapsed in the desert and only the return of his son with water had saved him. Strangely, James says nothing more about his father until they are separated at San Diego. As far as the narrative is concerned, Sylvester, after some water and some rest, recovered from his dehydration and exhaustion. Isaac Slover, who had collapsed at the same time, showed no serious aftereffects and would live for another twenty-five years.

Yet, there was apparently more wrong with Sylvester than momentary dehydration and exhaustion. Nathaniel Pryor, who was also with the party, later said Sylvester was "sick from the fatigue" of the march when they reached San Diego. Pryor thought he would recover, but James, given his emotional outburst, was not so optimistic. He gives no clue as to why he was so distraught about his father, but events of the next few weeks would prove his concern was justified.

The eight men were each put in a separate cell. James's

•

emotional state, as he describes it, is realistic enough for a man used to roaming the wilderness, now locked in an eight-by-ten-foot cell with barred doors and windows. Throughout the day he paced furiously back and forth across the cell. Occasionally, the guard at the door looked in, and Pattie thought he seemed extremely pleased at the fate of the prisoner.

It was worse when night came, for there was no light in the cell and to James it looked like "the darkness of the grave." He had been given blankets, and he spread them on the floor and lay down. He would try to fall asleep and find a few hours' escape, if not from prison, at least from his own thoughts. Instead, he lay there with his mind ranging everywhere, then finally returning, always, to the worries about his father. He closed his eyes, "but nature would have her way" and he could not sleep.

"At length," he said, there was a glimmer of daylight and he gave up the hopeless attempt to sleep. He looked through the barred window and saw, directly across from him, the governor standing in the doorway of his office. Apparently, he too was having difficulty sleeping. James watched him and wished he had a rifle with just one shot to fire at the governor. "But," he said, "wishes are not rifle balls and will not kill."

Later, after the church bell rang and the drum rolled to muster the soldiers at the *presidio*, a guard brought him something to eat. It looked like dried beans and corn cooked in rancid tallow, and after smelling it he refused to eat. That evening, when the guard returned with more of the same, Pattie handed him the untouched portion from that morning. The guard asked why he had not eaten; he said that he could barely stand to smell it, let alone eat it. The guard threw the food in his face and told him it was good enough for a brute like him. If the food was intended for brutes, Pattie said, then the guard should eat it himself. With that, the soldier left. Probably the food was better than Pattie claimed, for he also said, "My thoughts were too dark and

•

2 3 2

my mind too agitated to allow me appetite." Besides, he said, he felt sick.

The soldier with whom Pattie traded insults must have complained, for later that night the sergeant came to Pattie's cell. His name was José Antonio Bernardino Pico, and he was a small, good-humored man whom Pattie liked. Pico asked why he had not eaten, and Pattie explained that it was because the food was terrible and his stomach was unsettled. There was nothing Pico could do about the stomach, but he did order some better food.

James's immediate concern was for his father, and he asked Pico for information. The sergeant said he had visited the elder Pattie but had been unable to talk to him because Sylvester could not speak Spanish. The conversation then turned to James's family, and Pico asked about his mother and his brothers and sisters. The sergeant was particularly interested in how long it had been since he had heard from them and what he had been doing since he left home. James thought Pico was much affected by the story, and probably he was, for unknown to James, Pico's background gave him an understanding of the situation. James, the eldest in a family of nine children, was now trying to come to terms with the fact that his father was dying. He was not too different from Pico, the eldest son in a family of ten, whose father had died ten years before and left him in charge of the family.

While they talked, James felt better and was able to eat some food, but after Pico left him alone, all his problems returned. He spent another uncomfortable, sleepless night, and the next day was again unable to eat. That evening, however, Pico returned not only with food, but with his sister, whom James thought was a great beauty. She also asked about his past life, and he took full advantage of the opportunity to play on her sympathy. He broadly hinted he would like to leave California, as he was anxious to see his brothers and sisters from whom he had been separated for so long. He also claimed, dramatically, that separating him from his "old and infirm" father was like taking his life.

•

233

Señorita Pico promised to do what she could by praying and, which was probably more satisfying to James, by interceding with the governor. She also promised to supply him with everything he needed while he was in jail. She was as good as her word, and he was soon provided with a bed and a change of clothes. She even saw that he "suffered for nothing in regard to food or drink."

It was about this time that John Bradshaw, master of the ship *Franklin*, called on the American prisoners. Pattie, who called Bradshaw "a true hearted American," was deeply impressed by this show of sympathy and friendship. The conversation he related, however, indicated Bradshaw was less interested in showing sympathy than in the furs they had buried on the Colorado River. Was there a chance of recovering them, was Pattie willing to make the effort, and once the furs were brought in, was he willing to sell them to Bradshaw? Pattie, like the others whom Bradshaw had talked to individually, assured him he was willing to do business, and the ship's captain promised to do everything he could to secure the release of the prisoners. Bradshaw did obtain momentary freedom for Pattie, and he was able to talk briefly with his father. Sylvester seemed to be happy, for he told his son that a beautiful young lady visited him and treated him with great kindness.

Thus far, except for the melodrama, Pattie's outline of events is reasonable. The fact that the eight men were disarmed and put in jail is easily established. The fact that Echeandia was a suspicous and indecisive man, and that he was not in the best mental condition to handle this problem, is also easily shown. Yet, Pattie paints the overall scene in darker colors than it deserves.

Much of the darkness, however, was in Pattie's own mind. By stripping away his attitudes and looking only at the events he describes, it is clear that conditions were not so bad. Probably he did spend a night or two on the floor; probably the food was bad; and probably Pattie, sleepless, worried, and unable to eat, did exchange harsh words with an

•

insensitive soldier. Still, it all ended within a few days, and he was provided with a bed, clean clothes, and whatever food he wanted. Soon afterward he was also allowed out of jail long enough to talk with his father. Looked at in this light, his story does not vary greatly from that of Nathaniel Pryor, who said, "Their detention was but for a few days, and they fared sumptuously, for Mexican hospitality to strangers is great."

Eventually, however, Pattie's unhappiness at being jailed caused him to tell a wild, impossible story. While in his cell, he said, he received a note from his father, who said he was so desperately ill he could not recover and he wished to see his son one last time before he died. The note was written on pasteboard torn from a hat and was "written with a stick, and the ink was blood, drawn from his aged veins." Unwittingly, Pattie has already denied his own story by relating the conversation in which Sylvester told him he was being treated kindly and provided with whatever he needed.

Pattie's willingness to use this story clearly demonstrates his attitude toward Echeandia. For reasons that are never entirely clear, all his bitterness is aimed at the governor, and Pattie blamed him for all his problems in California. He thought that Echeandia was a "miserable republican despot" who was "fickle and infirm in purpose." There were many in California who would have agreed with him on that. Much less believable, however, was his attempt to portray him as a cruel tyrant who kept a dying man in a cold cell, refused to allow him to see his own son, and forced him to write a secret letter in blood. Not only does this violate Pattie's own evidence of good treatment, but it also disagrees with all other views of Echeandia. One man, who was well aware of the governor's faults, was still willing to admit he was incapable of harming anyone.

Pattie, because of his desire to revenge himself on Echeandia for some real or fancied wrong, has abdicated his role as a narrator of real events. His abdication leaves the field of narration to Nathaniel Pryor, who was also there and who

•

later gave his account. Pryor and Pattie were very different men, as was clearly shown by their later activities. Pattie eventually went back to the United States, where he wrote a book damning Californians in general and Echeandia in particular. Pryor, however, stayed in California, converted to Catholicism, became a citizen, and married into a prominent California family. The differences in their choices of ways of life are also reflected in their narratives.

Pryor's account of the arrival in California is much the same as Pattie's, but without bitterness. They were arrested, disarmed, and placed in jail, but it was only for a short time and they were treated well. They were questioned on their activities and their reasons for being in California, but Pryor easily dismissed this as "the usual routine of red tape, taking depositions, etc." He also agreed that a captain of a Boston vessel offered to buy their furs and promised them a better price than they could get in Santa Fe. They were also free, according to Pryor, to go to Mission San Luis Rey, forty miles away, to obtain horses for the trip to the Colorado River to bring back the furs.

The only problem was Sylvester Pattie, and here the two accounts begin to move apart. Sylvester, Pryor said, was ill when they reached San Diego, and since he could not make the trip back to the river, the rest of the party decided to wait until he recovered. While he was ill, Sylvester was treated with the utmost kindness, a claim that even James, in his bitterness, did not entirely deny. Sylvester, however, did not recover, but grew worse, until one day he called all of his companions together and announced he was dying. He also said that even his own wife and daughters could not have treated him better than the women of San Diego. These same women had been urging him to become a Catholic, and he was ready to agree. He said he knew little of Catholicism and had no time to learn, but he assumed that where he was going it would do him no harm. Thus, in the last days of his life Sylvester Pattie was baptized a Catholic with Don Pio

•

Pico and Doña Victoria Dominguez de Estudillo standing as sponsors.

James Pattie could not accept, or at least in the narrative he would not admit, that his father converted to Catholicism. Again, however, he slips when he reports a conversation he had with Señorita Pico. She came to sympathize with him and to assure him that his father, during his illness, would receive every possible attention. She also said that if it was the will of God to take him, she would see that he was buried decently "as if he were her own father." A decent burial to a California Catholic almost certainly would require prior conversion.

Pattie claims that during these last days of his father's life, they were kept in small cells on order from the governor. Pryor, however, denies this, and it is doubtful that Echeandia ever issued such an order. Jedediah Smith, even when he reappeared in Monterey after being ordered to leave, was given the freedom of the town. Surely, Echeandia gave the same freedom to the trappers in San Diego, particularly since the sick comrade and the promise of horses and a good market for their furs were enough to keep them from leaving.

Yet, it is possible that James remained in a small room, kept there not by a locked door but by his own health. He had not been sleeping, and despite the unlimited food and drink, he was not eating. It was at this time that he described himself as "so emaciated and feeble that I could hardly travel across my prison floor." It may have been a physical ailment, but more likely it was nervous exhaustion brought on by the trip, by the problems with the governor, and by his constant worries about his father.

On May 24, 1828, Sylvester Pattie died at the age of forty-five. James's immediate reaction was relief, for he thought that his father had not enjoyed life much since the death of his wife. Now he was free of it, and James said that he too expected and even hoped to soon join his mother and father. "I felt weak, and exhausted myself, and I expected to rejoin

•

him in a few days, and never be separated from him. Life was a burden of which I felt longed to be relieved."

Sylvester Pattie's funeral, according to Pryor, was "the grandest funeral San Diego had ever seen." The procession was led by a Franciscan father, followed by four acolytes dressed in white. The coffin came next, borne by four Californians and followed by James Pattie, the other trappers, several crew members from an American ship, and, finally, most of the residents of San Diego. Catholic rites were performed, and when the last words of the ceremony—dust to dust and ashes to ashes—were said, the grave was surrounded by kneeling women offering up prayers for Sylvester's soul.

James Pattie remembered it differently. On the day of the funeral he was taken from his dark cell by six soldiers. When he stepped outside, the light dazzled his eyes and made him so dizzy that he reeled when he tried to walk. In his version there is no priest and no procession. Instead, brief ceremonies were conducted by a lieutenant, and Pattie himself arrived at the burial site only in time to catch a fleeting glimpse of the coffin being lowered into the grave. His only comment on religion was the abrupt insertion of the statement "No prayers were said." His father's conversion to Catholicism was apparently a subject he preferred to ignore. Some time later, when James himself was given the opportunity to convert, he instantly and bitterly rejected it.

As soon as the funeral was over, Pattie returned to his room. His only hope, he said, was that his health was rapidly declining and he would soon be out of prison and free to "rejoin my father, and be at rest." Much to his amazement he lay down on his bed and fell asleep. After that he slept regularly, his appetite returned and with it his health. Whatever had been bothering him, physical or mental, had passed away with the death of his father.

•

CHAPTER

THIRTEEN

N THE DAYS JUST AFTER HIS FATHER'S death, James's life changed considerably. Whatever caused his stomach to turn at the sight of food, and whatever kept him awake night after night, was gone. He was able to sleep, his appetite was good, and his strength began to return. His only problem was boredom, for there was no one to talk to, no books to read, and nothing to do. His solution, finally, was to take up smoking again. Sergeant Pico brought him some cigars, and he amused himself for hours watching the smoke curl into the air.

He even had some money. The captains of the ships in the bay—Seth Rogers of the *Andes*, Aaron Williams of the *Clio*, and William H. Cunningham of the *Courier*—had sent it to him. Pattie said they gave it to him to provide for all the trappers in case of emergency. If the money was sent directly to him, however, it was probably less a recognition of his leadership than a gesture of condolence to a young man who had lost his father.

He also began to make peace with the governor. Echeandia had received letters written in English that he could not read. Since Pattie could read English and also could speak passable Spanish, he was asked to translate them. Pattie, although modestly disclaiming any real scholarship, said he had no real trouble in understanding the letters and conveying the message, in Spanish, to the governor. As a result

•

Echeandia thawed somewhat and began to ask Pattie about himself and about his travels.

When Pattie left the governor's office, he felt much better. In the future the governor would undoubtedly need his services again, and it would give him the opportunity to ingratiate himself. He was right, for in the next few days he was often summoned to the governor's office. Each time Echeandia greeted him kindly, asked after his health, and acted with the utmost civility. Pattie immediately took advantage of this to hint at the injustice that was being done to the Americans. Echeandia, whenever he could, ignored the hints, and when that was impossible, he hid behind evasive answers.

Finally, Pattie made a specific offer to the governor. If there were any doubts about the return of the Americans to San Diego, he said, Mexican soldiers could be sent to guard them. He also assured Echeandia that the trappers would be willing to indemnify him for any expenses and, beyond that, would also be very grateful. Echeandia listened to this plan, which stopped just short of offering a bribe, with more than the usual attention. He told Pattie he would think about it and inform him of the decision within a week.

Pattie assumed that the governor's only problem was what to do about the American trappers. Yet, at the same time Echeandia was faced with another major problem that also concerned an American. John Bradshaw, master of the ship *Franklin*, had reached San Diego shortly before Pattie arrived. At that time he had been granted all possible privileges, and his supercargo, Rufus Perkins, had been allowed to travel overland to trade with each mission. Sometime later, after the *Franklin* had gone north to Monterey, Echeandia received a message accusing Bradshaw of smuggling along the Baja California coast. When the ship returned to San Diego, sometime in June, Echeandia ordered Bradshaw to land his cargo and deposit it in a warehouse pending the outcome of an investigation. It was a problem that, for the moment at least, took precedence over that of Pattie and his fellow trappers.

•

In the course of the investigation Captain Bradshaw submitted several letters, which Pattie translated for the governor. Pattie, however, had neither the insight nor the patience to wait until the problem was solved. Instead, when he handed the governor the completed translations, he asked him if he had reached a decision on allowing the trappers to retrieve their furs. Echeandia, faced with the unwanted task of making a difficult decision about the *Franklin*, said no in what Pattie thought was "his surliest tone."

The curt dismissal angered Pattie. His first reaction was the recurring daydream of shooting the governor. "How earnestly I wished that he and I had been together in the wild woods, and I armed with my rifle." That being impossible, Pattie reached a more practical solution—he would refuse to translate any more letters for the governor.

He had three days for his anger to fester before the governor sent for him again. Echeandia was unaware that he had offended Pattie, for he greeted him as he always had. He gave him some letters to translate and Pattie, after glancing at them, asked if he could leave. Echeandia looked at him; Pattie thought he had the look of a wild beast in his eyes. He asked—Pattie thought it sounded like the growl of a wounded grizzly—why he would not translate the letters. Pattie told him he would no longer work voluntarily for his enemy.

Echeandia was angered, either by the message or by the tone in which it was delivered. He took his sword, and with the flat side of the blade knocked Pattie to the floor. Pattie was momentarily stunned, but recovered quickly enough to try to attack the governor. The guards, however, seized him, while Echeandia rained rich and surprisingly plentiful Spanish curses on him. Pattie, as he was dragged from the room, shouted insults about an officer and gentleman who would beat an unarmed man. His recurring violent daydream also returned, and he demanded a sword and the opportunity to meet the governor face-to-face. Instead, he was thrown in a cell.

•

Pattie's claim that he had been locked in a cell since his arrival in San Diego is doubtful, but surely it is true now. Echeandia, the governor-general of both Californias, however weak and vacillating, could hardly allow himself to be insulted by an insolent young foreigner. Nor could he ignore the attempted attack or the threat to fight him, face-to-face, with a sword. Undoubtedly, Pattie did spend the next week as he described—in a cell, without visitors, and again reduced to a twice-a-day ration of corn cooked in rancid tallow.

Pattie's story of how he and Echeandia both lost their tempers is a plausible account of an encounter between two men, each so preoccupied with his own problem that he is unable to see the other man's point of view. The story, too, goes far toward explaining the bitterness toward Echeandia that pervades Pattie's entire account of California.

It was Captain Bradshaw who finally broke the tension. Echeandia, in his investigation of the charges against Bradshaw, planned to question each crew member of the *Franklin*. Only Bradshaw spoke Spanish, and since the governor hoped to catch crew members in contradictory testimony, he would not allow the captain to interpret. The obvious choice for the position was Pattie, whom Echeandia said was entirely capable of doing it if he was in a good humor. If not, Echeandia told Bradshaw, he would rather deal with the devil than with James Pattie when he was in a bad mood. Bradshaw then asked for permission to approach Pattie on the subject.

Bradshaw first asked him what he had done to make the governor so angry. Pattie described the confrontation, but Bradshaw, instead of being shocked, thought it was uproariously funny. Finally, he told him why he had come, and Pattie said he was willing to do whatever he could to help. Bradshaw returned to the governor's office, and shortly thereafter Pattie was summoned. When he entered the office, Echeandia asked him if he had changed his mind and was now willing to translate. Pattie said he was always will-

•

243

ing to translate for a gentleman, trying to convey that he meant Bradshaw and not the governor. Echeandia either missed the innuendo or chose to ignore the pettiness, for he said nothing. Instead, he set a time to begin the testimony and told Pattie that he must translate truthfully and in good faith. Again, Pattie could not contain his insolence and told the governor that Americans, unlike Californians, were at a disadvantage, for it was their weakness to be unable to say anything but the truth. Echeandia, however, refused to react and only smiled and waved him away.

The next morning Pattie went to work as a translator. Echeandia began by questioning Captain Bradshaw about the voyage. Much of the questioning concerned business, trading, shipping, and the technicalities of entering and leaving foreign ports. Most of this was unfamiliar to Pattie, and consequently the translation dragged on interminably. After Bradshaw finished, Rufus Perkins, the supercargo, was called, and after him the various members of the crew. Before they appeared, Bradshaw took Pattie aside and asked him to translate the testimony of the crew in such a way that it agreed with that of the captain. Bradshaw said some of them were angry at him—a normal state for sailing-ship crews of the time—and he feared they might purposely give testimony to hurt him. Pattie agreed to do all he could "in honor" to help the American captain.

The taking of depositions lasted several more days. Finally, Pattie, who now seems much more subdued, again raised the question of retrieving the furs. Surprisingly, Echeandia, instead of being angry, said that as soon as the *Franklin* affair was settled, he would allow them to go. Pattie protested that if they waited too long, the spring flood down the Colorado would destroy the buried furs. Echeandia, however, refused to be pushed and said it was not in his power to grant permission at the present time.

Pattie again insists he was continually locked in a cell, but it is more likely that he was given the freedom of the town. He himself admits that after he finished his work as a

•

translator, he was allowed to spend the night on board the *Franklin*. It was a new experience, for he had never been on board an oceangoing vessel before. He prowled through the ship, examining the masts, the rigging, and the sails. When he was finished, he then went below decks to investigate.

Not only was the ship a strange, new thing, but so was the crew. Pattie's experience with his countrymen was almost entirely limited to his fellow Kentuckians and Missourians who were active in the southwestern fur trade. Few if any of them ever ended up on a sailing ship. Instead, ship crews in California waters came mostly from New England and were augmented by beached sailors of all nationalities who could be obtained, willingly or unwillingly, in various ports. At first, he had difficulty understanding their dialect, but when they began talking about what they would do to the governor —his own favorite daydream—he understood them well enough. The sailors described several things they would like to do, but tarring and feathering seemed to have the most support. Pattie, too, admitted it would be an enjoyable sight. But as always he was forced to return to reality, for, "the worst of it was, after all, the general was not in their power."

The conversation with the crew was only passing, and Pattie soon moved to the captain's quarters, a completely different world on a sailing ship. The three men—Pattie, Bradshaw, and Perkins—spent much of the night talking about the cruelties and oppressions of Governor Echeandia. Pattie also described the death of his father, for Bradshaw and Perkins had not been in port when it happened. Possibly it was sympathy that caused Bradshaw to make an offer. He said that if Echeandia tried to condemn the *Franklin*, he was going to slip anchor and run out of the harbor even at the risk of being sunk by the guns at the fort. If it came to that, he said, Pattie was welcome to sail with him. He even promised to find him a job when the ship reached Boston. Pattie thanked him but declined, for he did not want to desert the other trappers.

Not long after, the subject of retrieving the furs was finally

•

solved. Echeandia himself opened the subject by asking Pattie what guarantee they could give that all the trappers would return to San Diego. One choice was to leave a man behind as a hostage for the good conduct of the rest. Pattie, however, was unwilling to agree to this. He assumed that the governor was planning to send soldiers with them. Sometime during the trip, Pattie suspected, the trappers would rise, take all of the horses, and send the soldiers back to the general on foot. His faith in the self-control of his fellow Americans was not strong enough for him to offer a hostage. Instead, he said he could offer the governor no security.

Echeandia, who probably had already formed his own plan, ignored this and told the trappers to make their arrangements to return to the river. They needed horses to make the trip, and Antonio Peyri of Mission San Luis Rey had promised to furnish them. Some of the trappers, including Pattie, therefore rode to the mission on a road that ran through barren, brush-covered hills, devoid of any sign of life. The endless climbing of hills made the trip so tedious that it seemed much longer than the actual thirty miles. Finally, from the top of one hill, the mission itself could be seen in the distance. The most prominent feature was the large white main building. It was built in the form of a quadrangle, with the front part supported by arches and columns and one corner anchored by the massive church bell with its high bell tower. From here, all the minor defects were hidden and it looked more like a palace than a mission. Beyond the buildings, stretching off to the north, were the pastures covered with thousands of cattle, sheep, and horses, for at the time San Luis Rey had by far the largest flocks and herds of all the California missions.

San Luis Rey also had a reputation as the finest mission in California, and the man responsible was Father Antonio Peyri, who had been there since it was founded in 1798. At that time he was just twenty-nine years old, and in the days just after the founding he had lived in a brush hut. Now,

•

thirty years later, he presided over the large buildings, the flock and herds, and an Indian population of nearly three thousand, which, again, was by far the largest at any California mission.

Almost everyone who met Peyri liked and respected him, and Pattie was no exception. The missionary greeted him and invited him in to have some wine. A Frenchman, who was there shortly before Pattie, also had some of the wine produced at the mission and called it the best in California. Pattie's background, however, had not prepared him to appreciate good wine, and his only comment was the passing hint that he did not think it entirely proper for a holy man to drink it. Still, he was influenced enough by the signs of good taste—the pictures of saints, the glassware, and the furnishings—to be on his best behavior. He was careful, he said, "not to let any of my hunting phrases and back-woods dialect escape me."

Pattie, as usual, had to tell his story and answer questions about his long journey across the continent. Then they turned to the business of the horses and soon reached an agreement. Peyri would supply fourteen horses and mules— seven for riding, seven more for packing the furs. In exchange, the trappers, when they returned, would pay him twenty-five cents a day for each animal.

Sometime after the agreement was reached, the church bells rang and Father Peyri began to pray. He said the Lord's Prayer, and as he paused after each phrase, Pattie repeated it. When they were finished, Peyri asked him why he had prayed, and James said it was for the salvation of his soul. The father said he was surprised at the young man's piety, for he had been led to believe that Americans were not Christians. James assured him that in the United States there were churches everywhere, and that people read the Bible and believed it. Peyri, however, argued that Americans were in error, for they did not believe in the Immaculate Conception of the Virgin Mary. By now, the theological discussion was too deep for James, and he began to hedge. What

•

Americans in general believed about this he could not say. For himself, he said, he had not read the Bible enough to have formed an opinion. That, Peyri said, was obvious enough, and if he had read the Bible more, he would not have been led astray by Protestants. Unfortunately, the brief time before the trappers left for the Colorado River was not sufficient to show him the true way. Pattie admits that by now Peyri was laughing; although as he laughed, he also suggested that when Pattie returned he might care to be baptized. Pattie was very uncomfortable with this turn in the conversation, but fortunately Peyri soon went on to other topics. "Glad was I," Pattie said, "when he dismissed this subject, and began to chat about other matters. We had an excellent supper, and I was shown to my bed."

After the horses were obtained, the trappers returned to San Diego to make their final preparations. By now, it was early July, six weeks after Sylvester's death. Much of the time since then had been spent in taking depositions about the *Franklin*, and when that was completed, Echeandia, as he had promised, gave the trappers permission to get their furs. Pattie, apparently hoping to demonstrate the unreasonable length of time it took to reach a decision, has stretched out the narrative; by his dates it is now September. All other records, however, conclusively show that it is only July.

Pattie, as he envisioned the trip, assumed that once they were on their way, they could easily overwhelm the soldiers, take their horses, and never return to San Diego. Echeandia apparently assumed the same thing, for just before they left he announced a change in plans. He told them he was unable to spare the necessary soldiers to accompany them, and thus, to assure their return, he planned to keep one man in San Diego as a hostage. The man he chose was James Pattie.

Pattie, in describing his reaction to this announcement, again becomes melodramatic. Some of the other trappers, he said, wanted to abandon the expedition rather than leave him alone in California. Pattie, however, insisted they go, telling them that "I had no fear of anything, the general

•

could inflict, that I had little left, but life to relinquish." Despite the melodrama, Pattie may indeed have been worried, for he did not fully trust his companions' self-discipline or their ability to resist the temptation to escape now that there would be no supervision. Besides, the furs were in hostile Indian country, and it was entirely possible that all the trappers might be killed.

Even if he had these worries, however, he was in much better condition than he was willing to admit. Sometime before the others left, he had signed a promissory note to his fellow trapper Jesse Ferguson. It said, "For value received I promise to pay unto Jesse Ferguson two hundred and thirty seven dollars and seventy five cents when we get the fur in that is cashed on Red River and make sale of it as witness my hand and seal. Signed, James O. Pattie." Exactly how Ferguson obtained such an amount of money or why Pattie borrowed it is unclear. Probably, it was to be used to support him in San Diego while the others were gone. Two hundred and thirty-seven dollars and seventy-five cents should have done so handsomely.

At the same time, Pattie was given the opportunity to inform the United States government of his situation. The nearest American consul was John Coffin Jones, Jr., who was in Hawaii, and Captain Bradshaw, who was making plans to escape from San Diego, offered to deliver a message. Pattie wrote a letter in which he related the story of his imprisonment, the death of his father, and the names of all the party. He also asked that Jones inform the government of their plight. Eventually, by way of Hawaii and Massachusetts, the letter reached a St. Louis newspaper, which published the information a year after the letter was written. Somehow, the information also reached John Pattie and his family in Bracken County, for they asked Nicholas Coleman, their newly elected congressman, to look into the matter. All that, however, took time and had no immediate effect on Pattie in San Diego.

Not long after his fellow trappers left for the Colorado,

•

Pattie was involved in the final events of the *Franklin* affair. He again served as translator at a conference in which Bradshaw asked for his papers. Echeandia refused. Instead, the governor insisted the cargo of the *Franklin* be unloaded. Pattie, in his dramatic and belligerent fashion, said that Bradshaw refused to obey and stormed out of the governor's office. Bradshaw, however, was older and less hotheaded, and in reality he handled it much more smoothly. He promised Echeandia he would comply with the order and asked only that he be allowed to return to his ship to make arrangements.

At first Echeandia agreed to let him go aboard the *Franklin*, but later changed his mind and ordered him arrested before he could leave. Pattie claims he overheard the governor give this order and went to warn Bradshaw. He may again be promoting himself to a major role in events he only witnessed, but someone warned Bradshaw, for he escaped by taking to the ship's boat and ignoring the pointed rifles and threats of the squad of soldiers sent to arrest him.

That night Bradshaw changed the *Franklin*'s anchorage to a place near the French ship *Heros*. The captain of that ship, Auguste Duhaut-Cilly, now found himself innocently caught in the middle. A few days earlier, when the *Heros* arrived in San Diego, Echeandia had asked the French captain if he would have his ship's carpenter build a small boat. Duhaut-Cilly agreed, thinking that the governor needed it as a customs boat to meet incoming ships. Only later did he discover that Echeandia intended to use it to put a boarding party on the *Franklin*. Duhaut-Cilly, when he learned this, warned Bradshaw and also told his carpenter to delay the building as long as possible.

The morning after Bradshaw shifted anchorage, Echeandia appeared on the beach with a troop of horsemen. When Duhaut-Cilly went ashore, the governor asked for immediate delivery of the boat and the Frenchman began to delay. The boat had not yet been caulked, he said, and besides, he had been unable to find any oars for it. Echeandia then asked for

•

the use of one of the *Heros*'s own boats, but Duhaut-Cilly refused on the grounds that it would compromise him with the United States government. Through all these delays, he kept looking toward the *Franklin*, hoping it would slip anchor and leave port. It stayed, however, and Duhaut-Cilly could delay no longer. His carpenter caulked the boat, and the Californians found, somewhere in the *presidio*, some old galley oars left over from Spanish days. The oars, however, were thirty feet long and needed trimming to make them usable in a small boat. While Echeandia's own carpenters debated over whether to cut the excess off the handle or the blade, the *Franklin* suddenly set sail.

It was, Duhaut-Cilly said, an unbelievable sight. One moment the *Franklin* was sitting firmly at anchor. The next moment, without the appearance of any activity, it had slipped its anchor and was under full sail. The Frenchmen marveled at the ingenuity of Bradshaw in secretly rigging his ship to accomplish this, but gave no particulars on how it was done.

James Pattie apparently had a good place to view the action, for he gave an accurate account of the way Bradshaw ran out of port. As the *Franklin* passed the guns at the battery, the Californians fired about forty shots at the escaping ship. Bradshaw hove to long enough to fire a broadside at the battery, then sailed on. Pattie, during the action, was close enough to accurately assess the damage to the *Franklin*. Shots had entered the hull, he said, and the sails had been considerably cut up by grapeshot. Duhaut-Cilly, presumably more expert in naval matters, disagreed, and in his original journal said the *Franklin* suffered only minor damage. Later, however, he again saw the *Franklin* in Hawaii and found that the cannon fire had been more accurate than he thought. The ship, he said, had "received two balls in the hull and two others in the rigging, which necessitated changing the main and mizzen yards."

A week after the *Franklin* sailed, Echeandia held a final hearing on the case. Pattie gave a somewhat confused ac-

•

count of an earlier hearing in which the governor threatened him with death if he did not testify. Pattie, however, said that he considered Echeandia's threats to be those of an old woman and refused to answer any questions. Despite this the records of the final hearing show that Pattie was a willing witness. According to the report filed by Echeandia, Pattie, when asked to testify, stated simply and accurately that he knew beforehand that Bradshaw planned to leave port secretly and that he also planned to fire on the fort if they tried to stop him. By then, it made little difference, for after Echeandia filed his report the case was forgotten.

In the weeks after the *Franklin* sailed, Pattie waited alone in San Diego for the return of the other trappers. Again, he claims he was locked in prison and tortured, mentally if not physically. Each day, he said, Californians would come and tell him his companions would never return and that they had left him at the mercy of Governor Echeandia. They also told him that when the other trappers failed to return, the governor would execute him. Some said it would be by hanging, others said by using him for target practice, and still others said he would be burned alive.

There is no specific evidence to either support or deny Pattie's claim, and there may have been a few sadistic individuals who delighted in tormenting a frightened young man. Still, common sense based on the way other foreigners were treated in California makes this tale of horror almost impossible. Foreigners were often subject to the bureaucratic delays, confusions, and arbitrary decisions of California officials, but few were ever physically mistreated. Even those angered by the treatment they received from officials usually admitted they were treated kindly by individual Californians. Most likely, Pattie spent his time quietly in San Diego, his main enemy being boredom rather than an outraged population talking about burning him at the stake.

Finally, the other trappers returned from the river. They brought no furs with them, for the spring flood had already come down the river and the water had seeped into the pit

•

where the furs were cached. When the trappers dug them up, they found that all the furs had been ruined. They did bring back the traps they had buried, but the proceeds from these went mainly to pay for the horses and mules they had used. Pattie's opportunity to return home a moderately wealthy man based on his share of thirty thousand dollars in fur was gone.

CHAPTER

---•◆◆•---

F·O·U·R·T·E·E·N

AMES PATTIE, THROUGH ALL HIS YEARS IN the West, had one main hope—to make enough money so that he could return triumphantly to Kentucky, where, he imagined, his brothers and sisters were waiting for him to bring home a fortune. Several times he had come close, but each time something had intervened. He had hoped for a fortune with the sale of the furs buried on the Colorado River, but that dream disappeared when the others returned to San Diego without them. By then, he had been traveling for more than three years, his father was dead, he was still a long way from home, and he had almost nothing to show for all the years of trapping.

He was in a difficult position, and had he been more perceptive, he might have given an honest examination of his own emotions that would have heightened the impact of the narrative. Instead, he continued to build carefully a chronicle of mistreatment by the governor. The narrative, as happened once before when Pattie was troubled, began to disintegrate. In real life Pattie reached his lowest point in California; in the narrative he would perform his greatest feats.

Pattie insists that after the other trappers returned they were again disarmed, thrown into jail, and kept there for several months. By now, just four of the original eight were left. Sylvester was dead, and Edmund Russell had either dis-

·

appeared or died. He had been listed as a member of the party in Pattie's letter to Jones, but unlike the others he is never mentioned in any California records. Two other trappers, Isaac Slover and William Pope, had not returned from the Colorado River but had gone from there back to New Mexico. In the narrative Pattie claimed the two men refused to return for fear they would be thrown in jail, but Echeandia apparently knew of their intention, for he issued them a separate passport. Thus, by the end of 1828 the party in California had been reduced to Nathaniel Pryor, Jesse Ferguson, Richard Laughlin, and James Pattie. Given all the circumstances, it is highly unlikely that they spent any more time in jail. Yet, Pattie insists that it was not until just before Christmas that he was allowed out of prison.

The day after he was freed he met a man named James Lang. Lang, who was passing secretly through San Diego, said he was in California to hunt sea otters and also to do some smuggling. He also said he was willing to make Pattie and the other trappers an offer. He had a ship off the coast of Baja California, and if they would accompany him, he would furnish everything needed to hunt otters, would split the profits, and would even give them passage back to the United States. Pattie, and one other trapper, sneaked away from San Diego and traveled by night to meet Lang at Todos Santos Bay. When they arrived they found he had already been arrested, and they sneaked back to San Diego, again traveling by night.

The story is almost true. In December 1828 a man named Lang—Charles, not James—was arrested in a small boat off the coast of Baja California. Lang, whom Pattie portrayed as glibly describing profits in smuggling and otter hunting, was less articulate when he was arrested. He told the arresting officers a story of why he was in the boat, but his companion, an American named Winslow Lewis, told an entirely different story. Later, in the official investigation, Lang, faced with Lewis's contradiction, told still another story. He had come to California, he said, to establish a ranch, build a

•

house, and devote himself to farming. Even with time to think he was unable to invent an entirely convincing story, for as officials pointed out, his two trunks of dry goods and a barrel organ were better suited to illicit trading than to farming. The goods were confiscated and Lang was deported.

Certainly, Pattie knew Lang, for they were two Americans in a small foreign town at the same time. Yet, it is doubtful that Pattie was ever involved in Lang's smuggling venture. His story of how he was freed is unconvincing, his secretive trips at night are melodramatic, his time sequence is impossibly foreshortened, and his dates are demonstrably wrong. Furthermore, no hint of suspicion ever touched him, for in the official inquiry Pattie was never mentioned. He was there during the investigation, however, and quite likely he heard Lang's story and used it to reaffirm his own account of how Americans were treated in California. As always, he was unable to tell someone else's story without making himself a participant.

The story of Lang is only a minor aside to the high drama of how Pattie finally won his freedom. Having committed himself to a tale of long imprisonment by an unreasonable tyrant, he now needed a dramatic event to explain the governor's decision to give him freedom to travel throughout California. In response to this need, he created one of the best-known and least likely stories in the *Personal Narrative*.

The story is simple enough. Late in 1828, while Pattie was still in jail, a smallpox epidemic broke out in the northern part of California. As it worsened, and as it began to move toward San Diego, Echeandia became concerned. One day a soldier, passing the time in talk, asked one of the trappers if he knew anything to do to stop the epidemic. The trapper explained about vaccination and also said he thought that Sylvester Pattie had brought some vaccine from the copper mines. As a result James Pattie was called before the governor, who demanded that he begin vaccinating people. Pattie

•

refused until he and his companions were freed. Finally, the governor agreed, and Pattie began his vaccination program. Over the next several months he would travel from San Diego all the way to the Russian settlement at Fort Ross vaccinating some twenty-two thousand people.

Pattie's story, as he tells it, cannot stand against critical analysis, for there are too many inconsistencies, improbabilities, and outright falsehoods. His numbers are impossible, for by his claim he vaccinated more people than actually lived in California. His implication that vaccination was a complete mystery to Californians is wrong. Information on smallpox and its prevention had been available since the 1780s, and the first vaccine had reached there in 1817. His tale of how he happened to have vaccine with him is improbable, and his claim that he withheld it until he was given his freedom is inconsistent with his own story of spending eight months in jail at the mercy of the governor. Under such circumstances he could hardly have prevented its seizure, particularly since, at the time, the governor was actively searching for vaccine. On March 12, 1828, Echeandia asked all *presidio* commanders to do everything they could to obtain vaccine. Six weeks later he also wrote to Mexico begging for smallpox vaccine because there was none available in California.

The most telling fault, however, is the complete absence in contemporary records of any mention of what Pattie described as an epidemic that overwhelmed all of California. Yet, buried in those same records is enough information to show the real situation in California and to demonstrate how Pattie adapted it to his own needs.

A year before Pattie arrived in San Diego, a serious measles epidemic broke out in California. It began at San Gabriel and spread to all the other missions. By the time Pattie reached San Diego, however, the epidemic had ended there, and the only serious outbreaks were in the northern missions several hundred miles away. He was never at a mission

•

while this epidemic was at its height, but he did arrive soon after it ended. Undoubtedly, he heard of it, and it may have given him the basic idea for a story about an epidemic.

Pattie's epidemic, however, was not measles but small-pox. And if there is no indication of a major outbreak of that disease, there is considerable evidence to show that small-pox was present and that Echeandia was concerned enough to begin a program of vaccination. In 1828 both Santa Clara and San Jose missions reported cases, and Echeandia, in his letters of March and April, began searching for vaccine. Then, in late 1828, the Russian ship *Baikal* brought vaccine to California, leaving some at Monterey, the rest at San Diego. Shortly afterward, on January 12, 1829, Echeandia informed both Father Peyri at San Luis Rey and Father José Sanchez at San Gabriel that he was sending them some smallpox vaccine. The basic framework of Pattie's story is there; the only question is how far did he adapt it and how far did he invent his own role?

Quite likely, Pattie, who was in San Diego during this time, was no more than an observer. It is possible that he could have conducted a small-scale vaccination program, but even this is doubtful. The missionaries were responsible not only for the souls but also for the physical well-being of the Indians, and thus they had at least some basic knowledge of medicine. Besides, when Echeandia sent the vaccine to Father Sanchez at San Gabriel, he also included instructions on how to use it.

Even if the missionaries were unable to vaccinate, there were several men in California who were more qualified than Pattie to carry out such a program. In Los Angeles there was Joseph Chapman, an American, who was not only a carpenter, millwright, and boatbuilder, but an amateur doc-tor as well. At Santa Barbara, "Dr. Diego Borris," a New Yorker, had been baptized and appointed troop physician in 1824. Farther north, at San Francisco, William Richardson was already known to California officials as a man who had "some knowledge and moderate practice" in medicine and

•

surgery. All of these men had been in California for several years, were better known, and had more experience in medicine than Pattie.

The only real possibility left for Pattie is that he could have been a delivery boy who carried vaccine to the various missions. Even that is unlikely, for Echeandia, a governor, certainly had couriers available and had no need to turn to an American. Besides, he told Peyri and Sanchez he was sending the vaccine on January 12 and did not issue a travel permit to Pattie until six weeks later.

Throughout all this Pattie was in San Diego waiting for his permit and was in a position to hear of the vaccination program. The Californians, however, had no real need for him, and he was ignored. Later, it would have been easy to take what he had seen and heard and create the story of how he saved California from smallpox.

Behind all the heroics there is again the story of a man who made little impact. Instead of being ordered by the governor to vaccinate the people of California, it was Pattie himself who opened the question of his future. In February 1829 he requested permission to stay in California. Shortly afterward, Echeandia issued him a conditional permit that allowed him to travel freely throughout the area for one year. Ironically, given Pattie's account of his relations with the governor, the pass describes him as "not vicious . . . but of regular conduct."

After the permit was issued in the spring of 1829, Pattie, who had been in San Diego for almost a year, was finally free to see the rest of California. With his three fellow trappers, Pryor, Laughlin, and Ferguson, he left for Los Angeles with a letter of introduction to Antonio Rocha, who might be able to help the Americans establish themselves in that area.

The route north from San Diego took them to San Luis Rey, which Pattie had visited earlier. Although he did not vaccinate anyone, he did stop long enough to give a description of mission life. His facts are generally accurate, but in his bitterness he emphasized mostly the things of which he

•

disapproved. The mission itself, he said, was the largest and most flourishing in California and was filled with Indians who had been trained as blacksmiths, carpenters, shoemakers, and even musicians. Yet, most of the Indians had been brought into the mission against their will, baptized, and then put to work. Discipline was rigid and based on "applying the rod to those who fall short of the portion of labor assigned to them." The missionaries also had assumed the role of protector of women and, an hour after supper, locked up married women whose husbands were absent and all unmarried women above the age of nine. All this did little good, he said, for "I saw women in irons for misconduct and men in the stocks."

A day's travel north of San Luis Rey was the mission of San Juan Capistrano, which Pattie mistakenly called "St. John the Baptist." His faulty memory, or his flair for the dramatic, also caused him to describe it in a peculiar way. The mountains, according to Pattie, closed in upon the coast so closely that there was hardly room for the mission, and the ocean waves dashed directly upon the shore in front of it. Actually, the mission is several miles from the coast, and the Santa Ana Mountains behind it are twenty miles to the east. Still, while he was at Capistrano he did hear a fairly accurate story of the collapse of the church in the earthquake of 1812. This time he resisted the temptation to exaggerate or insert himself into the story and gave only a straightforward description of a past event. If anything, he understated it, for he gave the number killed as between twenty and thirty, when, in fact, more than forty were killed when the church collapsed.

Again, however, he found something of which he disapproved. The priest, he said, "was in the habit of indulging his love of wine and stronger liquors to such a degree, as to be often intoxicated." Such stories were common tales told by Americans, and only occasionally were they true. In this case there was little basis for the story. The two missionaries at San Juan Capistrano were José Barona and José Zalvidea,

•

and there is no other evidence that either man was given to excessive drinking. Zalvidea did have certain eccentricities, most notably taking solitary walks and arguing with the devil. Barona, by 1829, was old and broken in health. Six years before, he had had trouble with a soldier who tried to prevent his leaving the mission without a military escort. In the struggle Barona fell from his horse, and although he was not physically hurt, the insult and shock aggravated his already weakened health, and he never fully recovered. James Pattie, young and bitter against Catholics and Californians, could easily have seen an eccentric man, or an old, broken man, and leaped to the conclusion that the cause was drunkenness.

The four trappers stayed briefly at San Juan Capistrano, then continued on to Los Angeles to deliver the letter of introduction to Antonio Rocha, a man who understood the problems of trying to adapt to a foreign country. He was a Portuguese who in 1815 had arrived in California aboard the ship *Columbia,* which was bound for the Northwest Coast. When it put in briefly at Monterey, several men, including Rocha, jumped ship. Most of the others were later caught, but Rocha never was. Instead, he settled in California, and by 1829 was living near Los Angeles. He was friendly to the four Americans and allowed them to stay with him until they got settled.

Pattie never mentioned Rocha by name. Yet, in the account of his visit to Los Angeles, he gave details that show he spent at least some time at Rocha's new home. In the years just before Pattie arrived, the demand for hides and tallow by New England ship captains had placed a large emphasis on tha cattle industry in the Los Angeles basin. As a result Rocha, in 1828, had obtained a land grant to forty-four hundred acres of land west of the pueblo. The grant included the La Brea tar pits, just north of which Rocha built his home. It was these same tar pits that attracted all of Pattie's attention when he was in Los Angeles. He watched the liquid tar rise to the surface and make large bubbles that finally

•

burst with a loud noise. He also described the way those who lived in Los Angeles came to the pits to obtain tar. The pitch, in places where it had hardened, was broken off with an ax or some other tool, and carried to the pueblo. Here the chunks were placed on the dirt-covered roofs and the heat of the sun soon blended them into a tar-covered roof.

Three of the four Americans soon found work in Los Angeles. Pryor became a silversmith, while Laughlin and Ferguson went into the nearby mountains to work as lumbermen. These three were apparently content, for they settled here, and in the next few years would convert to Catholicism, become citizens, and marry into California families. James Pattie, however, would not or could not settle into this routine. Nathaniel Pryor claims Pattie soon left, intending to return to Kentucky. Pattie, however, claims he left Los Angeles to vaccinate Indians at the missions north of there. Although that claim could not possibly be true, his descriptions are such to verify his claim that he traveled by land at least as far north as Santa Barbara.

After he left Los Angeles Pattie stopped briefly at San Fernando Mission, but said little more than that it was "a fine place." At San Buenaventura, however, he heard the kind of story he liked to tell. Not long before his arrival two missionaries had left the mission "taking with them what gold and silver they could lay their hands on." He offered no names, but the two men were Antonio Ripoll and José Altamira, and their story was well known in California. In January 1828 they had secretly boarded a ship at Santa Barbara and left California for good. They had heard of the decree expelling Spaniards shortly before their flight, and that may have been the final, determining factor. Still, Ripoll, at least, had been thinking of leaving since the previous summer. In June 1828, when Duhaut-Cilly had visited him, he discovered that the Frenchman was carrying a draft for seven thousand francs, drawn on the English government. Ripoll offered to give Duhaut-Cilly piasters for the draft, since they could be more easily used in Europe. The Frenchman ac-

.

cepted, although at the time he had no idea why the missionary made the request. It was not until later, when he heard of the flight, that he understood.

Pattie was not the only one to accuse the missionaries of stealing whatever they could, for that story would be popular in California for years to come. It was Duhaut-Cilly, however, who gave the most intelligent account. When he sold the draft to Ripoll, the missionary told him that the money was his own, accumulated from the stipend of four hundred piasters a year given by the government. Duhaut-Cilly added, "I had too high an opinion of this missionary to believe it otherwise; and when some person told me that, on leaving, he had carried away large sums, I did not give credit to those injurious assertions." The fact that an investigation turned up no serious shortages at the mission bears out Duhaut-Cilly.

From San Buenaventura Pattie went to Santa Barbara, where he found several American ships in port. He went aboard to see the ship captains and "enjoyed the contrast of such society with that of the priests and Indians, among whom I had lately been." The presence of ships is undoubtedly true, for Santa Barbara was frequently visited by American traders. The implication, however, that he had to go aboard ship to escape the society of priests and Indians is less true, for by 1829 there was a surprising number of foreigners living in California.

Before 1821, when California was still part of the Spanish empire, it had been illegal for foreigners to even visit the area. Nonetheless, foreign ships seeking sea otter furs often touched the coast, and each time they did several crew members attempted to desert. Many were successful and, despite the law, Californians were hospitable. At the same time the missionaries discovered that these foreigners often possessed skills that were unavailable elsewhere in California. Consequently, they were allowed to stay, and by the time Spanish rule ended there were several dozen foreigners already living in California. In the next decade, under Mexico,

•

foreigners were allowed to settle, and by the time Pattie arrived there was a sizable foreign colony in California.

Several of the foreigners lived in San Diego even during the time that Pattie claimed he was a lonely American in a foreign jail. There was a Scotsman, a Frenchman, an Irishman, but the most prominent was an American, Henry Delano Fitch, a native of New Bedford, Massachusetts. Fitch had arrived in 1826, and within a year proposed to Josefa Carrillo and was accepted. Echeandia, however, also had hopes of marrying the same woman and used his power as governor to block the marriage for almost two years. Finally, in April 1829, Fitch and Señorita Carrillo secretly boarded a ship in San Diego and went to Valparaiso, where they were married. The story was an instant sensation in California, and Pattie could hardly have missed hearing it. In the narrative, however, he ignored it, quite likely because he realized it would seriously weaken his own account. Fitch, an American trader, in order to marry had successfully defied the governor by easily slipping away from San Diego. Pattie, however, was relating a story of how he was a lone American, who was unable to escape and who was constantly at the mercy of a governor who had absolute power.

Farther north, in the area between San Gabriel on the east and San Fernando on the west, the foreign population was even larger. More than a dozen men, their nationalities including Portuguese, French, Norwegian, English, and American, lived in or near Los Angeles. The oldest and best-known resident of the area was Joseph Chapman, who had arrived in 1818 aboard the pirate ship commanded by Hippolyte de Bouchard. Chapman was an American who had been pressed into service in Hawaii, but when Bouchard reached California and began to raid, he deserted. He was allowed to stay, and he worked as a carpenter, lumberman, and blacksmith. He had also built the gristmill at Mission Santa Inez and later built another mill at San Gabriel. By 1829 he owned and ran a vineyard near Los Angeles, served the community as an amateur doctor, and was recognized as

•

the most prominent foreigner in the area. Pattie's companion Nathaniel Pryor later remembered him as one of the first men he met in the Los Angeles area. Pattie, however, completely ignored Chapman.

At Santa Barbara, where Pattie went aboard the American ships to escape the constant company of Indians and priests, there was also a group of foreigners. They were not difficult to locate, for Alfred Robinson, who like Pattie visited Santa Barbara in 1829, met in quick order Daniel Hill, Robert Elwell, and William G. Dana. All of them were New England merchants who had been baptized Catholics, become citizens, and married California women. Dana had also begun expanding his activities beyond simple trading. He was involved in stock raising, farming, soap making, and also in sea otter hunting, by allowing those who could not obtain licenses to use his for a percentage of the catch. About the time Pattie arrived, he also had workmen building a thirty-three-ton schooner, which, when it was finished, would be christened the *Santa Barbara*.

Pattie ignored all the activities of Dana and the other Americans and concentrated instead on his loneliness. He visited the mission, on a hill northwest of town, and found "a fine view of the great deep." Looking out over the Pacific, he began to brood about the many hours he had spent looking at the ocean during "this long and lonely journey, through a country every way strange and foreign to me." Even his dark thoughts, however, could not contain the sense of wonder of a landlocked midwesterner who, for the first time, saw whales swimming and spouting water into the air.

In the narrative Pattie claims he left Santa Barbara and traveled by land to visit all the northern missions. Since he still insists that the main point of this trip was to vaccinate everyone in California, he could hardly have ignored them. Other evidence in the narrative, however, strongly suggests that he never saw these missions, and that he left Santa Barbara by sea rather than by land.

•

Until now, the *Personal Narrative* at least has borne out Pattie's claim to have visited the missions between San Diego and Santa Barbara. The story of vaccination is impossible, but beyond that Pattie gave a plausible account of the things he saw and heard and provided enough detail to demonstrate he had visited these places. Above Santa Barbara, however, the narrative changes completely. There is no longer even a superficial description, but only a list of the number of people vaccinated at each mission. Not only is there no detail, but the order of the missions also is confused; one is missing entirely and several others are misplaced. This, combined with Pattie's story of meeting ship captains in Santa Barbara, plus the story of a sea voyage that he later inserts into the narrative, is strong evidence that he traveled north by ship.

Pattie himself, once he finished his tale of vaccination, told his story of going to sea. He met the ship captain on shore and made arrangements with him to visit various ports in California. He gave no details as to the captain's name, the ship, or where it went. Instead, he described how, within an hour after sailing, he was seasick, and how it lasted for a week, during which time he could eat little or nothing. Finally, he recovered and "never enjoyed better health in my life," as they sailed from anchorage to anchorage. Pattie said the trip began and ended in Monterey, and possibly it did. Still, the absence of any real knowledge of the land north of Santa Barbara, and the solid detail on Monterey and San Francisco, where ships frequently anchored, indicate that all his travel in the north was by sea.

Sometime during his travel aboard ship he visited San Francisco Bay. While he was there, he took the opportunity to also visit the Russian settlement at Fort Ross. Months before, in San Diego, he said, the commander of the fort had invited him to come and vaccinate its inhabitants. The Russians, who had brought the vaccine to California, needed no help from Pattie. Still, the Russian ship *Baikal* had been in San Diego twice while Pattie was there, and he may well

•

have received an invitation to visit the fort. Certainly, his description of Fort Ross is too detailed to ignore.

Pattie's guides from San Francisco to the fort were two Kodiak Indians who had been brought from their home island in the Aleutians to hunt sea otters for the Russians. Pattie saw enough of their activities that he could give an accurate account of the way they hunted. They used a bidarka, which he described as a boat shaped like a canoe and made out of sea lion skin. The entire boat, including the top, was covered except for two small holes fore and aft. The hunters crawled into the boat, drew a waterproof cover over themselves and the hole to make the boat watertight. Then they went after otters, with the man in the stern steering while his partner in the bow darted a spear at any otters he saw. It was efficient enough, Pattie said, for "great numbers are thus taken."

The two Kodiak took him across the bay, then worked their way past the mouth of a big river that Pattie called by its Spanish name, Rio de San Francisco. They landed on the north edge of the bay at the mouth of Petaluma Creek and from there traveled overland to the fort. The country appealed to Pattie, who thought it was beautiful, "with a rich soil, well watered, and timbered." It was a long trip, and they did not reach Fort Ross until after dark. Rather than going into the fort, Pattie accompanied the men to their hut, where he was given something to eat and a sealskin on which to sleep.

The next morning he went to the fort, supposedly to vaccinate, but more logically to just look around. He was welcomed by the commander, Paul Shelikov, whose name Pattie, with his bad ear for foreign words, recorded as "Don Seraldo." For the next week he stayed at this "delightful place." He said little about the rectangular fort, with its twenty-foot plank walls and two gun turrets, or the large house of the commandant, or even the newly completed chapel. Instead, he concentrated mainly on the beauty of the surrounding country. The fort itself sat on high bluffs di-

.

rectly above the Pacific and in the midst of a valley filled with cattle. Beyond this valley, back from the ocean, was a heavily forested mountain. Thus far, the view is accurate, but Pattie again lifted his eyes too far and found, just beyond the fort, a nonexistent mountain "glittering with perpetual ice and snow." Even without snowcapped mountains, Pattie found it attractive and called its location "one of the most beautiful that I ever beheld." It was one of the few places in California that Pattie liked. It was also one of the few places where he was free of Spanish-speaking Californians.

After his week at Fort Ross Pattie returned to San Francisco, where almost immediately he began to rage about the Californians again. His anger, he claimed, was caused by a document given him by a missionary. It said, "I certify, that James O. Pattie has vaccinated all the Indians and whites on this coast, and to recompense him for the same, I give the said James O. Pattie my obligation for one thousand head of cattle, and land to pasture them; that is, 500 cows and 500 mules. This he is to receive after he becomes a Catholic, and a subject of this government. Given in the mission of St. Francisco on the 8th of July, in the year 1829." It was signed, "Juan Cabortes."

The document is strange, for although it cannot be accepted at face value, neither can it be totally dismissed. The faults are clear enough. The claim that he was being rewarded for a widespread vaccination program cannot be true. The missionary at San Francisco, where Pattie received the document, was Thomas Estenega, not Juan Cabortes. There was a missionary named Juan Cabot, but in 1829 he was at San Miguel, several hundred miles to the south. Furthermore, although it is conceivable Pattie might have been given some mission stock, a missionary had no right to grant land. About the only portion that is accurate is that such a grant would have carried with it the requirement that he become a Catholic and a subject of the Mexican government.

Yet, for all the inaccuracies, the document cannot be ignored. On three other occasions—one in New Mexico and twice in California—Pattie has either quoted or mentioned a document, and each time they have shown up in the records. In none of these cases has he invented the document, but each time he has revised and adapted it to suit his own purpose. Given this, some kind of document probably existed, although it need not have been very close to what is quoted in the narrative. Probably it did no more than promise him something in exchange for becoming a Catholic and a citizen of Mexico.

The strangest thing, however, is not the document, but Pattie's reaction. When he saw that he had to become a Catholic and a citizen of Mexico, he said, "I was struck dumb. My anger choked me." He kept quiet, for the priest, he said, inaccurately, "had the power to hang me if I insulted him." The missionary, however, apparently read his displeasure and asked what was wrong. Pattie said he was being treated unjustly and that he wished he was back in the United States where a man must pay his debts without adding whimsical conditions. As far as being a Catholic, he said, "I would not change my present opinions for all the money his mission was worth." Citizenship in "the society and companionship of such a band of robbers" also had no appeal.

After hearing this, the priest ordered him to leave, and Pattie, as he went, feared he might be attacked by one of the missionary's attendants, who serve him like "a good biddable dog." The overly dramatic confrontation between Pattie and the priest probably did not occur exactly as it was described. Still, it demonstrates an attitude toward Catholicism and Mexican citizenship that is entirely out of keeping with the kind of American who went west.

Such requirements were always part of obtaining land in the Spanish colonies and later in the Republic of Mexico. Hundreds of Americans, their consciences eased by the refusal to take the matter seriously, had already made the nec-

•

essary conversion to obtain land. Most of them came from backgrounds that were almost identical to that of James Pattie.

Before the Louisiana Purchase in 1803, Americans could obtain land in the territory west of the Mississippi by paying lip service to Spanish law. Large numbers of Kentuckians took advantage of this and moved west, led by Daniel Morgan Boone, the Patties' friend and neighbor on the Big Piney while James was growing up. After the Louisiana Purchase such requirements were forgotten, but in the early 1820s, about the time Pattie came of age, the opportunity arose again. Moses Austin, who had earlier moved to Missouri while it was still Spanish, made arrangements for Americans to move into Texas. After his death his son Stephen carried out the project and took large numbers of Americans, many of them from Missouri, into Mexican territory. Again, they were required to convert to Catholicism and become citizens, and, again, they did so without objection and without taking it too seriously.

The same thing was happening in California, and there was little objection to such requirements. By 1829 several Americans had already become citizens, and in the next few years they would be joined by several others. All three of Pattie's fellow trappers, whom he had left in Los Angeles, would settle easily into California life. Two other members of the party, William Pope and Isaac Slover, had returned to New Mexico, where they also became Catholics and citizens of Mexico. Later, both would return to California and fit easily into its society. Of the six surviving members of the party, only Pattie rejected the opportunity to settle in Mexican territory. Apparently, he was one of the few men at the time who took either his religion or citizenship seriously enough to place it ahead of obtaining land.

By now, Pattie had made up his mind to leave California and find his way back to Kentucky. He went to Monterey, which despite Echeandia's long residence in San Diego, was still the capital and the place where most foreign merchants

•

made their headquarters. It was also usually the first and last port visited by American ships, and as such was the ideal place to arrange passage out of California. There was no regular sailing schedule, however, and a passenger could only wait, sometimes for months, until a ship captain finished his trading and was ready to sail.

Monterey was a pleasant place to wait, for it was a town with an ideal location. On one side lay the ocean, on the others were hills covered with forests of pine and live oak. There were several lakes that in winter were filled with ducks and geese, and the woods held enough game to satisfy any hunter. The forest was also full of grizzly bears, and Pattie was intrigued by the way the Californians went about killing them.

They hunted the grizzly, he said, by killing an old horse and building a scaffold over its carcass. Then, armed with a gun or lance, they waited for the bear to approach and either shot it or tried to run it through with the lance. Sometimes they succeeded, but other times a man was knocked off the platform and forced into hand-to-hand combat with a wounded grizzly. Some of those who had wrestled with a bear and survived told Pattie they had no real desire for a rematch. For once, Pattie, despite his claim that Californians were cowards, was forced to admit they had done something he could not match. In describing personal combat with a bear, he said, "I do not speak for myself in this matter, as I never came so near as to take the *close hug* with one in my life."

Monterey had not only a pleasant location, but by California standards it was a large town with a sizable foreign population. Many were the representatives of the various companies engaged in the hide-and-tallow trade, and many were naturalized citizens who had married into California families. Earlier, when Pattie was describing his vaccination program, he had carefully ignored the foreigners and portrayed himself as a lonely traveler in a foreign land. Now, with that story finished, he said that in Monterey he met "a

.

great number of acquaintances, both American and English."
It was this group of foreigners who first told him of a revolution that had broken out in California.

The revolution began on the night of November 12 when a small band of soldiers, in a bloodless coup, took control of the *presidio* of Monterey. Two days later they summoned Joaquin Solis from a nearby ranch to take command of the revolutionary force. Solis had first come to California in 1825 as a member of a band of convicts. He was no ordinary prisoner, however, but a man who during the wars of independence in Mexico had been the chief lieutenant of Vicente Gomez, who was known as *"el capador,"* the gelder. Gomez was a thief, an assassin, and a man who tortured any Spaniard—man, woman, or child—who fell into his hands. Yet, his services to the cause of independence were so great that, like Solis, his only punishment had been banishment to California. A few years after his arrival, however, he had been killed in a brawl, and when the revolution began in Monterey it was his lieutenant, Joaquin Solis, who took charge.

Pattie was elated when he heard of the revolt aginst Echeandia. The rebels promised foreigners great advantages in trading if they would help, and Pattie was instantly ready to join the cause. He donated part of his meager funds and was even willing to accompany the rebel army when it marched against the governor. He hoped to make that old recurrent dream of having "one shot at the general with my rifle" come true.

Several other foreigners, many of them with experience in Latin American revolutions, advised him against any rash actions. The best policy, they said, was to give some advice and a little money to those now in control, but to withhold any active participation until they saw who was going to win. Pattie, after his hot temper cooled down, took their advice.

Solis, once he was in command, issued a proclamation in which he justified the actions of the rebels and accused the governor of various wrongs. The foreigners in Monterey lis-

•

tened and more or less approved it out of "motives of courtesy." Solis then marched on San Francisco, and since his force was the only sizable group of armed men in the area, he had little trouble convincing others to declare in favor of the revolution. With the north subdued, he returned to Monterey and began preparations to march south. In the meantime Governor Echeandia had heard of the revolt and moved troops north to Santa Barbara, where he planned to meet the rebel army.

Soon after Solis's army left for the south, foreigners in Monterey became suspicious of his real intentions. One of the leading American residents, John Rogers Cooper, was married to the daughter of Ignacio Vallejo, who recently had retired from the army after fifty years' service in California. The old soldier told his son-in-law that what Solis was saying in private was directly opposite to his public statements. Publicly, he had promised foreigners full trading rights, but privately he was saying that they would either have to swear allegiance to his government or he would drive them out.

Cooper and several others, who had already vaguely approved of Solis, now decided it was time to demonstrate their good will toward Echeandia. They sent him a message warning him of the revolt, although by then he had already marched north and fortified Santa Barbara. Still, the message gave the foreigners a foot in each camp, and they sat back to wait for the outcome of the battle in the south. If the governor won, Pattie realized he would end up on the side of Echeandia, and in a rare burst of irony he called him "my old acquaintance from San Diego, for whom I bore such good will."

Finally, a messenger arrived and Pattie heard the story of the battle. Solis and his rebel army had arrived before the fortifications at Santa Barbara, and for three days faced Echeandia's troops. Then, having fired all their ammunition and used up all their supplies, the rebel army retreated with the loss of one horse. Pattie heard, too, that during the battle cannonballs, by the time they reached the enemy, were so

•

spent they could be caught by hand. Another man who was there—a Scots doctor—wrote, "You would have laughed . . . The two parties were in sight of each other for nearly two days, and exchanged shots, but at such a distance that there. was no chance of my assistance being needed."

As Solis retreated toward Monterey, Pattie, again with a certain irony, described the reaction of the populace. Solis's name was "exalted to the skies," and he was praised for his ability to organize an army, for his skill in preventing useless slaughter, and especially for his talent in conducting a retreat without losing a man. John Rogers Cooper and some of the other foreigners were experienced and cynical men who knew that such empty praise would not keep a retreating army from looting. It was time for them to take an active role, and Cooper, according to Pattie, rolled out a barrel of rum and invited all Solis's supporters to celebrate his victorious retreat. Then, when they were drunk, they were all locked up and the foreigners took control of Monterey.

Thus far, Pattie's version of the revolution, except for his incorrect dates and some minor inconsistencies, is reasonably accurate. Not only does he cast himself in a minor role, but also his description of events, the things he saw and heard, and his mention of the role played by Cooper and Ignacio Vallejo all agree with other accounts. When Solis's retreating army approached Monterey, however, Pattie could no longer contain himself.

His story is that before Solis reached Monterey, a group of thirty-nine foreigners formed into a military force with Cooper as commander and James Pattie himself as orderly sergeant. They built a large fortification on which they mounted a cannon loaded with grapeshot and ball. When Solis's army appeared, Cooper ordered them to surrender, and most of the common soldiers complied. Solis and six others, however, fled, and according to Pattie, he was chosen to lead the pursuit. They caught up with the six men, killed one of them, and forced the others to surrender. Among them was Solis, who walked up to Pattie and offered him his

•

sword. Pattie said he refused to accept it, and instead led the rebel leader back to the fort.

Except for the fact that Cooper's house served as headquarters for those opposing Solis, there is little truth in this story. Individual members of the retreating and disorganized army straggled into Monterey, were pardoned, and allowed to return to their posts at the *presidio*. The only rebels who did not surrender were eight or ten leaders, including Solis, who went into hiding near his ranch. Eventually, he was captured by a party led not by James Pattie, but by Antonio Avila, one of the convicts who had accompanied Solis to California. He agreed to capture him in exchange for a promise that he would be allowed to return to Mexico. The agreement was made, Solis was captured, but the promise was never kept and Avila was forced to stay in California.

When Pattie finished the tale of the Solis revolt, he was almost done with his story of California. The things he saw and described—his own arrest, the *Franklin* affair, the arrest of Charles Lang, the smallpox vaccination, and the Solis revolt—were all real events. Yet, he constantly twisted the evidence, dramatized it, and built his own role at the expense of reality, until his account of California becomes the most distorted part of the narrative. There is more to Pattie's distortion, however, than simply making himself the hero, or inventing exciting, melodramatic stories to sell books.

Pattie had come west seeking his fortune, and the *Personal Narrative* is a story of fortunes won and lost. A fortune in furs, taken on the Gila, was stolen by Apache; another fortune in furs, taken on the Colorado, was confiscated by the governor of New Mexico; another fortune, this one from the Santa Rita copper mines, was lost when a clerk absconded; still another fortune in furs was destroyed by the spring flood on the Colorado River. By the time Pattie was ready to leave California, everything had turned sour. His father was dead, the last hope for a fortune had disappeared, and Pattie was almost broke. He could, like the other trappers, have stayed in California and obtained a large grant of land. Some strange quirk in his own makeup, however, prevented that. Besides, California land could not be carried back to Kentucky, where, he thought, his brothers and sisters were waiting for him to return with a fortune. Later, on his way home, he expressed his unhappiness because he could bring "to them nothing but poverty."

There was one last hope of salvaging something if Pattie could make a claim against the Mexican government. And in the days just before he left California, Pattie was advised to do just that. The advice came from John Coffin Jones, Jr., the American consul in Hawaii, who arrived in Monterey in late March 1830. Jones told Pattie he should make out a statement as to the value of the lost property and take it to the American minister in Mexico City. It was probable, Jones said, that the Mexican government could be forced to pay for both the loss of the furs and for Pattie's unjust imprisonment. Pattie, therefore, wrote his version of what happened and began to collect material relative to his case. He also wrote his three companions in Los Angeles, telling them of his plans and asking them, if called upon to testify, to tell the story "exactly as it took place."

Pattie, however, was making a claim against the government, and like most men he was not as interested in exactly what happened as he was in winning his case. And the basis, if not the exact facts, of his claim was later incorporated into the *Personal Narrative*. He had innocently arrived in California, and through the arbitrary and unjust actions of the governor, he had lost all of his property. Despite the injustices, he had still rendered valuable service to Mexico by single-handedly ending a smallpox epidemic, by fighting in a revolution on the side of established government, and by capturing, again single-handedly, the rebel general. Any reasonable man, reading all this, could see that James Pattie should be recompensed for his services to Mexico.

•

CHAPTER

FIFTEEN

N LATE MARCH 1830 THE AMERICAN SHIP *Volunteer* arrived in Monterey after a six-week passage from Honolulu. The captain and owner was John Coffin Jones, Jr., who was also the American consul at Oahu. He planned to spend several weeks trading in California before sailing south to San Blas and Mazatlán in Mexico. While he was in Monterey he reached an agreement with the government to transport Joaquin Solis and several other leaders of the rebellion back to Mexico for trial. Jones also agreed to give James Pattie passage to San Blas, the first leg of the long trip back to Kentucky.

By now, it was five years since Pattie, young and inexperienced, had left Missouri with his father. It was also two years since he had arrived in California, where he had his most difficult time and his worst experiences. His troubles were clearly reflected in the *Personal Narrative;* when he writes of California he is always bitter, his dates are constantly wrong, and his stories are usually distorted. When Jones arrived in Monterey, however, with his promise of a passage out of California and his suggestion of a claim against the Mexican government, Pattie was able to pull himself together. From here to the end of the narrative, most of his bitterness is gone, his stories are more subdued, and his dates are generally accurate.

Before he left California, Pattie was even able to have a

•

last interview with Echeandia that did not end with them shouting at each other. Echeandia had long lived in San Diego, but the revolt at the capital had finally forced him to move north and take up residence at Monterey. Pattie, after he drew up his list of complaints, went with Jones to present them to the governor. Echeandia, as usual, was polite, and, as usual, Pattie was hostile, at least in the beginning. Again, he claimed he could read the governor's innermost thoughts, for he said he grew pale with fear when Pattie, backed by the American consul, arrived to demand an accounting.

The conversation, as reported by Pattie himself, indicates that Echeandia had no particular fears. He freely granted Pattie a passport to leave California and asked only why he was going by way of Mexico City instead of New Mexico. Pattie told him of his plan to file a claim in Mexico, and gave the governor a list of his complaints. Echeandia read it, admitted the facts were correct, but said there was no basis for a claim because, as governor, he was simply enforcing the laws of Mexico. Beyond that, the interview was mostly an argument about whether or not a passport was needed to travel in the United States; whether Echeandia had due cause to consider them spies; and why Echeandia had torn up Sylvester Pattie's permit. It was all ground that had been covered before without agreement, and no agreement was reached this time. Still, no one became angry, no one shouted, and, later, when Echeandia found that Pattie was traveling on the same ship as Solis and the other prisoners, he made a joke about the company Pattie was keeping. It clearly opened the way for a sharp rejoinder, but Pattie passed it off with a light remark of his own.

There were still several weeks before the *Volunteer* sailed, and Pattie was free to do whatever he wanted. It was about this time that he met William S. Hinckley, who, like Jones, had arrived in California on board the *Volunteer*. Hinckley was a few years younger than Pattie, but he, too, had seen something of the world and had spent the last few years as a trader in Hawaii. He was a handsome and intelligent man

•

who, when he returned to California in later years, became highly popular with the Californians. He was known for his good humor, his practical jokes, and his conversation, which sometimes became reckless when he had too much to drink. He also was known to tell grizzly bear stories that his listeners did not always fully believe. It was a trait that gave him much in common with James Pattie. Hinckley also was waiting for the *Volunteer* to sail to San Blas, where he planned to leave the ship, cross Mexico to Vera Cruz, and catch another ship that would take him back to his native Massachusetts. Pattie planned to follow the same route as far as Vera Cruz, and thus they would be traveling together for several months.

Fortunately, the two young men, Hinckley at twenty-three and Pattie at twenty-six, got along well together. Soon after Hinckley's arrival, Pattie took him to San Carlos Mission, where a three-day festival was in progress. There were a great many activities, but the high point of the festival was the bear and bull fight. The fights were held in a confined pen, where a grizzly bear and a fighting bull were tied together with a fifteen-foot length of rope. Usually, it was the bull that charged first, and sometimes it managed to kill the bear on the first thrust. More often, it missed and was then torn apart by the bear. All a victorious animal won was the right to face more opponents until finally its stamina was gone and it was killed. Hinckley had never seen anything like it before and was absorbed in the fighting in which fourteen bulls were used before the last of the five bears was killed. Pattie, however, was a bit bored, for he had been in the country long enough to have seen such fights before.

After the festival at San Carlos, Pattie and Hinckley returned to Monterey. There were still a few weeks left and Pattie went sea otter hunting with a Portuguese companion. They spent ten days hunting along the coast and took enough otters so that when the furs were sold, Pattie's share came to three hundred dollars. It was not the fortune he had

•

hoped to find in the West, but it was enough to defray expenses on the way home.

He also had another opportunity to make money, but he passed it up. John Rogers Cooper badly wanted to buy his rifle, and after the sea otter hunt, Pattie had no more use for it. He could not bring himself to sell it, however, for it was a "tried friend" who could not be bartered for money. Instead, he simply gave it to Cooper, and with that gesture he announced his retirement from fur trapping. He was on his way home, and carrying a rifle all the way to Kentucky would be a nuisance. Besides, he could always buy another rifle if he decided to go trapping again. All that is immensely practical, but it does not take into account the fur trapper's feeling for his rifle. It was not just an inanimate object, not just a weapon or a tool of the trade, but a companion who, more often than not, even bore a name given by the trapper. Pattie, although he never mentions a name for his rifle, certainly felt this way. He had carried it for five years, and by now it was a "tried friend" who could not be sold, but must be given away. In surrendering his rifle, Pattie, consciously or not, indicated he never again intended to be in a position where he needed the support of his friend.

It was now almost time to leave, but before he went Pattie looked back over his experiences and offered a reprise of his attitude toward California. Despite "the misery and suffering of various kinds" he had endured, he was forced to admit it was some of the best country he had ever seen. Yet, he added, "the inhabitants are equally calculated to excite dislike, and even the stronger feelings of disgust and hatred." The priests, he said, were all-powerful, the Indians were held in abject slavery, kept at work by rigid supervision, which "led them at times to rebel, and endeavor to escape their yoke." Pattie's view, influenced by his real and imagined troubles in California, is clearly bigoted. These comments have brought down on him the wrath of latter-day historians, who quote from this section to prove the bigotry of

•

Pattie in particular, and sometimes of Americans of that period in general. These remarks, too, are only one paragraph long, and had that paragraph, with its easily quoted statements of intolerance, been omitted, the attitude toward the *Personal Narrative* might have been very different.

In early May Pattie received his passport from Echeandia, and on the morning of May 9, 1830, sailed from Monterey on board the *Volunteer*. The voyage was easy, and Jones, the captain, was happy with the "pleasant passage of only 9 days." The passage, however, was not so pleasant for Joaquin Solis and the other prisoners, who were put in irons, then chained to a long iron bar in the hold. Not only did they fear what awaited them in Mexico, but as soon as the ship was at sea, they were seasick and began alternating groans, prayers, and vomiting. Pattie apparently had found his sea legs on his earlier trip, for he was not sick this time. Still, he remembered the feeling well enough to have some sympathy for the prisoners, whose sounds of misery he could hear throughout the entire nine days.

The *Volunteer* put into port at San Blas to unload the prisoners, and Pattie, in company with William Hinckley, went ashore to begin preparations for the land trip across Mexico. They spent the next three days in San Blas, which in Spanish days had been a shipbuilding center and the major port for supplying the California colonies. It had never been very satisfactory, however, and by now had begun to decline, at least in part because of its poor location. The city stood on a small hill above the surrounding swamplands, but the slight elevation did little to ease the heat or the attacks of mosquitoes and tiny, almost invisible, sand flies, which could inflict a painful bite. Pattie found it warm, others who were there at the same time of year found it hot and humid. The daytime temperature almost always went above ninety degrees, and at night it rarely dropped below eighty. The only thing that tempered the heat was the sea breeze, which usually began to blow in midmorning, setting off a flurry of activity that lasted until the breeze died in midafternoon.

•

Pattie was not the only one making travel preparations, for it was the time of year that citizens of San Blas began their annual exodus from the city. In early June the rainy season began, and the weather became hotter and more humid, the sea breeze quit entirely, and the invasion of mosquitoes and sand flies reached its peak. Consequently, in late May everyone who could began the move into the interior. Windows were boarded up, doors were locked, and the road to the inland city of Tepic was filled with traffic. The wealthy rode horseback, their baggage following on mules, while the poor loaded their possessions, their old people, and their smallest children on the family mule and joined the exodus on foot. By the first of June the city was almost abandoned.

Pattie followed the same route as the exodus from San Blas to Tepic. Just outside the port city the road crossed a swampy area filled with salt beds, then entered a heavy tropical forest, so full of trees, vines, and undergrowth that it was impossible to even see the ground. The road passed several villages of thatched huts with high conical roofs, then began the steep climb toward Tepic. Pattie and his companions traveled slowly, keeping a constant watch for bandits, for they had been told there were "thousands upon this route." Despite the ominous warnings, however, no one offered them any harm.

After three days they reached Tepic, where they rested for a day. Compared with San Blas it was a pleasant place to stop, for although it could be hot during the day, it was three thousand feet high, and thus cooled off considerably at night. Besides, during the hottest part of the day, from after dinner to four in the afternoon, there was nothing to do but join in the siesta, for the streets of Tepic were completely deserted.

It took eight days to travel the 140 miles from Tepic to Guadalajara. They passed several small villages, and on the streets, as well as along the highway between towns, they ran into large numbers of beggars. The beggars stood by the side of the road, often with a dog or small child to lead them

•

285

into the path of an approaching traveler. They stood block-
ing the road and asked for alms, not for themselves, but for
a saint whose image was hung around their neck. At first,
Pattie gave them small sums, but eventually he found there
were so many that he began to refuse. Besides, he soon became suspicious that many of these beggars varied their
source of income by "a dexterous management of their fin-
gers." Thus, he closed his purse to the demands of the various saints.

After eight days on the road the Americans reached Guadalajara. They were stopped at the entrance to the city by
customs officials who carefully searched their baggage. A
traveler in Mexico at this time normally expected a search
that, depending on the whim of the official, ranged from a
cursory glance to a detailed scrutiny of even the smallest
item. One man, exasperated by a thorough search by a pomp-
ous official, finally opened the cover of his watch so it too
might be searched. The announced purpose of the custom-
houses at both the entrance and exit to a city was to prevent
smuggling, but despite the careful search, Pattie found more
contraband trade in Guadalajara than anywhere else he had
been.

Guadalajara, with its seventy thousand people, was the
largest city Pattie had ever seen, and apparently he had difficulty absorbing it all. Although he spent three days there,
he said nothing of the city's prominent features—the cathedral, the many churches, the mint, the national hospital, the
palacio, or even the booths of the leatherworkers, who were
well known for the quality of their work. He did, however,
after his long absence from civilization, enjoy an evening at
the theater, but said nothing except "the actresses appeared
young and beautiful, and danced and sung charmingly." Another man who visited the same theater about the same time
added more details. The boxes for wealthy patrons, he said,
were quite good, and were filled with ladies dressed in the
latest fashions from France and England. It could have been
an English theater except for the incessant smoking of cigars,

•

even by women in balldresses decorated with ostrich plumes.

When Pattie and Hinckley left Guadalajara, they again went through customs, showing their passports, having their baggage searched, and obtaining a statement listing all property, including the trunks and all of the contents. A traveler did well to check the list, for any goods that were not on it would be confiscated at the next custom station.

The road east from Guadalajara toward Mexico City passed through a well-populated area, and while traveling through it, Pattie met a Mexican army officer who demanded to see his passport. Pattie and his companions felt the officer had no authority to make the demand, but since they were foreigners and he was leading a squad of soldiers, they showed the passports.

Pattie, however, could not let it go at that but began to bait the officer by asking questions "that might perhaps have seemed rude." He innocently asked the officer's rank and received a civil reply—he was a first lieutenant. Pattie then asked where he was going and again the answer was civil— he was on his way to Mexico City to assume a new command. Apparently, Pattie's questions had begun to irritate him, for he added that this new command would take him to Texas to find Americans who refused to obey Mexican law. When he found them, he said, he would teach them how to behave.

Pattie, always quick to take offense, saw both contempt and implied insult in the officer's answer. Although he knew it was unwise for a stranger to make rude remarks, he told the officer he and his men should be careful when they were among Americans. They would find, he said, that unlike Mexicans, Americans would not hide behind a house and while looking the other way, fire their guns around a corner. At this, the officer lost his temper and Pattie quieted down. "I did not try," he said, "to irritate him any further." Possibly Pattie was belatedly showing some good sense. Possibly, too, he could not think of anything more insulting than

•

what he had already said. Fortunately, the officer angrily rode off and left them alone.

That night they stayed in a *mesón*, or Mexican inn. Others who traveled through Mexico at this time found that accommodations in such inns were usually poor. They were built in the shape of a quadrangle, with a central courtyard that was entered through a small passageway that led from the street. Inside, a key bearer, who accepted no responsibility other than opening doors, unlocked the rooms that faced into the courtyard. The rooms were windowless, and light came in only when the door was open. Not only did travelers find them dark but also dirty and flea-infested. One man, when he arrived at a *mesón*, found the room so dirty he hired a man to clean it out, not with a broom but with a shovel.

Pattie, who had been traveling for five years, had few complaints. He paid his two reals, or twenty-five cents, and was shown into a room by the old man who kept the keys. If it was dark and dirty, he did not think it worth a comment. The only problem he noticed was that there was nowhere to buy food at the inn, and he had to look elsewhere. Even that was a minor problem, for a short walk through the passageway led to a large number of street vendors selling all varieties of food. Throughout the trip Pattie found this the easiest way to obtain his meals.

That evening after supper two Englishmen arrived at the inn. One of them was a young English merchant named Edward Perry, who was also bound for Vera Cruz, where, like Pattie, he planned to find a ship headed for New Orleans. More immediately, however, the two Englishmen were in a hurry to reach Mexico City, for the feast of Corpus Christi, the greatest Catholic festival of the year, was about to begin. Pattie and Hinckley readily joined them, "as we were desirous to lose the sight of nothing curious." Late on the eve of Corpus Christi, they arrived in Mexico City.

Mexico City, with its 150,000 population swollen by thousands more who had come for the festival, was even larger and more crowded than Guadalajara. The best place to

•

stay in the capital was the Sociedad Grande, which, unlike village inns, had more than just sleeping rooms. There were billiard tables, dining rooms, coffee rooms, even ice cream and candy shops. Pattie, however, did not stay there, probably because it was already full on the eve of Mexico City's biggest festival. Instead, he stayed in an inn run by an Englishman who, like those in the small towns, furnished only rooms with beds. The innkeeper did have a supply of liquor, but offered no meals, and that night Pattie and his companions found food in a coffeehouse.

The next morning they were awakened by the ringing of bells and went into the street to see the festival. During Corpus Christi the small image of Nuestra Señora de los Remedios was brought into the city from its church in a small nearby village. The fiesta always came at the beginning of the rainy season, and Nuestra Señora was believed to assure the rain. The procession that accompanied her into the city was brilliant, and one resident said that visitors who arrived during the festival—as Pattie did—received a mistaken idea about the wealth of Mexico City.

Nuestra Señora rode in the presidential carriage, escorted by troops, to a small church within the city limits. The next day she was taken to the cathedral in an even larger procession. It was led by a regiment of cavalry followed by high government and church officials, each carrying lighted candles. Then came the various religious orders, more soldiers, groups of Indians, and finally, just before Nuestra Señora de los Remedios, a group of Indian girls strewing roses in her path. The small image itself, now carried by four men, rode under a canopy of richly textured cloth and was surrounded by gilded ornaments. As she passed, those in the streets kneeled, while those in the windows showered her with roses. One visitor estimated that the procession itself contained forty thousand people, ten thousand of whom were soldiers.

During the festival, Nuestro Amo, Our Master the Host, was also often carried through the city. When it passed,

•

those in the street fell to their knees and crossed themselves. One woman, watching from her window as the Host went by, saw an instant change in the crowd below. People had been talking, arguing, and shouting, and two men were fighting, when the Host approached. They all dropped to their knees, the two fighting men side by side, and the street was totally silent until the Host was gone. Then the street noises again rose to her window.

Pattie had his own problems with the passing of the Host. One evening he and his friends were on their way back to the inn as the procession approached and they, like the rest of the crowd, knelt. Pattie, however, was wearing white pants and was very put out at having to kneel in the dirty street. After this he learned to listen for the tinkling bell that announced the coming of the Host and would duck into the nearest doorway to avoid kneeling.

Pattie was somewhat confused in his only other description of events during Corpus Christi. On the first morning, when he stepped from the inn, he saw three biers being carried through the street. The bearers, guarded by a band of soldiers, were begging money to pay for the burial. Although this may have been part of the religious festivities, someone told Pattie that the biers contained the bodies of three men who had been murdered the night before. He believed the story, for he thought he could actually see blood dripping from the biers. The men had been murdered, he heard, at the Alameda, and nothing would do but for the travelers to visit it.

The Alameda was a beautiful promenade, heavily shaded by elm and aspen trees. There were walkways and a carriage road that circled the edge just outside the stone walls. Pattie found thousands there, for the Alameda was always jammed with people of all classes during a festival. Ladies, however, never alighted from their carriages, and gentlemen remained on their horses and rode around the promenade. Those on foot, those seated on the stone benches built into the walls, and those sitting among the trees and shrubs were of a differ-

•

ent class. It was here that the *léperos,* the large drifting population of Mexico City, congregated during the feasts. They had no permanent homes, but slept where they could, sometimes under cover, sometimes in the open air. They begged alms in the streets, responding to donations with an astonishing number of blessings and prayers. Many, too, were accomplished pickpockets, and the stories of sleight of hand surpassed stories told of their colleagues in London and Paris.

The implied danger of visiting the Alameda, particularly late at night, was a thrill that Pattie and his companions, all of them young men, could hardly pass up. They spent several nights wandering through the Alameda, where they could see, half-hidden by the shrubs, groups of "men and women of the lowest order" playing cards. Pattie, who since he arrived in Mexico had been filled with stories of robberies and murders, expected the card games to erupt into violence at any moment. Instead, "notwithstanding the danger really to be apprehended from visiting the place after certain hours, my two companions and myself spent several evenings in it without being molested in the slightest degree."

Despite this, Pattie's fears were not entirely imaginary, for Mexico City did have a reputation for violence. A few years after his visit, Fanny Calderon de la Barca took up residence in Mexico City. Although as the wife of the Spanish minister she led a sheltered life in one of the better neighborhoods, she mentions a surprising number of murders, one of which occurred just below her balcony. Such killings, however, usually arose when two *léperos* quarreled, according to Pattie because of jealousy, according to Fanny Calderon because of drunkenness. Usually, as Pattie discovered, a foreigner who minded his own business could walk the streets unmolested.

Pattie's closest brush with a *lépero* came one evening at the theater. Like most Mexican theaters, it was divided into classes—the boxes and the pit. The wealthy sat in the boxes, which were arranged in the form of a large horseshoe with

·

the open end narrowing as it reached the stage. These boxes were rented by the year, some for as much as five hundred dollars, and Pattie had no access to them. In the center of the horseshoe was the pit. In the front part, toward the stage, there were seats, but again these were for gentlemen and were leased by the year. Behind them was an area where the rest of the people, including casual visitors like Pattie, could stand during the performance. Most visitors said less of the happenings on the stage than of those in the boxes around them. Again, the thing that attracted most attention was the constant smoking of both men and women, and one man found the theater so smoky he could barely see across it. Another watched through the haze as men lit and relit cigars with flint and steel and thought the house looked as if it was full of fireflies.

Pattie described none of this, for his attention was captured by another event. He was standing in the dense crowd of the pit when he noticed that his watch was gone. Whoever stole it was adept, for he was completely unaware that it had been taken. Pattie, usually so willing to vent his anger in writing if not in fact, simply shrugged it off, saying it was impossible to even look for it in a crowd that was so dense he could hardly move.

Pattie, who had little experience with city life and entertainments, used his time in Mexico City to the fullest. Not only did he attend the theater in the evening and prowl the Alameda late at night, but he also found things to fill his days. One day he obtained a horse and rode around the entire Valley of Mexico. He had read, somewhere, enough of the Spanish conquest to have in his mind the image of Mexico City surrounded by a large lake. He could find no lake, only low, flat land cut by a canal that carried off water that came into the valley. Not only did the canal drain the valley, but it was used by hundreds of Indians in canoes who brought fruits, vegetables, and flowers to the markets in Mexico City. Off to the southeast, as he rode around the valley, were

.

the snow-covered summits of Iztaccihuatl and Popocatepetl, the latter an active volcano. Pattie knew this and could not resist adding that it was "continually sending up proof of the existence of an unceasing fire within." Actually, the smoke sent up by Popocatepetl could not be seen from the valley but only from the edge of the crater itself.

There was also business to be taken care of in Mexico City. Before Pattie left California he had written out a statement of losses suffered because of the actions of Echeandia. John Coffin Jones had told him to present the statement to the American minister in Mexico City, who could probably force the Mexican government to pay for the losses. Thus, Pattie, who was now nearly out of money, took his carefully prepared statement and went to see Anthony Butler, the American chargé d'affaires.

Butler was not entirely surprised to see Pattie, for as soon as he identified himself, Butler showed him a letter from Washington, D.C., concerning the case of James and Sylvester Pattie. Somehow, Pattie got the idea it was from President Andrew Jackson to the president of Mexico. Actually, it was from Martin Van Buren, the secretary of state, to Anthony Butler, the chargé d'affaires, but it did concern the two Patties. Sometime earlier, after the Twenty-first Congress began its first session in December 1829, Van Buren had received a letter from Nicholas Coleman, a newly elected congressman from Kentucky. Coleman informed the secretary of state that members of Sylvester and James Pattie's family who resided in his district had reason to believe that the two had been imprisoned in California. He asked the State Department to do whatever it could to obtain their release. At the same time two other men, Mr. Buckner and Mr. Taylor of Paris, Kentucky, had also contacted the State Department with information that Richard Laughlin of Bourbon County was also being held prisoner in California. They, too, asked for help from the government. Van Buren, therefore, in January 1830, wrote to Butler recommending

.

"in a special manner to your care and attention, the case of these citizens of the United States, that your best exertions be promptly employed toward effecting their discharge."

Pattie, after he saw the letter, had reason to hope that his claim would be seriously pushed by the American government. Not only had Jones, the American consul, told him he had a good case, but now no less a man than the secretary of state had shown a personal interest. It was not to be, however, for unknown to Pattie, Anthony Butler was not the man to take care of it.

Butler, who had only recently arrived in Mexico, had been appointed to the post of chargé d'affaires by Andrew Jackson, under whom he had served during the Battle of New Orleans. Most of those who knew Butler had little respect for him. The American consul in Mexico City. with whom he had quarreled, charged him with immorality; Sam Houston, with whom he had also quarreled, claimed he was a gambler, a swindler, and a man who had squandered his wife's property, then abandoned her. John Quincy Adams, who later read some of Butler's dispatches from Mexico, said they demonstrated both his vanity and his lack of moral principle. Even Andrew Jackson, who appointed him and kept him in Mexico for five years, eventually reached the conclusion that he was a scamp and a liar.

Pattie knew none of this, nor did it bear directly on his case. Butler's personality and his reasons for being in Mexico, however, kept him from doing much for Pattie. Butler had long been a speculator in Texas lands, and once he reached Mexico, he spent most of his time in various intrigues designed to obtain Texas for the United States. Much of the rest of the business of the United States he ignored, as he did also the case of James Pattie.

The letter from Van Buren about Pattie, written in January, went unanswered until April 10, for according to Butler, it had not arrived until the day before because of "a most extraordinary delay." Possibly it was delayed en route, but since another letter sent separately from Washington was

•

also delayed, the problem was probably in Butler's office in Mexico City. Finally, however, he answered, saying briefly that the subject would be "immediately attended to and the result communicated as early as possible." After that, there was no more mention of the case in Butler's correspondence until after Pattie himself arrived in Mexico City. By then, James Pattie was obviously free, and he told Butler that Sylvester had died and that the others had voluntarily stayed in California. The problem had solved itself, and Butler wrote to Van Buren suggesting he inform Congressman Coleman that he had taken care of the situation.

Even while Pattie was in Mexico City, Butler did little for him. He looked at the written complaint and asked several questions about the lost property. Beyond that, he told Pattie he was only a chargé d'affaires and could do nothing. He suggested that he continue on to the United States and present his case there. Others in the embassy told Pattie they did not think he had much chance of recovering anything, although Butler, always thinking big, told him to go to Washington and lay the matter before the president of the United States.

Butler did, however, arrange an audience with the president of Mexico, Anastasio Bustamente. Pattie went to the National Palace, "a splendid building," although much marked by the recent revolution against President Vicente Guerrero. He was ushered into the office of the president, "a man of plain and gentlemanly manners, possessing great talent." Bustamente had been elected vice-president of Mexico the year before, but after the flight of Guerrero he had taken over the office of the president on New Year's Day, 1830.

The two men talked briefly of California, of the revolution against Echeandia, and of James Pattie's role in it. Eventually, they reached the story of Pattie's imprisonment, and Bustamente appeared to be surprised. Either Butler had ignored his instructions to vigorously press the case, or Bustamente found it momentarily convenient to pretend he knew nothing about it. After hearing Pattie's account, the

•

president told him he had been informed by others that Echeandia had acted illegally in several cases, and he had been ordered back to Mexico to answer for his conduct. If Pattie, with his strong dislike for the California governor, hoped that this meant Echeandia would now have his own difficulties, he was to be disappointed. Several months earlier Bustamente had appointed Manuel Victoria as the new governor of California. Echeandia, however, did not return to Mexico, but stayed in California, and when Victoria was driven out by a revolution, he reassumed the office of governor. Finally, in 1833, he did return to Mexico, but by then Bustamente had been expelled from office in another revolution, and Echeandia settled down to a long, quiet life in Mexico.

Pattie was somewhat surprised that the president would discuss Echeandia's status with him. Finally, he came to the conclusion that it was Bustamente's way of showing that he did not approve of cruel and unjust treatment of Americans. It was a good performance, for Pattie came away satisfied that the president was entirely innocent of any wrongdoing. As with Butler, Pattie had received sympathy, but so far he had found no one who would accept the responsibility for doing anything about it.

After the interviews Pattie wrote to his former companions in California, telling them of his failure in Mexico City and of his intention to go on to the United States. He also added a personal note telling Richard Laughlin to write a letter home. He had learned from Butler that Laughlin's parents were worried and "desirous to see or hear from you." Laughlin may have written home, but he never went back to Bourbon County, for he lived out the rest of his life in California.

Finally, there was no more to be done in Mexico City, and Pattie and his companions began the trip across the mountains to Vera Cruz. They went by carriage in company with a French woman traveling alone, a wealthy Irishman with his Spanish wife, and a Mexican woman traveling with her

•

husband, an officer who was violently opposed to former President Guerrero. The company was friendly and the trip was easy until the second afternoon, when they met a band of about fifty armed men. Those in the carriage thought they were soldiers searching for bandits who had robbed and killed several people a few days before. Instead, they turned out to be the bandits, or, as they claimed, followers of the Guerrero cause, which badly needed money. At first they acted like beggars, politely pleading for money, but at the same time carefully surrounding the carriage. Once in place they drew weapons and demanded that the men hand over their arms. They were experienced highway robbers, for they had positioned themselves so well that Pattie—and the others—quickly recognized "that opposition would be unavailing." They took what they wanted, although they were kind enough to leave Pattie his trunk full of clothes.

The bandits—or Guerrero supporters—also recognized the Mexican officer as an enemy. They dragged him from the carriage and hanged him from a tree despite the pleas of his wife. Then they ordered the carriage to drive on, and they were instantly obeyed. Most of the travelers had escaped without too much damage, but they were reminded of the danger they had faced by the agony of the woman whose husband had been murdered. Finally, when they reached Jalapa, she was left behind.

Shortly after they had left Mexico City, they had crossed the Continental Divide at almost eleven thousand feet. Since then, the road had steadily descended toward the east. Other travelers sometimes complained of the road, but Pattie, after years of traveling through roadless wilderness, thought it was excellent. Much of it was paved, and it frequently cut through the points of mountains to impressively demonstrate the labor and expense that had gone into its construction.

At Jalapa, Pattie reached a city that was almost universally praised by travelers. It sat in a beautiful valley, and the white, many-towered buildings contrasted vividly with the

•

dark green of the surrounding mountains. The town was famous for the medicinal jalap, which came from the root of a plant dug from nearby mountainsides and brought into the city to be sold along with the fruits and vegetables.

Pattie arrived during the rainy season, a time when Jalapa was always crowded with people from the lowlands. As San Blas on the Pacific was deserted in the summer, so too was Vera Cruz on the Atlantic. All those who could afford the trip left the seaport city to escape the heat. Not only was Jalapa, at five thousand feet elevation, cool, but it was also healthy, while in Vera Cruz yellow fever increased dramatically during each rainy season. Some travelers, if they knew beforehand that their ship was not ready to sail, stayed in the mountains until the last possible moment before going to Vera Cruz. Pattie, however, stayed only briefly before going on to the coastal city.

Not far from Jalapa the road descended from the mountains into a tropical forest filled with palm trees, dense vegetation, and flocks of parrots. Other times of the year it was a pleasant excursion, but during the rainy season the intense heat began here and grew worse as the traveler approached Vera Cruz. Pattie said nothing of this stretch of road, not even describing the famous bridge across the Río Antigua. It had been built in Spanish times and called the Puente del Rey, but in the years just before Pattie crossed it, the name had changed, in rapid succession, from Puente del Rey, to the Puente Imperial, finally to the Puente Nacional. Most of those who saw the arched stone bridge across the deep ravine described it with the same word—"magnificent."

Soon after they arrived in Vera Cruz, Hinckley boarded a boat for New York, but Pattie and his English friend, Edward Perry, spent almost a month waiting for a ship to take them to New Orleans. During this time Pattie stayed with Isaac Stone, an American merchant of the firm Stone, Cullen, and Company, and also temporarily the United States consul at Vera Cruz. A few years earlier another traveler had stayed

•

with an American consul and was quite happy with his accommodations, undoubtedly much like those enjoyed by Pattie. He had a large, comfortable room with high ceilings, but more important, the house was well suited to the hot climate. Thick stone walls kept out the heat, and the interior courtyards were heavily shaded. Pattie again says nothing of his impression of Vera Cruz, quite likely because he saw little of the city. The intense heat and the annual yellow fever epidemic of the rainy season usually discouraged visitors from wandering around the town.

Pattie by now was also broke and discouraged. His feelings at the time, he said, were that "the prospect, which the future offered me, was dark. It seemed as if misfortune had set her seal upon all that concerned my destiny." He had no money to pay his fare to New Orleans, but finally Isaac Stone, the consul, arranged for a free passage on board the *United States.* Samuel Creaghead, the ship's captain and owner, in 1830 was sailing exclusively for Stone's company, and thus it was easy for the consul to make arrangements. On July 17 Pattie was on board the *United States* as it sailed from Vera Cruz toward New Orleans.

Once again, as he had done when he sailed from California, Pattie summed up his feelings as he left Mexico, the country "where I had seen and suffered so much." His "dreams of success in those points considered most important by my fellow men, were vanished forever." The worst part, however, was the charity he had to accept to get home. After all "my endurance of toil, hunger, thirst and imprisonment"; after all the encounters with fierce animals and "fiercer men"; after all the "danger, want and misery," he was indebted to Isaac Stone for the passage home.

Two weeks later the *United States* reached the mouth of the Mississippi, marked by the large amount of muddy water pouring into the gulf. Pattie, who earlier in California had been amazed by his first sight of a sailing vessel, now affected the pose of an old salt. "The wind," he said, "had not

•

299

been entirely favorable. It blew a stiff breeze from a direction which compelled us to run within five points and a half of the wind."

It took two days to ascend the Mississippi from its mouth to the city of New Orleans. As the boat slowly made its way upriver, Pattie's mind raced ahead to the upper waters of the Mississippi where he had spent his childhood. He imagined the home where he had lived, happily, with his mother and father and all his brothers and sisters. He remembered, too, the house, heavily shaded by trees and surrounded by paths over which he bounded as a child. All that had long since disappeared, but it was still alive in his mind for "years and change have no place in such meditation."

At New Orleans he was jolted back to reality. Edward Perry casually asked him if he had booked passage on a steamboat to Kentucky. When Pattie said no, Perry, who had made arrangements to travel on the *Cora*, suggested Pattie do the same. Momentarily, Pattie forgot his financial situation, for he accompanied the Englishman toward the steamboat. Before he reached it, however, he thought to ask how much it would cost. When he found that passage as far as Louisville was forty dollars, he mumbled an excuse about having another appointment and promised Perry he would see about it later. When he was alone, he counted out his small amount of money and found that he could not afford a cabin. In fact, he could not even afford deck passage.

He went back aboard the *United States* and found Captain Creaghead in conversation with another ship captain who was planning to sail to Vera Cruz. He needed someone to accompany him and help sell both the cargo and the ship itself. Creaghead pointed out Pattie as a man who could speak Spanish and who was also badly in need of money. After some conversation the captain offered Pattie a job and a percentage of the profits. Pattie promised to think it over and to give his answer the next day.

He spent the rest of the day wandering through the streets of New Orleans. Most travelers found much to see in the

•

city—the cathedral, the Big Bone Museum, the marketplace, the large number of black slaves in the streets, and the white population, at least half of whom spoke French rather than English. Pattie, his mind on other things and having already seen five years' worth of strange sights, saw nothing worth mentioning.

That night, as he had promised, he met Perry, who again insisted he accompany him to the *Cora* to make arrangements for his passage. Pattie had run out of excuses and finally had to admit that he had no money. He also told Perry of his plan to go back to Vera Cruz. The Englishman argued strongly against the plan, pointing out that Pattie would arrive back in Vera Cruz at the very height of the yellow fever season. He also said that if it were only a question of money, he was willing to pay for the passage himself. Pattie, already sensitive to the charity he had taken from Stone, refused, saying that as a traveler in a foreign country, Perry needed all his funds. The Englishman then asked if there was someone in New Orleans who could lend him money, but Pattie said he knew no one in the city. After that they parted, each going to his separate lodgings.

The next morning Perry arrived at Pattie's boardinghouse with a companion, the United States senator from Louisiana, Josiah Johnston, who also planned to travel on the *Cora*. It was a fortunate meeting, for Johnston was not only an influential man, but also one who knew several members of the Pattie family. Johnston, who was the same age as Pattie's father, had grown up in Washington, Kentucky, just fifteen miles from where the Patties lived. So, too, had his much younger half-brother, Albert Sidney Johnston, who was the same age as James Pattie. By 1830 all the Johnston children were gone, but their father, John Johnston, still lived in Washington, where he had been for more than forty years.

Johnston surprised Pattie by telling him he knew some of his family, and also told him that after being absent for so long he should immediately go to see them. Pattie, again embarrassed by his lack of money, was evasive, but Johnston

•

was aware of the problem and insisted that he be allowed to pay the fare. Finally, Pattie agreed to accept the money as a loan rather than a gift, and with it he made his arrangements for a cabin on board the *Cora*.

It was the first steamboat he had ever been on, and he found it as exciting as the first sailing ship he had visited in San Diego Bay. But as the *Cora* ascended the river, taking Pattie toward Kentucky, the excitement gave way to depression. Senator Johnston continually asked him questions about his travels, but he did not give very satisfactory answers. His mind was on other things, for as he neared home he began to realize that his thoughts of happier days with his family were part of a dream that was not dead. He was thinking of home, he said, but then he added, "Home did I say? I have none." His mother was dead and buried somewhere along the Big Piney River, his father was dead and buried more than a thousand miles away in a foreign country. He felt guilty, too, for as the eldest son he should have taken over the responsibility of a parent to his brothers and sisters. Instead, "I . . . shall carry to them nothing but poverty, and the withering remembrances of an unhappy wanderer, upon whom misfortune seems to have stamped its inexorable seal."

At Cincinnati Senator Johnston introduced Pattie to Timothy Flint, until recently the editor of the *Western Monthly Review*, and a writer who was well known for his interest in the West. Pattie, apparently in a hurry to reach home, spent only a few days there, but made some kind of arrangement to return to Cincinnati and work his story into publishable form. The *Cincinnati Advertiser and Ohio Gazette* also noted his passage through the city briefly and anonymously. He was "a passenger who arrived here yesterday, from Vera Cruz, in the schr. *United States*." For all the travel, for all the experiences in the past five years, the paper was interested only in his comments on the Mexican situation, and Pattie satisfied them with some secondhand stories he had heard at the consulate in Vera Cruz.

•

A few days later he arrived in Augusta. Walking through town toward his grandfather's house, he saw several people he knew, but they did not recognize him. As he approached the house, he found that the large grove of trees had all been cut down and the stream that flowed beneath them had almost dried up. His grandmother was an old woman now, and his grandfather, "the vigorous and undaunted hunter," was almost unrecognizable. John Pattie, in a feeble voice, asked question after question concerning the fate of his eldest son, Sylvester.

Most of the brothers and sisters, whom he had pictured as waiting for his return with the family fortune, had gone off on their own. One little boy—just a baby when Pattie left— was still there, but he had no memory of his oldest brother. A sister, Jennie, was there, too, but she was just a child when he had left. Now she was a married woman with a child of her own. Her husband, Edwin Collins, was a total stranger, but he invited Pattie into his home. The two tried to overcome the strangeness by calling each other "brother," but Pattie at least could not make the word convey any true feeling.

Pattie was home, and he was ready to end his story. Before he did, he looked back over his five years in the West and warned those who wished to follow him that from his experience he could draw only one conclusion. It was, he said, to stay home in "peace and privacy," and not to wander away "to see the habitations, and endure the inhospitality of strangers." All he had obtained in his travels was this: "The freshness, the visions, the hopes of my youthful days are all vanished, and can never return. If any one of my years has felt, *that the fashion of the world passeth away,* and that all below the sun is vanity, it is I."

Here ended the *Personal Narrative* of James O. Pattie.

EPILOGUE

THE SEARCH FOR JAMES PATTIE

"This man, Ohio Pattie . . . left my camp in the Sierra Nevada Mountains, amidst the deep snows of the terrible winter of 1849–50. . . . I suppose he perished in the deep snows, or was killed by the Indians."

—WILLIAM WALDO

"[Andrew Jackson Raney] in March, 1853 . . . went over to Rag Canon, there being only one settler there at the time, who was a Frenchman, by the name of James Ohio Patti."

—*History of Napa and Lake Counties, California*

"In 1883 a man whose name I cannot recall, apparently trustworthy, while visiting my library, stated that his wife was a niece of Pattie, and that the latter had spent some time at her residence in San Diego in late years, or at least since 1850."

—H. H. BANCROFT

T WAS ON THE LAST DAY OF AUGUST 1830 that Pattie, for the first time in more than five years, awakened to find he was no longer a traveler. On his way back to Kentucky, he had reentered the United States at New Orleans. Custom officials, as usual, had met the boat, and as part of their examination they asked each passenger to state his occupation. For Pattie it was a somewhat tricky question. During the past five years he claimed to have been many things—fur trapper, prison guard, heir to a mining empire, interpreter for the governor of California, public health doctor, sea otter hunter, and orderly sergeant in a counterrevolutionary army. When he reached New Orleans, however, none of these seemed entirely appropriate, and he finally listed his occupation simply as "traveller." A month later, when he arrived at his grandfather's home in Bracken County, even that claim was gone.

Pattie's account in the *Personal Narrative* ended with his arrival at his grandfather's house in Augusta the day before. As he brought it to a close, he constantly dwelled on his growing depression and the hopelessness of his situation. Some of this, certainly, was for dramatic effect, but it is still a fair enough reflection of the mind of an ambitious young man who had returned home with nothing.

The depression, the hopelessness, cannot have passed away immediately, for during those first days back in

•

Bracken County his situation was not good. He was twenty-six years old, and he was broke. In fact, he had been broke since Vera Cruz and had reached Kentucky only through the charity of Isaac Stone and Josiah Johnston. He had no real occupation, and none of the experiences of the past five years —almost all the years of his adult life—had prepared him to live in a small Kentucky town.

There was, however, some improvement in his immediate daily life. He had long been living among strangers, and now he was surrounded by people he had known since his childhood. There was his grandfather, still a wealthy man, with his seven slaves and his 130 acres of land. He was old and feeble, or so James thought on his return, but he had enough strength left to live through the winter, another summer, and well into the next winter. There was also his grandmother, Ann Pattie, whom James thought was "tottering under the burden and decline of old age." She, even more than her husband, fooled him, for eight years later she was still alive and capable of making a ninety-mile trip from Augusta to Franklin for a visit. She did not die until sometime in 1840. Beyond Augusta, spread across Bracken and Mason counties, were also several aunts and uncles ranging from his aunt Sally Howard, well past fifty, to Leland Pattie, his uncle, who was only a few years older than James himself. There were also innumerable cousins and, most important of all, his sister Jennie Collins, who had taken him into her home upon his return.

Beyond the relatives, there were friends and acquaintances who had lived in Augusta long enough to have watched not just James, but his father as well, grow up and leave home. Surely, they were interested in what had happened to two hometown boys in the West, and just as surely in a small town, there was a time in September 1830 when nothing else was talked about. The stories they heard, their reactions to them, and the changes they saw in Pattie have not, however, survived.

Except for a few old men like John Pattie, and a few trav-

•

elers like James Pattie, none of those living in Bracken County had any real knowledge of the frontier. Most of them were farmers whose main object was to turn as much land as possible into tobacco fields. One of the first things Pattie noticed on his return was the disappearance of the last vestige of wilderness, the large trees that had once shaded the lower part of Bracken Creek. Compared with where he had been, there was no serious hunting and no serious Indian danger, for the big game, and with it the Indians, had long since disappeared from Bracken County.

These differences made his days much more predictable. For five years he had been traveling, sometimes through Indian land, sometimes through desert, and always in a foreign country. He often exaggerated his isolation and danger, but anyone who trapped the Southwest in those years knew something of exhaustion, thirst, hunger, fear, and loneliness. In Augusta—for James, at least—such things no longer existed. He did not have to awaken each morning and wonder where the next meal would come from, what the day's travel would bring, and whether the Apache, or the Papago, or the Mohave, or some unknown tribe of Indians would kill him before the day was over.

If anything, life in Augusta by 1830 was all too predictable. The town had seven hundred people, and like the surrounding area of Bracken and Mason counties, it had entered a period of quiet stability. The great growth that first brought John Pattie to Augusta forty years before was over, as was the drain of population to the West, which twenty years before had drawn Sylvester and his family to Missouri. Augusta no longer excited much interest even among travelers along the Ohio River. Earlier in the century, when it lay near the edge of civilization, travelers moving slowly downstream in keelboats often stopped to look over the town. By 1830 a new group of travelers, anxious to see the new West, hurried down the Ohio in steamboats that stopped only at the major ports—Pittsburgh, Wheeling, Cincinnati, and Louisville. If they noticed Augusta at all, it was

•

as just another small river town that the boat hurried by without stopping. Those who rode the local boats that stopped at Augusta usually had seen so many riverfront towns that they saw nothing special about this one.

If Augusta was just another small Kentucky town to travelers, it was still a pleasant place to live in 1830. The *Lexington Reporter* recently had noted the town's "delightful position" on the Ohio, and Timothy Flint, in his survey of the entire Mississippi Valley, had thought it worth singling out for a brief comment. The thing that attracted this attention, however, was not the location of the town, or the large, stone winery, or the courthouse in the large public square, but rather the college located on the east side of town. The school, a descendant of the old Bracken Academy, had been opened by the Methodists in 1825 under the new name of Augusta College. By 1830 it had more than one hundred students and a campus with four buildings—the president's home, two dormitories, and a classroom building. Timothy Flint was impressed by its president, Joseph Tomlinson, and said the college showed great promise for the future.

Apparently, James Pattie thought so, too, for he enrolled as a student at Augusta College. Before he went west, he probably had spent some time at the old Bracken Academy, and thus had some idea of what to expect. Still, it was a very different life from the one he had been leading. One magazine proudly pointed out that the college had adopted regulations to control the expenses and habits of the students. Furthermore, it said, the town of Augusta offered few opportunities to indulge in vice or extravagancies, and thus there were few colleges where morality and religion were more pronounced. To keep it that way, the faculty made frequent reports to parents and guardians on students' "health, habits, and proficienty." Pattie left no account of life at Augusta College, which is unfortunate, for what a man who had roamed the West, sometimes with Old Bill Williams, or Peg-Leg Smith, thought of this would be worth knowing.

Certain questions rush immediately to mind. How was he

•

accepted? In age he was almost a decade older than his class-mates, in experience far older. Was he a hero to them, a man who could tell stories of strange experiences in an almost unknown country? Or was he, faced with students' frequent cruel demand for conformity, treated as an outsider who talked of things that were unimportant, irrelevant, and prob-ably not true anyway?

How, too, did he react to his courses at Augusta College? There was no long list of electives to choose from, but rather a set program organized into the fields of English, Latin, Greek, mathematics, and history. Within each field the yearly course of study was also spelled out, and in both Greek and Latin specific authors were assigned in specific years. How, then, did the man who wrote an account of a long, difficult journey react to Xenophon's *Anabasis*? What did the man who filled his own account with stories he had collected think of Herodotus's history? How well did he do in the course in geography, a field in which he had consider-able knowledge? Finally, did he ever succeed in passing the course entitled "Elements of Chronology"? The questions are endless, fascinating, and also unanswerable.

The college carefully controlled the students both in what they studied and how they behaved, but James Pattie may have escaped some of this. Most students, many from as far away as Louisiana and Mississippi, lived in boardinghouses, where for $2.50 a week they were given food, lodging, wash-ing, lights, fuel, and servants. Pattie, who was older, proba-bly did not live here, but rather stayed with members of his family, possibly even his grandfather, who lived just a few blocks from the campus.

It was here, late in 1831, that John Pattie died at the age of eighty-one. A few months later his son Leland, as executor of the will, inventoried the property. The most valuable items were the slaves—a boy named Thornton, three girls, Ann, Henrietta, and Harriet, and two women, Rachel and Aggy. Rachel, worth three hundred dollars, was the most valuable, while Aggy was worth only fifty dollars. Aggy was

•

an old woman, who fifty years before, in 1781, had accompanied John Pattie on his migration from Virginia to Kentucky. Besides the slaves, there was the livestock, which consisted of a small herd of nine cattle, twelve hogs, thirteen sheep, twenty-seven geese, and three horses. As this was Kentucky, the horses were carefully described as a sorrel mare, a chestnut sorrel horse, and a young bay mare. There was farm equipment, a plow and harrow, a wagon, a log chain, a pitchfork, bee stands, and a broken mattock worth only twelve cents. Finally, there were the personal items, ranging from a cornish cupboard worth fifteen dollars to a coffee mill valued at seventy-five cents. When it was all totaled up it came to slightly more than twelve hundred dollars, which, when added to the land, made an impressive inheritance.

Six years before, John Pattie had taken care of its distribution in his will. He made provisions for his wife, arranged cash payments to several daughters and their children, and then divided the land and slaves between his sons John, Jr., and Leland. Sylvester, his eldest son, was alive when the will was written, but he went unmentioned. So did all of Sylvester's children, some of whom were living with their grandfather when he wrote his will. Later, when James returned home, John Pattie added a codicil to the will. In it he gave Leland another slave, but said nothing about his grandson. Quite likely Sylvester at some time in the past—possibly when he was raising money to outfit an expedition to the West—had taken his share of the inheritance. However it was arranged, James inherited nothing.

About the time John Pattie died in late 1831, the *Personal Narrative of James O. Pattie* was published in Cincinnati. Although E. H. Flint, Timothy's son, was both a publisher and printer, he was not involved in the first edition. Instead, it was sent across the street to the firm of Williamson and Wood at 177 Main Street, and the firm's junior partner, John H. Wood, was listed as both printer and publisher. At the time the facilities at Flint's printshop were probably taxed

•

to capacity by his father's two-volume *History and Geography of the Mississippi Valley*, which would appear shortly after the *Personal Narrative*. Once that was out of the way, a second edition of the narrative was published using the same plates, but this time with E. H. Flint as the publisher.

The purpose of printing a second edition was apparently to return publication rights to Flint, rather than because there was any great demand for the book. There are no indications of how well it sold, but even with Flint's name on the title page, it made no impression on the reviewers. Soon after it was published, there was a brief notice by William Gallagher, editor of the *Cincinnati Mirror*. He said he had read only a portion of the book, but had found it interesting and might, in the future, print some extracts. Since the *Mirror* was financed by the same John H. Wood who published Pattie's narrative, Gallagher's mention may have been based more on editorial discretion than on true interest. At least he did not keep his promise to print extracts.

Gallagher's halfhearted notice of the narrative, however, was better than the absolute silence in other quarters. None of the national magazines, many of which had reviewed Flint's earlier books, took any notice. By the time the second edition appeared in 1833, Timothy Flint himself was editor of the *Knickerbocker*, but still the narrative was ignored. Even in the West, except for the brief notice in the *Mirror*, the major publications greeted it with silence.

The only long notice of the *Personal Narrative* was written by the naturalist Constantine Rafinesque. Most of the article was simply a summary of the country described by Pattie, but Rafinesque did comment briefly on the narrative. The most important thing, he said, was that although trappers had been wandering the interior of America for years, they rarely wrote accounts of the country they had visited or the discoveries they had made. The narrative, then, provided a definite service to geography and other sciences, for despite the sometimes fabulous stories, the geography and basic descriptions were sound. The article made almost no

•

impact in the United States, however, for although Rafinesque often wrote for American magazines, he chose to write
this review in French and to publish it in the French *Bulletin
de la Société de Géographie*. It was never translated into
English, and never appeared in the United States. Ironically,
the book in which Pattie rearranged his adventures to make
himself more noticeable suffered the same fate as its author
—no one paid much attention.

About the time the second edition appeared, whatever relationship Pattie had established with Timothy Flint ended
when Flint moved east. Flint, throughout much of his life,
had been in poor health, and he often tried to improve it by
moving from place to place. During 1833 it had declined
again, and hurrying his departure was a serious cholera epidemic along the Ohio River. Finally, during a brief respite in
the epidemic in mid-June, Flint left Cincinnati to go to New
York, where he would be briefly the editor of the *Knickerbocker*.

It was also in June 1833 that James Pattie appeared on the
tax list of Bracken County, Kentucky. If he had profited sub-
stantially from the *Personal Narrative*, it was not reflected
there, for he owned no land, no slaves, and his only taxable
property was two horses valued at seventy-five dollars. This
was the last time he would appear on the tax books, and it is
the last sure sighting of James Pattie in any records.

It was not until seventeen years later, during the California gold rush, that there was another report of James Pattie.
The story was told by William Waldo, who said that Pattie
"left my camp in the Sierra Nevada Mountains, amidst the
deep snows of the terrible winter of 1849–50; and his sister,
whom I met in Missouri eleven years after, told me that that
was the last account she had ever received concerning him.
I suppose he perished in the deep snows, or was killed by the
Indians." Waldo's version is the most frequently used story
of Pattie's death, but it is not automatically acceptable. If
James Pattie must face the tests of analysis, so, too, must
William Waldo.

•

3 1 3

In the first test—the opportunity to know something of Pattie other than what he read in the narrative—Waldo does very well. His older brother, David Waldo, had known the Patties since they left for the West. He had arrived in Missouri in 1820 and, like Sylvester, had been a lumberman along the Gasconade watershed. He had also served in Gasconade County as the assessor, the treasurer, and the court clerk. On the day in 1825 that Sylvester filed his deed with the court, the clerk who signed it was David Waldo. In later years both David and his brother were involved in the Santa Fe trade with many of those who had known the Patties in New Mexico. Finally, in 1856, after his return from California, William Waldo appeared before the Osage County, Missouri, court on the same day as Hardy Keeney. Since Keeney was married to one of James Pattie's sisters, it establishes Waldo's opportunity to have known this sister and to have discussed the fate of Pattie with her.

The opportunity to hear a story and the ability to remember it correctly are, however, two different things. And in the second category Waldo does not do as well. In his recollections he admitted he had never kept a diary or other written record and was writing entirely from memory. Still, he said, "my memory is clear and fresh and to recall those I knew and with whom I acted in the past, and the incidents of an active and adventurous career, is, for the moment at least, almost to live life over again."

The recollections, however, do not bear this out. He was an old man when he wrote them, and he often confused one generation with another. He assigned Lilburn Boggs activities that rightfully belonged to his son, and he identified S. S. Pratte as a brother rather than a son of Bernard Pratte. He also was confused in his accounts of the deaths of various people. S. S. Pratte, whose death he placed on the Gila, actually died on the Platte, and Alexander Le Grand, who he said died in the Texas War of Independence, was still alive years later. In themselves these are minor, isolated facts, but they demonstrate both the faultiness of his memory and his

•

willingness to relate, with complete assurance, stories that never happened.

His memory is even worse when he combines the isolated items into a connected story. The account of Jedediah Smith's travels is riddled with mistakes. Smith, in his wanderings, was often captured by Indians and just as often escaped; he and Isaac Galbraith were the only survivors of the Mohave attack; on other occasions Smith was the sole survivor of an Indian massacre; and according to Waldo, Smith made the entire trip from San Francisco to the Columbia River by himself. The stories all have some vague basis in the actual events of Smith's life, but they have clearly undergone considerable modification in Waldo's mind.

The same is true of his brief account of Pattie's expedition to California. The party left Missouri, he said, and after much suffering reached California, where they were thrown into prison. Then, he added, "seven died during their captivity; others, after a confinement of several years, were liberated." Again, there is some basis in fact, but again there is much revision in the telling.

The question, then, is whether Waldo could have been so wrong so often and still been right about the last days of James Pattie. It is not very likely. Even Waldo seems to have thought he went too far with the Pattie story, for in the original manuscript he included a sentence that was later deleted from the published version. Immediately after this story, just after he said of Pattie, "I suppose he perished in the deep snows, or was killed by the Indians," Waldo added, "but I am afraid you will cry, 'Enough, hold on, no more.'— so I will close." It is a fair-enough assessment of a critical reader's reaction.

Beyond that, doubt is also cast on the story by the lack of any supporting evidence. None of the other sources, the records, the reminiscences collected by H. H. Bancroft, the various censuses, or the index to newspapers and records, give even the vaguest hint that Pattie was in California in 1849. Presumably, there were others in Waldo's camp who would

•

have known Pattie and would have known of his disappearance, yet the story survives nowhere else. Certainly, Pattie could have returned to California, then disappeared without leaving a record. Still, the story would be more believable if it did not rest entirely on the testimony of William Waldo, who was confused on so many other items.

There is one other point worth developing, for even if Waldo is believed, he does not actually account for the death of Pattie. Waldo says only that he never saw him again after he left camp and adds, "I suppose he perished in the deep snows, or was killed by the Indians." It is just as logical to assume he left camp, possibly to escape Waldo's confused stories, and survived the trip out of the mountains. Thus, the way is paved for the next sighting of Pattie in California.

The story was told by Andrew Jackson Raney and was reported in a history of Napa County, California, published in 1881. Raney had come to California in 1849, spent some time in the mines, then went to Napa County to farm. In March 1853 he moved to Rag Canyon, where there was only one other settler, "a Frenchman, by the name of James Ohio Patti." It was all Raney says, and he offers no clue as to how "Patti" got there or how long he stayed.

Again, the story is not entirely believable. Raney was born and raised in Lexington, Kentucky; the real James Pattie in nearby Augusta, and it is inconceivable that Raney could mistake a fellow Kentuckian for "a Frenchman." There is also, again, a complete absence of other evidence, and this time it is more serious for Raney's story concerns a specific place where specific records can be checked. If Pattie ever lived in Napa County, he did not appear on the land maps, did not buy or sell property, get married, appear in court, file a will, or do anything else that would place his name on records in the county recorder's office. Again, it is possible he squatted on land in Rag Canyon for a few years, then moved on, but the story has its own flaws and is entirely unsubstantiated.

There was still one more reported sighting of James Pattie

•

in California. In 1883 "a man whose name I cannot recall" visited Bancroft's library and told the historian that his wife was a niece of Pattie's. He also said that Pattie had spent some time at her home in San Diego, "in late years, at least since 1850." Strangely enough, although the story comes from the vaguest of all possible sources, it is worth considering, for Pattie did have a niece in California at the time. Her name was Nancy Norris, and she was the daughter of one of Pattie's younger brothers. She had married Elias Norris in Missouri, moved to Kansas in the early 1860s, then on to California in the late 1870s. In 1880 she lived not in San Diego, but in Sonoma County.

The story can be checked this far but no further. Bancroft's source promised to talk to his wife and send a more definite statement, but it never arrived. Possibly he forgot; possibly he found that he was mistaken. Certainly, there was no such tradition within the Norris family. In later years one of Nancy's sons, Thomas Norris, became prominent in California historical circles, and on one occasion actually began a history of California. The unfinished manuscript, now in the Bancroft Library, contains his account of the Pattie expedition to California. His material, however, was taken almost entirely from Bancroft's version in *The History of California*. Norris was aware that James Pattie was his great-uncle, he was aware of the importance of Pattie to California, and he was vitally interested in California history. If he had knowledge from his family of Pattie's later life, he surely would have taken this opportunity to speak out. Instead, he said nothing.

From this material—Waldo, Raney, and "a man whose name I cannot recall"—it is possible to construct a theory that Pattie later returned to California to live. The theory, however, is weak, for it is based on three stories, each with its own flaws and each unsubstantiated by outside sources. Fitting them together only weakens them, for it creates for Pattie an improbable ghostlike life in which he moved from place to place, never stayed long, never owned property, and

•

never made the slightest mark on the records. The weakest part of the theory—weak to the point of causing collapse—is its inability to account for the missing seventeen years between the time Pattie appeared on the tax list of 1833 and the time he was supposedly seen in William Waldo's camp in the winter of 1849–50.

Those familiar with the wide variety of research sources available know it is not easy for anyone to completely disappear. It is not particularly difficult to give at least a brief account of the other members of Pattie's family during these same seventeen years. His grandfather died in 1831, his grandmother in 1840. His uncle Leland lived in Bracken County until 1851, then moved to Grant County, Kentucky, where he died of a heart attack in 1858. His other uncle, John, Jr., moved west to Ohio County, Kentucky, and lived there until his death in 1870. Apparently, he remembered his nephew, for just before his death one of his new grandsons was christened James O. Pattie.

James's brothers and sisters are also easily followed. John, the eldest after James, frequently appeared in the records of Gasconade and Osage counties, Missouri, from 1830 to 1850. Three other brothers—Thomas, William, and Roland—also lived there, although both Roland and Thomas died in Missouri during the 1840s. Thomas, much younger than James, was impressed enough by his brother's accomplishments that he named his first son James. Two of the three sisters—Sarah, who married Hamilton Stewart, and Julia Ann, who married Hardy Keeney—also lived most of their adult lives in Missouri. Julia kept the family legend alive, for she named one of her sons Sylvester, and he in turn named his son James O. Keeney. The third sister, Jennie, never went back to Missouri, but instead married Edwin Collins in Kentucky. He soon died, and by 1840 she was living as a widow in Cincinnati's fifth ward. Later she remarried and would live until 1900. She had no sons, but she did her share to keep the legend alive by naming one of her daughters Jacova, after Pattie's New Mexican heroine.

•

Thus, the records account for all the surviving children of Sylvester and Polly Pattie except one—their eldest son, James. Although the most logical place to find a man is near other members of his family, Pattie appears in none of these records. Nor does he appear when the search is expanded to surrounding counties or to bigger cities—Lexington, Frankfort, Cincinnati, Louisville, or St. Louis. An even wider check into other places he might have gone reveals nothing. It is impossible, of course, to look at every record for every part of the United States over a period of twenty years. Still, the available indexes to the federal census and to the territorial and state censuses now cover a surprisingly large part of the United States in the years 1830 to 1850. They reveal several James Patties—or Pattys—ranging from Pennsylvania to Arkansas. A closer look at each specific entry, however, shows that in all cases they are either much too young or too old to be James O. Pattie. He might have been missed, for the census was taken only once every ten years, but the fact remains that every other member of his family can be located.

Two theories to explain this strange disappearance come to mind. Possibly he had a serious difference with his family —maybe even over his grandfather's will—and thus broke off all relations. This is not very likely, however, for between 1840 and 1870 several different members of the family, in a clear show of respect, named their children after him. Possibly, then, the depression that marks the last pages of the narrative became so bad that he cut himself off from human contact and lived as a hermit. The stories told by Waldo, Raney, and the unremembered man suggest just that. Again, it is unlikely, for Pattie did not disappear immediately after his return, but was still in Bracken County three years later. Not only did he have time to recover, but he was also attending college, which, at least then, was a sign that he had some goal in mind. The later occupations of other Augusta College graduates—lawyers, judges, doctors, businessmen, ministers, college presidents—indicate the kind of thing Pattie

•

might be expected to do. Surely, he did not attend college to become a hermit.

The search, then, has led from a look at various stories told in California, to a re-creation of the lives of other family members, to a sometimes frantic search in indexes, and finally to the building and dismantling of various theories. Such methods have their advantages, for sometimes they suddenly encounter the trail in a most unexpected place. When they will not work—as in this case—there is nothing to do but return to the beginning of the last trail. And in Pattie's case that beginning is at the last sure sighting in Bracken County in the summer of 1833.

It had not been a pleasant summer, for the Ohio River Valley was caught in the midst of a severe epidemic. Since 1831 Americans had watched cholera spread west from Asia, across Russia, Poland, and Western Europe, until it reached England. There had been little fear in the United States, however, for cholera had never appeared there, and in the past it had always been associated with the crowded, poverty-stricken areas of Asia and Europe. Then, in mid-June 1832, word reached New York City that cholera had broken out in Quebec and Montreal. Almost immediately it spread down the Hudson into New York and west across the state to Buffalo. From Buffalo, troops under Winfield Scott left to go west to fight in the Blackhawk War. Cholera broke out on board the steamboat, and by the time they reached Chicago one officer and fifty-one men were dead, and eighty more were ill. There was panic among the rest of the soldiers and many of them deserted to escape the cholera. Their fate was described in a letter to the *Philadelphia Enquirer*: "Of the deserters scattered all over the country, some have died in the woods, and others have been devoured by the wolves. Their straggling survivors are occasionally seen marching, some of them know not whither, with their knapsacks on their backs, shunned by the terrified inhabitants as the source of mortal pestilence." Yet they were not shunned entirely, for the disease spread throughout the West.

•

Edward Mansfield, a Cincinnatian, had been in New York when the epidemic broke out along the Hudson. After it eased, in the fall of 1832, he started his trip back to Cincinnati. At Pittsburgh, however, he found that cholera had spread the whole length of the Ohio River. Several cases had been reported in Pittsburgh and several more downriver at Wheeling. Later, when his boat was anchored at Marietta Island, another steamboat anchored nearby. The captain said he had several cases of cholera on board, and he had stopped to bury one of the dead on the island. There was sudden panic on Mansfield's boat, and the captain and crew immediately raised anchor and ran downriver. Finally, in December 1832, Mansfield reached Cincinnati. By then it was cold, there was snow on the ground, and the cholera had died out.

Despite all this, the west and the south survived surprisingly well in 1832, for cholera did not arrive until late summer, and it seemed to die out with the coming of winter. It had not disappeared, however, but was only lying dormant, for in the spring of 1833 it broke out even more severely. In May it reappeared in Cincinnati, and a month later Timothy Flint decided to leave the city permanently. He wrote, "I left . . . in the dim haze of early dawn, when the steps of a solitary person along the pavement sounded, as if echoing in a sepulchre, and when it required little stretch of fancy to imagine, in the morning mists, the terrible pestilence setting down upon my house."

Cincinnati's epidemic, however, was mild compared with that which struck Kentucky in the summer of 1833. Cholera appeared suddenly, on May 29, at Maysville, less than twenty miles from Pattie's home in Augusta. The disease was easily recognizable, for its symptoms were too obvious and too spectacular to be missed or ignored. It began with diarrhea, severe vomiting, and painful cramps. The victim's face became blue and pinched with dehydration, the extremities cold and dark in color, and the skin on the hands and feet drawn and puckered. The symptoms appeared suddenly,

•

and after their appearance death could occur within a day or even within a few hours.

The appearance of cholera in Maysville came as a surprise, for most people still believed that the disease occurred only in unhealthy places or among the derelicts of society. Maysville, however, had a healthy location, and the first cases appeared in some of the best homes in town. By noon on May 29 there was news of other cases; by late afternoon rumors of several more. By the time the day was over, twenty cases had been verified and twelve of the victims had died. By the next day the death toll had reached twenty.

Those who had not yet been stricken fled the city, and within forty-eight hours it was almost deserted. It was impossible for the *Maysville Eagle* to publish that week, but two weeks later it was finally able to put out an extra. Nine-tenths of the city's population, it said, was gone, and those who had stayed behind were frightened. "Each one looks as though the next hour was that allotted for his destruction." A man who returned to Maysville about this time wrote, "We have just returned from the country, where we have been since the first. . . . The stores are still shut, and not more than one-tenth of the inhabitants in town. We are among the first in. The cholera is raging through the country —there have been several deaths around us. . . . Four families within a stone's throw of us, lost nineteen in two or three days."

The cholera spread quickly from Maysville to the rest of Kentucky, and by mid-June the list of stricken towns was long—among them Washington, Georgetown, Versailles, Bardstown, Shelbyville, Simpsonville, and Paris. In Flemingsburg, not far from Maysville, one-sixth of the population had died. Nearby, the village of Eliza, with almost one hundred houses, had been abandoned and three bodies left behind unburied. Even farmers abandoned their crops and fled. In mid-June one man said, "Should the excitement not cease in a week, the crops will not be cut."

The worst place, however, was the city of Lexington, with

•

a population of six thousand people. Although at least half of them fled at the first signs of cholera, the death toll climbed until it reached thirty per day on June 8, 9, 10, and 11. Again, the streets were deserted, the stores closed, and for six weeks there was almost no communication with the surrounding countryside. Hospitals were not operating, for nurses could not be hired at any price. Of the city's doctors, three had died, three more had fled, and most of the others at some time during the epidemic were themselves ill with cholera. One man wrote from Lexington, "I do assure you we have seen and heard enough . . . to strike terror to the strongest nerve. . . . It is useless for any one to attempt to guess how many have fallen. . . . On yesterday and today it has been impossible to get coffins or rough boxes made sufficiently soon to put them away."

Most of the news of cholera concerned the big cities, for they were both the best known and had lost the largest number of people. Still, Pattie's hometown did not escape, for in early July, Augusta, small as it was, was listed in a national publication as one of the places severely affected by cholera. At the same time serious epidemics were reported in all the surrounding settlements, including the Lower Blue Licks, where one man had lost every member of his family.

Finally, in late July and early August, despite sporadic outbreaks, the number of cholera cases began to decline. By then, it had affected almost all of Kentucky, particularly that stretch between Cincinnati, Ohio, and Maysville and inland to Lexington. In all the towns of this area, it had left behind a staggering number of victims. The *Niles Weekly Register* said, "The mysterious and terrible cholera, has passed over most parts of the state, and, in some, decimated the people in ten or twelve days—and then retired as if appeased with the sacrifice made. Many of the best and most valued inhabitants of Kentucky have fallen victims to this disease."

In November 1833, after the cholera epidemic was over, the Patties held a long-delayed auction to dispose of the effects of John Pattie, who had died almost two years before.

•

It was mostly a family affair, for Ann Pattie, his widow, bought the geese, his daughter Betsy Collins the furniture, and his grandson Whitfield Craig the hogs and the colt. Most of the farm equipment—the red heifer, the wagon, the plow, and the log chain—went to his son Leland.

His grandson James bought nothing. Possibly James had gone elsewhere that day; possibly he was outbid; or possibly he did not want the cow and calf or the "blind mare" that was sold out of the family. Still, six months before he had been in Bracken County; six months later, when the next tax list was prepared, he was not. He never again appeared in the records of that county, he was not in any future list of graduates of Augusta College, and he never showed up in the records of Missouri, where all his brothers and sisters lived.

Was he then, even at the time the auction was held in November, already dead? He was last seen in the midst of the cholera epidemic of 1833, and there is no sure record of him after it was over. That, plus the staggering death rates in Kentucky, makes such a suggestion entirely plausible.

There is no specific document to verify Pattie's death, but in the cholera epidemic of 1833, that is not particularly surprising. Kentucky did not keep death records at the time, and the surest source of information on those who died is the county will book. Pattie, however, was still a young man, not quite thirty, whose property consisted of two horses worth seventy-five dollars. Before the epidemic he had no reason to write a will, and if cholera struck without warning and caused death within hours, as it often did, there would have been no time to write a will. Also, in the confusion and panic of the epidemic, there was little hope of keeping track of the dead. Towns were abandoned, newspapers suspended publication, and people fled, leaving behind those who were dying. Those who joined the exodus were shunned as they moved into new places, and many of them finally died alone in the woods.

Even if Pattie died in Augusta, there may well have been no record, for even those who died at home were hurried

•

into the grave: "The dead could not be buried fast enough, nor could coffins be had to meet half the demand. Many of the victims were consigned to trunks and boxes, or wrapped in the bedclothes upon which they had just expired, placed in carts, and hurried off for burial without a prayer being said and no attendant but the driver. The grave-yards were choked. Coffined and uncoffined dead were laid at the gates in confused heaps to wait their turn to be deposited in the long, shallow trenches, which were hastily dug for the necessities of the occasion."

Whatever happened, James Pattie, "traveller," was seen no more after that final appearance on the Bracken County, Kentucky, tax list in the summer of 1833.

ACKNOWLEDGMENTS

Many people have contributed to the making of this book. During my research and travels hundreds of anonymous people—librarians, museum workers, park rangers, local historians, fellow researchers, sometimes even passing strangers—offered directions without which I would have been lost.

Cynnie and Jack Barrows and Mary Ann and Dick Shaffer showed a constant enthusiasm for my work which helped me more than I suspect they ever knew. Jim Holliday read the entire manuscript, made penetrating comments, and offered encouragement at a time when it was badly needed. Carole Hicke, a friend and fellow worker in history, also read the completed manuscript, gave encouragement, and made invaluable suggestions.

The book was guided along the various stages from manuscript to finished work by my agent Fred Hill, my editor Donald Knox, and his assistant, Naomi Grady. Their very professional abilities, their enthusiasm, their advice, suggestions, and cheerful answers to my frequent questions considerably eased my own tasks.

The deepest and longest-standing contribution to this work is that of my wife, Ann, and my daughters, Dayle and Denise. Not only did they uncomplainingly live with me—and various ghostly members of the Pattie family—during the writing of the book, they also spent a week camped in the rain tracing out fur trapper routes through the Gila Wilderness. It was indeed above and beyond the call of duty.

·

327

NOTES

The following abbreviations have been used in the notes:

CHSQ	*California Historical Society Quarterly.*
EWT	Thwaites, Reuben Gold. *Early Western Travels.* 32 vols. Cleveland: Arthur H. Clark Company, 1904–7.
HC	Bancroft, Hubert Howe. *History of California.* 7 vols. San Francisco: The History Company, 1886–90.
HSSCP	Historical Society of Southern California. *Publications.*
KHO	*Kansas Historical Quarterly.*
MHR	*Missouri Historical Review.*
MHSB	Missouri Historical Society. *Bulletin.*
MHSC	Missouri Historical Society. *Collections.*
MMFT	Hafen, Leroy. *The Mountain Men and the Fur Trade of the Far West.* 10 vols. Glendale, California: Arthur H. Clark Company, 1965–72.
NDHQ	*North Dakota Historical Quarterly.*
NH	*Nebraska History.*
NMHR	*New Mexico Historical Review.*
NSHST	Nebraska State Historical Society. *Transactions.*
OHSQ	*Oregon Historical Society Quarterly.*
PN	Pattie, James O. *The Personal Narrative of James O. Pattie.* Page citations are from the edition by William Goetzmann. Philadelphia and New York: J. P. Lippincott Company, 1962.
SDHC	*South Dakota Historical Collections.*
SWHQ	*Southwest Historical Collections.*
USGS	United States Geological Survey.
WWA	Morgan, Dale. *The West of William Ashley.* Denver: Old West Publishing Company, 1964.

•

PROLOGUE
pp. 1–20

Most of the material in the Prologue will be fully developed later, at which
time specific and detailed notes will be given. Therefore, I have
cited only major sources and given an indication of other things
to come. In cases where I plan no further development, however,
I have given full citations.

Page 1. This excerpt is from Henrik Ibsen, *Peer Gynt*, newly translated
from the Norwegian by Michael Meyer (Garden City: Anchor
Books, Doubleday and Co., Inc., 1963), 8.

Pages 2–3. Pattie's return home is described in *PN*, 228–30. This part of
the narrative is borne out by several other sources that will be
fully cited in the proper place. Also, the younger Pattie has generally been referred to as James Ohio Pattie, almost as if his name
were "Jamesohio." In my research, however, I have noted that he
always gave his own name—even on the title page of the *PN*—as
James or James O. In line with his obvious preference, and for the
sake of simplicity, I have referred to him throughout as James.

Pages 3–4. The story of the Patties on the Gila is from *PN*, 51–54. Pattie's
dates are sometimes suspect, but other times they are surprisingly accurate. In this case he is a year off, as he places these
events in 1825, instead of 1826. See *WWA*, 306. As Morgan points
out, beyond the mistake in year, the daily dates hold up very
well. I have found additional evidence that gives me confidence
that the dates are relatively accurate at this point.

Page 5. Flint's bookstore is described in E. H. Flint's ad in *The Cincinnati
Directory for 1829* (Cincinnati: Robinson and Fairbank, 1829).
The description of Flint's office is from James Stuart, *Three Years
in North America* (1833; reprint, New York: Arno Press, 1974),
2:275.

•

Pages 5–6. For background on Flint, see James K. Folsom, *Timothy Flint* (New York: Twayne Publishers, 1965), and John E. Kirkpatrick, *Timothy Flint* (Cleveland: Arthur H. Clark Company, 1911). Frances Trollope's attitude is in *Domestic Manners of the Americans* (New York: Dodd, Mead and Company, n.d.), 1: 124–25.

Page 6. Van Buren's letter is in U.S. Department of State, Diplomatic Instructions, National Archives Record Group 59, M97, Reel 9, pp. 175–76. The story will be developed more fully in a later chapter.

Pages 7–8. Flint's description of how he checked on Pattie is in *PN*, 1–2. Willard's story is from "Inland Trade with New Mexico," an appendix to *PN*. Willard's presence in New Mexico is established by R. W. H. Hardy, *Travels in the Interior of Mexico* (London: H. Colburn and R. Bentley, 1829), 477, and his residence in Cincinnati by the city directories of 1831, 1834, and 1836–37. James Glenn is in the 1829 and 1831 city directories. The trading permit can be found in the Museum of New Mexico, New Mexican Archives (photocopy, Bancroft Library, University of California, Berkeley), and in David Weber, *The Extranjeros* (Santa Fe: Stagecoach Press, 1967), 32.

Page 8. The first revival of Pattie's narrative was in 1847, when a writer using the name Ben Bilson published a book of his adventures entitled *The Hunters of Kentucky*. In fact, it was nothing but a pirated version of the *Personal Narrative* with the name "Pattie" changed to "Bilson" on both the title page and in the text. In 1860 the story was again revived as an article entitled, erroneously, "The First Overland Trip to California," which appeared in the June issue of *Harper's New Monthly Magazine*. This time the author, J. T. Headley, used Pattie's name as one of the participants, but nowhere did he mention the *Personal Narrative*, and he left the impression that the article was his own work. Instead, it is only a summary of the narrative to which the author adds nothing of his own. The narrative was finally reprinted in full with Pattie listed as author by Reuben Gold Thwaites as volume 18 of his *Early Western Travels* in 1905. Another edition was published, with Milo Quaife as editor, in 1930, and still another, with William Goetzmann as editor, in 1962.

Page 9. The magazine editor's comment is in the *Cincinnati Mirror* (May 12, 1832), 1:131.

Pages 9–10. See W. J. Ghent, "James Ohio Pattie," *Dictionary of American Biography* (New York: Charles Scribner's Sons, 1934), 14:310–11. One mention of Pattie as an illiterate trapper is in T. H. Watkins, *The Grand Colorado* (n.p.: American West Publishing Company, 1969), 68. Flint is also given blame—or credit—for abetting the lying biography of Jim Beckwourth. Whatever editorial sins Flint must answer for, that book is not among them, for he was long since dead when it was written.

•

Page 10. Flint describes his role in *PN*, 2. The promissory note is a manuscript in the Bancroft Library; the letter is in Vallejo Collections,
30:85, Bancroft Library, and reprinted in Robert G. Cleland, *This
Reckless Breed of Men* (New York: Alfred A. Knopf, Inc., 1950),
207–8.
Pages 10–11. Pattie's background and his stories in the narrative will be
cited fully when they are developed in later chapters.
Pages 12–14. The preface is *PN*, 1–4, the introduction, *PN*, 5–9. Flint's
specific quote on Kentuckians is p. 3. Like most writers, Flint
could work both sides of an issue, and in *The Shoshone Valley*, a
novel published in 1830, he took the opposite point of view in
describing trappers.
Pages 14–16. The similarities and differences of *Francis Berrian* and *PN*
are developed in chapter six. See also Frederick S. Stimson, "Francis Berrian; Hispanic Influence on American Romanticism," *His-
pania* 42 (December 1959): 511–16, and C. M. Lombard,
"Timothy Flint, Early American Disciple of French Romanticism," *Revue de Littérature Comparée* 26 (Avril-Juin 1962):
276–82.
Pages 16–17. The accounts of Yount, Smith, and Pryor can be found in
Charles Camp, *George Yount* (Denver: Old West Publishing
Company, 1966); "Sketches from the Life of Peg Leg Smith,"
Hutchings California Magazine 5 (1860–61); and Stephen Foster,
"A Sketch of Some of the Earliest Kentucky Pioneers of Los An-
geles," *HSSCP* (1887), 30–35. Material on Echeandia is from var-
ious manuscript records in the Bancroft Library that will be cited
fully at a later time.
Page 19. The five pictures in the narrative appeared in both the 1831
and 1833 editions, and were reproduced in later editions of the
PN by Reuben Gold Thwaites (1905) and Milo Quaife (1930).
For material on William Woodruff, the engraver, see David
McNally Stauffer, *American Engravers Upon Copper and
Steel* (New York: The Grolier Club of the City of New York,
1907), 1:295 and 2:560–62; and Walter Sutton, *The Western
Book Trade* (Columbus, Ohio: Ohio State University Press,
1958), 80. Woodruff also appears in Cincinnati directories of the
time.

CHAPTER ONE
pp. 21–47

Page 22. James Pattie's reminiscences of his home are in *PN*, 226. His
comments on his mother's death and his father's reaction are on
p. 8.
Pages 22–23. The marriage of Sylvester Pattie and Polly Hubbard is in
Mason County, Kentucky, Marriage Records, 1797–1803.

•

Thomas Hubbard's property is from Mason County Tax Book, 1802.

Page 23. John Pattie's property is from Bracken County Tax Book, 1802. His appointment as a judge is in Bracken County Court Order Book A, p. 2, and his appointment as a trustee for Bracken Academy is in William Littell, *A Digest of the Statute Laws of Kentucky* (Frankfort, Kentucky: Kendall and Russell, 1822), 2:242. When Pattie arrived on the Ohio River, the area was still part of Mason County, and he first appears in its Tax Book in 1794. His request to dam Bracken Creek so that he can built a gristmill is in Mason County Court Order Book B, p. 65.

Pages 23–24. Material on Bracken Academy is most readily available in Walter H. Rankin, *Augusta College* (Frankfort: Roberts Printing Company, 1957). Augusta College was a direct descendant of Bracken Academy. The letter used to speculate on Sylvester's education is Sylvester Pattie to William Clark, September 26, 1813, Clark Papers, Missouri Historical Society, St. Louis.

Page 24. The Patties migrated to Kentucky with the Upper Spotsylvania Baptist Church. See George Ranck, *The Travelling Church* (Louisville, Kentucky: Press of Baptist Book Concern, 1891). A firsthand account of the trip, which specifically mentions John Pattie as a member, is in Draper MSS, 11 CC 279–283 (photocopy, University of California, Berkeley, Library).

Page 25. There is much material on the siege of Bryant's Station, the Battle of Blue Licks, and the activities of the relief party. See Reuben T. Durrett, "Bryant's Station," and "The Battle of Blue Licks," in Filson Club Publication no. 12 (1897). The specific claim that John Pattie was part of the relief party is in *PN*, 5–6. I have not automatically accepted it, but the time, place, and people involved are such as to lend substantial weight to the claim. The fact that John's wife, Ann Pattie, was at Craig's Station at the time is clearly established by her own statement in Annie Walker Burns Bell, *Revolutionary War Pensions of Soldiers Who Settled in Fayette County, Kentucky* (Washington, D.C.: Annie Walker Burns Bell, 1936), 38.

Pages 25–26. See John Bakeless, *Daniel Boone* (New York: William Morrow and Company, 1939), and Patricia Jahns, *The Violent Years, Simon Kenton and the Ohio-Kentucky Frontier* (New York: Hastings House, 1962).

Page 26. Sylvester's purchase of land from his father is in Bracken County Deed Book C, p. 233. Jesse Thomas is listed as bondsman in the original marriage record. For his later career, see J. F. Snyder, "Forgotten Statesmen of Illinois," Illinois State Historical Society Publication no. 9 (1904), 514–25. Material on both Thomas and Pattie in the militia is in G. Glenn Clift, *The "Corn Stalk" Militia of Kentucky, 1792–1811* (Frankfort: Kentucky Historical Society, 1957), 127.

•

333

Page 27. Sylvester's land and slaves are listed in the Bracken County Tax Books from 1803 to 1811.

Page 27. For the recruiting of John Colter at Maysville, see Donald Jackson, ed., *Letters of the Lewis and Clark Expedition* (Urbana: University of Illinois Press, 1962), 125.

Page 27. The birth date of James Pattie will be discussed in a later chapter. The other children's birth dates were determined from various later censuses.

Pages 27–28. There are several editions of Zadok Cramer's *The Navigator*. I used the 1814 edition that is reprinted in Ethel C. Leahy, *Who's Who on the Ohio River* (Cincinnati: E. C. Leahy Publishing Company, 1931). Material on the *New Orleans* is also from Leahy, 307.

Pages 28–29. Pattie's sale of property is in Bracken County Deed Book D, pp. 131, 184. Harle and Hubbard's sale of property is in Mason County Deed Book M, p. 35.

Pages 29–30. The most detailed view of the war in Missouri is Kate L. Gregg, "The War of 1812 on the Missouri Frontier," *MHR* 33 (October 1938): 3–22; (January 1939): 184–202; and (April 1939): 326–48.

Pages 30–32. Sylvester Pattie appears in rosters of Missouri militia published in Louis Houck, *A History of Missouri* (Chicago: R. R. Donnelley and Sons, 1908), 3:106, and Clarence E. Carter, ed., *Territorial Papers of the United States* (Washington, D.C.: U.S. Government Printing Office, 1951), 14:791. His letter is Sylvester Pattie to William Clark, September 26, 1813, Clark Papers, Missouri Historical Society, St. Louis. The other letters written by Pattie appeared in the *Missouri Gazette*, October 2, 1813. Timothy Flint's version of Sylvester's military career is in *PN*, 6–7.

Page 32. Pattie's appointment and his assignment to Hight's company, as well as Hight's role as advocate general, is in Houck, 3:106, and Carter, 14:791.

Page 33. Material on Daniel Morgan Boone is from John Bakeless, *Daniel Boone*; Ella Hazel Spraker, *The Boone Family* (Rutland, Vermont: The Tuttle Company, 1922); and John K. Hulston, "Daniel Boone's Sons in Missouri," *MHR* 41 (July 1947): 361–72.

Pages 34–35. Pattie and Boone's trip into the Ozarks can be found in several printed sources. The best is R. A. Campbell, *Campbell's Gazetteer* (St. Louis: R. A. Campbell, 1875), 619. See also Howard L. Conard, *Encyclopedia of the History of Missouri* (Louisville: Southern History Company, 1901), 177; Nathan Parker, *Missouri as It Is in 1867* (Philadelphia: J. P. Lippincott Company, 1867), 404; and *A Reminiscent History of the Ozark Region* (Cape Girardeau, Missouri: Ramfre Press 1956), 32. All these sources are somewhat vague and confused, and Pattie's name ranges from "Petit" to "Paddy," but contemporary records make it clear it

•

could only be Sylvester Pattie. There is much material on early frontier hunters. Among the best contemporary accounts, however, is Henry Schoolcraft, *Journal of a Tour into the Interior of Missouri and Arkansaw* (London: Sir Richard Phillips and Company, 1821).

Page 35. The location of the mill is from Conard, *Encyclopedia*, and from the USGS Big Piney and Waynesville 1:62,500 maps. I also visited the area and camped on Paddy Creek in the fall of 1976.

Page 36. The story of Johnson, Dulle, and Cullen appears in several sources, the best being Campbell, 455. The 1819 Franklin County Tax Book bears out the story to the extent of listing Johnson and Dulle, but not Cullen.

Page 36. General material on the role of mills and millers can be found in Priscilla Ann Evans, "Merchant Gristmills and Communities, 1820–1880; An Economic Relationship," *MHR* 68 (April 1974): 317–26. The specific comments by John Bradbury are from his *Travels in the Interior of America* (London: Sherwood, Neely and James, 1819), as reprinted in *EWT* 5:313.

Page 37. The possibilities in the lumber industry in postwar Missouri are mentioned in *PN*, 8, and confirmed by John Shaw, "Personal Narrative," State Historical Society of Wisconsin 2 (1855): 225.

Page 37. The promissory note is in the Leonard Papers, Western Historical Manuscripts Collection, University of Missouri, Columbia, Missouri. For more on Hiram Scott, see Merrill J. Mattes, "Hiram Scott," *NH* 26 (1945): 127–62, and "Hiram Scott," *MMFT* 1: 355–66.

Pages 37–38. A copy of the Franklin County Tax Book is in the State Historical Society of Missouri, Columbia. The establishment of Boone's mill and its location can be found in Gasconade County Deed Book A, pp. 33 and 69. The 1820 tax list is in Goodspeed's *History of Franklin, Jefferson, Washington, Crawford, and Gasconade Counties, Missouri* (Chicago: Goodspeed Publishing Company, 1888), 638.

Page 38. Material on early life in the Ozarks is drawn from many sources. The most valuable are Schoolcraft, Bradbury, and Lennis L. Broadfoot, *Pioneers of the Ozarks* (Caldwell, Idaho: Caxton Printers, 1944).

Pages 38–39. For the organization of Gasconade County, see Goodspeed, 623–26. The various appointments of Sylvester Pattie are from Gasconade County Circuit Court Records, Book A, pp. 17, 20–21, and 25.

Pages 39–40. As indicated in the text, there are no specific records on Polly Pattie's death, the only mention being James's statement in *PN*, 8.

Page 40. For the activities of the Missouri Fur Company, see Richard Oglseby, "Manuel Lisa," *MMFT* 5:179–201, and John C. Luttig, *Journal of a Fur Trading Expedition on the Upper Missouri,*

•

1812–1813 (New York: Argosy-Antiquarian Ltd., 1964). For
Baird, see Frank B. Golley, "James Baird, Early Santa Fe trader,"
MHSB 15 (April 1959): 171–93. See also Rex W. Strickland,
"James Baird," *MMFT* 3:27–37.

Page 41. For the opening of the Santa Fe trade and all that followed, see
Louise Barry, "Kansas Before 1854; a Revised Annals," *KHQ* 27
(Autumn 1961): 497–543.

Pages 41–42. The best source for Ashley as well as the whole western
scene of the 1820s is *WWA*. Ashley's service in the War of 1812
and his gunpowder years are on p. xix. There is additional material on these early years in Harrison C. Dale, *The Ashley-Smith
Explorations and the Discovery of a Central Route to the
Pacific, 1822–1829* (Glendale: Arthur H. Clark Company, 1941),
58–59.

Page 42. The sale of Pattie's mill is in Gasconade County Deed Book A, p.
32. In order that the deed may serve as a mortgage, it is made out
from the Drolettes to Pattie, rather than vice versa. Thus, Pattie
is listed in the index as the grantor rather than the grantee.

Page 43. "Begged so earnestly" is in *PN*, 9.

Pages 43–45. James's version of the start of the trip is in *PN*, 11–12. As
indicated in the text, I have serious doubts as to its accuracy. I
have worked out my own interpretation after examining the various activities of those involved in the French company. See
David J. Weber, "Sylvestre S. Pratte," *MMFT* 6:359–70; Ray Mattison, "Jean Pierre Cabanne, Sr.," *MMFT* 2:69–73; Janet Le-
Compte, "Pierre Chouteau, Jr.," *MMFT* 9:91–123; Frederick
Billon, *Annals of St. Louis* (St. Louis: n.p., 1886); and particularly
David Weber, *The Taos Trappers* (Norman: University of Oklahoma Press, 1971), 82–97. I also have examined the Chouteau
Collection and other appropriate papers in the Missouri Historical Society, St. Louis. Although I found no mention of the Patties,
if, as I suggest, there was an informal agreement, there need be
nothing in writing. One fact stands out clearly—however the
arrangements were made, James and Sylvester did indeed accompany S. S. Pratte.

Pages 45–46. The type of outfit put together by Pattie and the fact that it
was purchased in St. Louis is in *PN*, 11. Unlike the plan, this
material makes sense, given time and place, and I have accepted
it as accurate. General information on St. Louis in these years is
from Billon; Richard Edwards and M. Hopewell, *Edward's Great
West* (St. Louis: Edwards Monthly, 1860); John L. Paxon, *St. Louis
Directory and Register of 1821*; and the bits and pieces contained
over many years in the *MHR*. The fact that Hawken supposedly
witchproofed his rifles is from Vance Randolph, *Ozark Supersti-
tions* (New York: Columbia University Press, 1947), 294.

Pages 46–47. The deed filed in Gasconade County is in Deed Book A, p.
32. The unanswered letter is from the postmaster's advertise-
ment in the *Missouri Republican*, October 10, 1825.

•

Page 50. Dale Morgan in *WWA*, 306, has established that the Pratte party went west in 1825 rather than 1824. Additional confirmation is offered by the fact that on October 18, 1824, Sylvester was still in Missouri, for on that date he served as a juror in the assault and battery case of David Mafari (State of Missouri, Second Circuit Court, Gasconade County, Book A, pp. 31–33). Once the necessary correction is made, the *PN* fits well into other known activities, and the individual dates, at least in the beginning, are reasonably accurate.

Pages 50–51. Pattie says little about this portion of the trip. The description of the route, as well as the weather, is from Kate L. Gregg, ed., *The Road to Santa Fe* (Albuquerque: University of New Mexico Press, 1952). It contains the diary of George Sibley, who was only a few days behind the Patties.

Page 52. For a description of a typical young frontiersman at the age of fourteen, see Schoolcraft, *Journal*, 49–50.

Page 52. Pattie's "begging" is in *PN*, 9. Bancroft's remark is in *HC* 3:162. Pattie gives his age, by implication, in *PN*, 6. Later, however, when passing through customs in New Orleans, in August 1830, he lists his age as twenty-three, rather than twenty-six. See National Archives, Record Group 36, Passenger Lists, New Orleans, August 2, 1830. (Pattie is on the list of the ship *United States*, which docked the previous day.) It is apparently in error, for the births of the other children, established by various records, are: Julia, 1805; John, 1807; Sarah, 1809; and Jennie, 1810. Since Sylvester and Polly were married in 1802, the logical place to put James is in late 1803 or early 1804, which would be consistent with his claim in the *PN*.

Page 53. Scattered comments in the *PN* are: love of rifle, p. 9; never seen a beaver, p. 21; never been alone in the woods, p. 49.

Pages 53–54. Comment that he was "at school" is in *PN*, 9. For material on Missouri education at the time, see Margaret McMillan and Monica Cook Morris, "Education Opportunities in Early Missouri," *MHR* 33 (April 1939): 307–25, and (July 1939): 477–98. Pattie's description of his return home is in *PN*, 229–30.

Pages 54ff. The general atmosphere at the bluffs has been pieced together from Paul Wilhelm, Duke of Wuerttemberg, "First Journey to North America in the Years 1822 to 1824," *SDHC* 19 (1938): 7–462; Russell Reid and Clell G. Gannon, "Journal of the Atkinson-O'Fallon Expedition," *NDHQ* 4 (October 1929): 5–56; Edgar B. Wesley, ed., "Diary of James Kennerly, 1823–26," *MHSC* 6 (October 1928): 41–97; Edgar B. Wesley, "Life at Fort Atkinson," *NH* 30 (December 1949): 348–58; W. H. Eller, "Old Fort Atkinson," *NSHST* 4 (1892): 18–29; Virgil Ney, "Prairie General and Colo-

•

nels at Cantonment Missouri and Fort Atkinson," *NH* 56 (Spring 1975): 51–76; and Richard E. Jensen, "Bellevue, the First Twenty Years," *NH* 56 (Fall 1975): 339–74.

Page 56. "One visitor" is in Wilhelm, 348–56.

Pages 56–58. Material on Joseph Robidoux is in Merrill J. Mattes, "Joseph Robidoux," *MMFT* 8: 287–314. The various sightings on the river are, 1806, Bernard DeVoto, ed., *Journals of Lewis and Clark* (New York: Antiquarian Press, 1959), 5:386; 1812, Luttig, *Journal*, 34; 1819 and 1822, *WWA*, L, 10. For Cabanne, see Ray H. Mattison, "Jean Pierre Cabanne, Sr.," *MMFT* 2:69–73. Robidoux's claim that he never wanted to be an employee is in *WWA*, 154. The visitor is again Wilhelm, 348. Kennerly's comment is in *MHSC*, 6: 70–71.

Pages 58–61. General biographical material is in Merrill J. Mattes, "John Dougherty," *MMFT* 8:113–41, and Aubrey Haines, "John Colter," *MMFT* 8:73–85. In recounting the story of John Colter, however, I have purposely followed the version of Thomas James in *Three Years Among the Mexicans and Indians* (New York: The Citadel Press, 1966), 52–65. James accompanied Dougherty on the trip with Colter and therefore it is logical to assume that what James heard is also what Dougherty heard.

Pages 61–62. For Joshua Pilcher, see John E. Sunder, *Joshua Pilcher, Fur Trader and Indian Agent* (Norman: University of Oklahoma Press, 1968), and Ray H. Mattison, "Joshua Pilcher," *MMFT* 4: 251–60.

Pages 62–66. The clearest and most intelligent look at William Ashley and the events along the Missouri in 1822–23 is in Dale Morgan, *Jedediah Smith and the Opening of the West* (Indianapolis: The Bobbs-Merrill Company, Inc., 1953). The basic documents are in *WWA*, and the best firsthand account is in Charles Camp, ed., *James Clyman, American Frontiersman* (Portland: Champoeg Press, 1960).

Pages 66–68. Events concerning Smith's party and the return of Clyman, Fitzpatrick, et al., are well handled in Morgan, *Jedediah Smith*; Camp, *James Clyman*; and Leroy Hafen, *Broken Hand: The Life of Thomas Fitzpatrick* (Denver: Old West Publishing Company, 1973).

Page 69. The suggestion that Branch and Stone accompanied Pratte to New Mexico is made by both Janet LeCompte, "Alexander K. Branch," *MMFT*, 4:62, and Camp, *James Clyman*, 311. Neither has clear proof, but given the time element and the later associates of the two men in New Mexico, I feel it is a valid claim.

Page 69. Information on the various trips of the Robidoux to New Mexico is in Weber, *Taos Trappers*, 85. The letter concerning Mexican officials at Council Bluffs is from James W. Covington, "Correspondence between Mexican Officials at Santa Fe and Officials in Missouri: 1823–1825," *MHSB* 16 (October 1959): 29

•

Page 72. The date of the keelboat's arrival is from *PN*, 11, and is confirmed by Kennerly in his diary, *MHSC* 6: 78.

Page 72. Because of the frequent confusion between Sylvester Pattie and Sylvestre Pratte, I have purposely referred to the latter as S. S. Pratte. Cabanne's attitude toward Pratte can be found in David J. Weber, "Sylvestre S. Pratte," *MMFT* 6:359–70. The specific quote is on p. 362.

Pages 72–73. The description of the trip from the bluffs to Pratte's camp is, of course, Pattie's. I have, however, checked it against and obtained additional material from Edwin James, *Account of an Expedition from Pittsburgh to the Rocky Mountains* (Philadelphia: H. C. Carey and I. Lea, 1823), 1:427–28; and Harlan M. Fuller and Leroy R. Hafen, eds., *The Journal of Captain John R. Bell* (Glendale: Arthur H. Clark Company, 1957), 103–24 (hereafter cited as Bell). Both men were with the Long expedition when it traveled this same route in 1820. I have used the USGS 1:250,000 maps (Fremont and Broken Bow), and then also drove the route in the fall of 1976.

Page 73. My refusal to accept Pattie's claim of visiting a Pawnee village is based on the absence of such a village in either James or Bell, and on Waldo R. Wedel, *An Introduction to Pawnee Archaeology* (Washington, D.C.: U.S. Government Printing Office, 1936). Wedel gives a careful description of all Pawnee sites, and I consider his failure to mention one in this area to be conclusive.

Page 74. The date August 6 is from the *PN*, 15. It is here that Reuben Gold Thwaites, in his 1905 edition of the *PN* (*EWT* 18:42), wrote a footnote that would determine much of the later attitude toward Pattie. Thwaites counted up all "the next days" and decided the date should be August 8 instead. Thwaites therefore implied that all the dates were inaccurate, and added, "There is no indication that Pattie kept a journal. . . ." Pattie may, however, have counted arrival and departure dates both as a day in camp and a day on the trail, thus making it come out right. Even if Thwaites is right, it is too minor an error for such a sweeping generalization.

Pages 74–77. Material on the Pawnee and the Pawnee villages is from Bell, James, Wedel, as well as George Hyde, *The Pawnee Indians* (Norman: University of Oklahoma Press, 1951, 1974), and Gene Weltfish, *The Lost Universe* (New York: Basic Books, 1965).

Page 77. All the above accounts are unanimous in placing the Skidi village on the Loup rather than the main fork of the Platte. Specific locations of the villages are in Wedel, 25–27, 36–38.

Pages 77–78. A contemporary account of the Indians in Washington, D.C.,

•

is in Thomas L. McKenney and James Hall, *The Indian Tribes of North America*, Frederick Webb Hodge, ed. (Edinburgh: John Grant, 1933), 1:201–17. Good secondary accounts are in James D. Horan, *The McKenney-Hall Portrait Gallery of American Indians* (New York: Crown Publishers, 1972), 43–49, and Katherine C. Turner, *Red Man Calling on the Great White Father* (Norman: University of Oklahoma Press, 1951), 48–58. Although there were several Pawnee in the delegation, Petalesharo is clearly identified as the only Skidi. The specific comment on the cannon foundary is in Horan, p. 46.

Page 78. The *National Intelligencer*'s story was on January 29, 1821.

Page 79. All the above sources have a version of the rescue of the Comanche girl, as do both Hyde and Weltfish. All, however, rest on James, 1:358–59; Bell, 119–20; and McKenney and Hall, 1:-205–6. Some sources call Petalesharo's father Old Knife, but the contemporaries, James and Bell, and the students of the Pawnee, Hyde and Weltfish, are unanimous in calling him Knife Chief.

Page 80. I have followed Turner, 55–57, and Horan, 48, on the presentation of the medal, but have parted company on the translation. A careful reading of McKenney and Hall, 1:208, indicates McKenney's version is more wishful thinking than a true translation.

Pages 80–81. Cooper's description of Petalesharo and his admission that he was the basis for Hard-Heart is in James Franklin Beard, ed., *The Letters and Journal of James Fenimore Cooper* (Cambridge: Belknap Press of Harvard University Press, 1960), 1:199. For a detailed study of the writing of *The Prairie*, and of Cooper's use of Petalesharo, see Orm Overland, *The Making and Meaning of an American Classic, James Fenimore Cooper's "The Prairie"* (New York: Humanities Press, 1973).

Pages 81–82. Pattie's description of the return of the raiders and the celebration is in *PN*, 15–16; his version of the captive boy is in *PN*, 16–18. It should be compared with McKenney and Hall, 1: 208–9, and James, 1:359–60. See also the *Missouri Gazette*, June 19, 1818.

Page 82. For specifics on the 1827 sacrifice, and for general material on all sacrificial events, see Dorothy V. Jones, "John Dougherty and the Pawnee Rite of Human Sacrifice: April, 1827," *MHR* 63 (April 1969): 293–316; and Melburn D. Thurman, "The Skidi Pawnee Morning Star Sacrifice of 1827," *NH* 51 (Fall 1970): 269–80.

Page 83. The letter placing Papin with Pratte in the summer of 1825 is in *MMFT* 6:362.

CHAPTER FOUR
pp. 85–104

Pattie's version of the trip across the plains is in *PN*, 19–38. His vague and sometimes confused geography, and the lack of any other

•

340

contemporary travel in the area, have made it difficult to determine the party's route. I have worked out my version, after considerable trial and error, on the various USGS 1:250,000 maps of the Great Plains. The three key factors are: (1) they started at the Loup, not the main Platte; (2) they camped under what is now called Castle Rock in Gove County, Kansas; and (3) they crossed the sand dunes south of the Arkansas to reach the Cimarron. With these as beginning, middle, and end, it is possible to work out a route with fewer problems than any other possibility. After establishing it on maps, I drove the entire route in 1976 and saw no reason to change my mind.

Page 86. Long's account is in Bell, 124–25, and James, 1:450–55.

Page 86. For location of the Skidi village on the Loup, see the note for p. 77. The lack of a rise in the Missouri is from the Atkinson-O'Fallon Journal under entry of June 25; see *NDHQ* 4:25. It also mentions the hot, dry weather, as does George Sibley in Kate Gregg, *Road to Santa Fe*.

Page 88. For the Republican Pawnee village, as well as Pike and Melgares's route, see Donald Jackson, ed., *The Journals of Zebulon Montgomery Pike* (Norman: University of Oklahoma Press, 1966), 1: 325–27.

Page 89. The Atkinson-O'Fallon Journal, *NDHQ* 4:40–41, reported rain on the Missouri just below the mouth of the Yellowstone on August 15 and 16; Sibley, in Gregg, *Road to Santa Fe*, reported it on the Arkansas at about ninety-eight degrees from the night of August 16 to the morning of August 18. These reports lend considerable weight to the relative accuracy of Pattie's dates.

Page 91. Apparently, they went overland from the Republican to the Prairie Dog Fork, for Pattie says, on the first night, that they camped by water. It is a strange comment if they followed the Republican to the mouth of the Prairie Dog Fork.

Page 91. There is material on the history of buffalo stands in David A. Dary, *The Buffalo Book* (New York: Avon Books, 1975), 106ff.

Pages 92–93. Other accounts of travel along the Prairie Dog Fork are well correlated in George A. Root and Russell K. Hickman, "Pikes Peak Express Companies: Part II—Solomon and Republican Route," *KHQ* 13 (November 1944): 211–42. See also Leroy Hafen, ed., *Overland Routes to the Gold Fields, 1859* (Glendale: Arthur H. Clark Company, 1942), 233–62, 285–97. There is a compilation of prairie dog accounts in Theo. H. Scheffer, "Historical Encounters and Accounts of the Plains Prairie Dog," *KHQ* 13 (November 1945), 527–37. The author is shocked by Pattie's comparison of the prairie dog to the Norwegian rat, finding it both "odious" and "inaccurate."

Pages 94–95. For a classic example of counting slain Indians by the hundreds, see T. D. Bonner, *The Life and Adventures of James P. Beckwourth* (1856; reprint, New York: Alfred A. Knopf, Inc., 1931).

•

Page 96. Pattie's description of Rock Castle is in *PN*, 27–28. The account of Lt. J. R. Fitch, of the survey party, is in Mrs. Frank C. Montgomery, "Fort Wallace and Its Relation to the Frontier," Kansas State Historical Society *Collections*, 17 (1926–28): 192. See also Warren G. Hodson and Kenneth D. Wahl, *Geology and Groundwater Resources of Gove County, Kansas* (Topeka: University of Kansas, 1960), which gives a precise location and also contains a picture on p. 14.

Page 96. For Sibley's rate of travel and the specific quote, see Kate Gregg, *Road to Santa Fe*, 77. Those wishing to follow the route from Prairie Dog Fork to Castle Rock should see USGS 1:250,000 Goodland and Scott City maps.

Pages 97–98. Pattie's account of the attack on the horse herd and the aftermath is in *PN*, 28–29. The story of Hugh Glass is covered in John Myers Myers, *Pirate, Pawnee, and Mountain Man* (Boston: Little, Brown and Company, 1963).

Page 99. Pattie's description of the wounds is in *PN*, 29. Yount's is in Charles Camp, ed., *George C. Yount* (Denver: Old West Publishing Company, 1966), 199. Yount also told the same story to Richard Henry Dana in 1859, for Dana in his journal gave a cryptic account that included the phrase "Neck open, wind pipe open, one flank gone." See "Letters and Journal of Richard Henry Dana, Jr., 1859–60," in John Haskell Kemble, ed., *Two Years Before the Mast* (Los Angeles: Ward Ritchie Press, 1964), 447. Charles Camp, in his original editing of the Yount chronicle in *CHSQ* (1923) 2:24–33, noted the similarities, as did J. Cecil Alter in *Jim Bridger* (1925; reprint, Norman: The University of Oklahoma Press, 1962), 41–42. Both men were hampered by the assumption that Pattie was describing events of 1824 rather than 1825. Camp, in the later book edition, was aware of Dale Morgan's correction of the dates and thus dropped the earlier footnote. Newspaper accounts that Pattie might have seen are *Missouri Republican*, June 13, 1825, and *Missouri Intelligencer*, June 18, 1825.

Page 99. The account of Glass's later years is from Lewis Dutton, who passed it on to George Yount, who later repeated it in his chronicles. See Camp, *Yount*, 205. See also Rex Strickland, "Lewis Dutton," *MMFT* 9:149. Dutton's story, however, is confused, and assigning an exact date based solely on it is impossible. Pattie's story of the litter is in *PN*, 29–30; Yount's is in Camp, 200.

Page 100. Pattie's bear count, *PN*, 30. Although Pattie says they followed the Smoky Hill to its source, that is clearly impossible. Not only is the distance too far, but it also would take them too far west to follow the route south of the Arkansas as it is described by Pattie. The Smoky Hill and its tributaries are intermittent, with several springs giving the false appearance as the source of the river. See Edward Bradley and Charlton R. Johnson, *Ground-Water Resources of the Ladder Creek Area in Kansas* (Topeka:

•

University of Kansas, 1957), 50. See also USGS 1:250,000 Scott City map. Based on these, and on what has gone before and comes later in the *PN*, the most logical route is up the Smoky Hill, then up Ladder Creek to a point just north of Scott City, Kansas. From here, they went due south and reached the Arkansas just west of Garden City, Kansas.

Page 101. Story of the calf, *PN*, 30–31.

Pages 101–4. Pattie's account of the meeting with Indians is in *PN*, 31–36. His descriptions as well as the relations between the Ute and Comanche hold up well when checked against Jean Louis Berlandier, *The Indians of Texas in 1830*, John C. Ewers, ed. (Washington, D.C.: Smithsonian Institution Press, 1969); Rupert N. Richardson, *The Comanche Barrier to South Plains Settlement* (Glendale: Arthur H. Clark Company, 1933), 55; and Ernest Wallace and E. Adamson Hoebel, *The Comanches* (Norman, Oklahoma: n.p., 1952), 3–5, 83, 277–79. Frederick Webb Hodge, *Handbook of American Indians North of Mexico* (Washington, D.C.: U.S. Government Printing Office, 1912), 1:594, points out the varied use of the term "Ietan."

Page 104. The quotes from Pattie are in *PN*, 36–37.

Page 104. The quotation on the burial of goods is from Thomas Forsyth to Secretary of War, St. Louis, October 24, 1831, in 22nd Cong., 1st sess., Sen. Doc. 90 (Ser. 213), p. 76. Pattie's quote is in *PN*, 38.

CHAPTER FIVE
pp. 105–119

Pages 106ff. Pattie's account of Taos is in *PN*, 38–39. I have checked it, when possible, against the travelers' accounts of Alfred Pike, *Prose Sketches and Poems*, David J. Weber, ed. (Albuquerque: Calvin Horn Publisher, 1967), and Lewis H. Garrard, *Wah-To-Yah and the Taos Trail* (Norman: University of Oklahoma Press, 1955), as well as the documentary evidence in Ralph Emerson Twitchell, *The Spanish Archives of New Mexico* (n.p.: Torch Press, 1914). The specific quote on p. 106 is from Pike, 147–48, and the description of the *alcalde*'s home is on p. 237.

Page 107. "One traveler" is Garrard, 174, 180.

Pages 108–9. The experiences of the Glenn-Fowler party are in Jacob Fowler, *The Journal of Jacob Fowler*, edited by Elliot Coues; further edited by Raymond and Mary Lund Settle and Harry R. Stevens (Lincoln: University of Nebraska Press, 1970). The story of Paul is on pp. 92–93.

Page 109. The "hot mess" is from Garrard, 175.

Pages 110–11. General material on trappers in Taos is from Weber, *Taos Trappers*. For the road survey party's arrival, see Kate Gregg, *Road to Santa Fe*, 130. Specific comments on Mexican com-

•

plaints about Taos are in H. Bailey Carrol and J. Villasana Haggard, *Three New Mexico Chronicles* (Albuquerque: Quivira Society, 1942), 65–66, 71–72.

Page 111. The road to Santa Fe is described by Pike, 101, 183; Carrol and Haggard, 31, 173; and Kate Gregg, 132–34.

Pages 111ff. Pattie's account of Santa Fe is in *PN*, 40–46. Thomas James's comments are in *Three Years Among the Indians and Mexicans*, 146–47.

Page 112. Pattie's comments on the license are in *PN*, 46.

Pages 112–13. General description of Santa Fe is from Ralph Emerson Twitchell, *The Leading Facts of New Mexican History* (Albuquerque: Horn and Wallace, 1963), 2:146–59; James, 147–59; Pike, 184–85; and Josiah Gregg, *Commerce of the Prairies* (1844; reprint, New York: J. P. Lippincott Company, 1962), 1:73–74. The description of the celebration and the specific quote are in James, 154–56.

Pages 113–14. On the fandango, see Pike, 148, and Josiah Gregg, 1:128–29. Pattie's description of a fandango is in *PN*, 46. The fact that one dance was the *valse despacio* is based on similarities of Pattie's account with a description in Twitchell, *Leading Facts*, 2:161–62. Pattie calls the music "slow and charming," Twitchell, "slow and somewhat mournful." It's all a matter of interpretation.

Pages 114–15. Pattie's story of the rescue is in *PN*, 40–45.

Page 115. Specific citations are Twitchell, 2:26–31, and Bancroft, 315. "Another historian" is Lansing Bloom in "New Mexico Under Mexican Administration," *Old Santa Fe*, 1 (January 1914): 245.

Pages 115–16. The story of the governor's daughter in Chihuahua is in John Sibley, "Historical Sketches of the Several Indian Tribes in Louisiana South of the Arkansas River and Between the Mississippi and Rio Grande," *American State Papers, Class II, Indian Affairs*, (Washington, D.C.: Gales and Seaton, 1834), 1:724. One of the few sensible attempts to analyze the two stories is in Folsom, *Timothy Flint*, 116–18. Many of his points are well taken, but he, too, is hampered by the assumption that the events occurred in 1824. His final conclusion—that Flint heard a second-hand account of Pattie's rescue—is rendered impossible when the dates are corrected, for Flint's book was published before the event supposedly occurred.

Page 116. The story Pike heard makes up the major portion of "Inroad of the Nabajo," in *Prose Sketches*, 147–62. For an analysis of the historical validity, the identity of the storyteller, see the notes by the editor, David J. Weber. I have been more interested in the story as Pattie might have heard it than in the actual expedition.

Pages 116–18. The story of Pattie and Jacova in the coffeehouse is in *PN*, 45–46. The retelling of the story is clearly my own.

Page 118. Material on the Chavez ranch and biographical material on the family is in Twitchell, *Leading Facts*, 2:25.

•

Page 122. There is a good description of the Chavez ranch in A. Wislizenus, *Memoir of a Tour to Northern Mexico* (Glorieta, New
Mexico: Rio Grande Press, 1969), 35.

Page 122. The fact that Williams was one of these men is based on the
date he left Taos and the direction he traveled. There is other
convincing material to come—specifically, the fact that he originally planned to stay until June, but actually returned in late
February. As will be seen later, it fits well with Pattie's description of what happened to these seven men. For now, see Kate
Gregg, *Road to Santa Fe*, 114, 132.

Pages 122–23. Basic sources for Williams are Alpheus Favour, *Old Bill
Williams* (Norman: University of Oklahoma Press, 1962), and
Frederick E. Voelker, "William Sherley (Old Bill) Williams,"
MMFT 8:365–94. There are some surprising areas of major difference, particularly concerning the period when Williams was supposedly a preacher. Voelker ignores it, but I find Favour's
account, which includes the period as a preacher, to be more
convincing. The comment of Williams's mother is in Favour, 43.

Pages 123–24. Williams's claim as to his origin is in Matthew C. Field,
Prairie and Mountain Sketches, Kate L. Gregg and John Francis
McDermott, eds. (Norman: University of Oklahoma Press, 1957),
191. Descriptions of Williams are from Pike, *Prose Sketches*, 34–
35; and George Ruxton, *Life in the Far West*, Leroy Hafen, ed.
(Norman: University of Oklahoma Press, 1951), 113.

Page 124. Material on the road down the west bank of the Rio Grande, as
well as descriptions of wildlife, campgrounds, etc., are from
W. H. Emory, *Notes of a Military Reconnoissance* (Washington,
D.C.: Wendell and Benthuysen Printers, 1848), 48–51. See also
"Journal of Captain A. R. Johnston," in Emory, 567–614.

Pages 125–26. Information on horse trading in Socorro is mentioned by
both Emory and Johnston. The specific quote is from Johnston,
570. Both men also comment on Indian troubles, and the specific
story of the man afraid to fish is from Johnston, 569–70. The
story of the Indians spotted by the guide is in Emory, 52.

Page 126. Pattie's description of the route south of Socorro is in *PN*, 47–
48; Emory's, 52–59; and Johnston's, 572–78.

Page 126. Pattie's accuracy will be shown in the pages that follow. It is
worth noting here, however, that National Forest Rangers Bill
Rogers and Joe Janes, who are familiar with both the country and
the *PN*, have more respect for Pattie's accuracy than do many
historians. For a similar conclusion, see Elizabeth Fleming Mc-
Farland, *Forever Frontier* (Albuquerque: University of New Mexico Press, 1967), 33.

Pages 126–27. Pattie's description of the general route is in *PN*, 48–49.

•

My own conclusions are based on the USGS 1:250,000 Clifton and Silver City maps. I also have used the Gila National Forest map. It has no topographical lines, but I have notes on the wide and narrow points in the river based on material supplied by Joe Janes in the summer of 1974.

Pages 127–28. Pattie's story of his encounter with the lion is in *PN*, 49.

Pages 129–30. Pattie's description of the "desertion" and aftermath is in *PN*, 49–50. The quotation on Williams being "stoically deaf" is from Ruxton, *Life*, 114–15. Christmas festival is from Kate Gregg, *Road to Santa Fe*, 134–35. A "fine American horse," is in "Sketches from the Life of Peg Leg Smith," *Hutchings California Magazine* 5 (1860): 321.

Pages 130–31. Pattie's description of the San Francisco is in *PN*, 50–51. His claim that the country is unexplored is in *PN*, p. 46, and that he named it, p. 50. See, however, John L. Kessel, "Campaigning on the Upper Gila, 1756," *NMHR* 46 (1971): 137. Strangely, the Apache National Forest, through which the San Francisco flows, accepts Pattie's claim in a pamphlet entitled "A Proposal, Blue Range Wilderness," p. 3. For the relationship of the headwaters of the various rivers, see USGS 1:250,000 Clifton and Saint Johns maps.

Pages 131–32. Pattie's story of the return of the seven is in *PN*, 52. Material on Williams's activities is from Kate Gregg, *Road to Santa Fe*, as follows: return to Santa Fe, p. 152; his intention to return in June, p. 132; and his gambling in Taos, p. 155.

Pages 132ff. In tracing the party's descent of the Gila, I have again used the USGS 1:250,000 maps (Clifton, Silver City, Mesa, Tucson, and Phoenix). I have also closely checked it against Emory, *Notes*. Those using Emory should be aware that many river names have changed since his report. See Ross Calvin, *Lieutenant Emory Reports* (Albuquerque: University of New Mexico Press, 1951), for details and a map. Again, I traveled much of the route in 1974 and 1976.

Pages 132–33. Pattie's bear story is in *PN*, 52–53. Emory, p. 66, locates these caves—complete with bear sign—near what he called San Carlos Creek, but what is now Bonita Creek.

Page 133. Pattie quotation is in *PN*, 54.

Pages 133–34. The descent of the Gila is in *PN*, 54–55.

Pages 134–35. The place where they were forced away from the Gila is where Coolidge Dam now stands. A trip to the dam, a look at a topographic map, or a reading of Emory, 71–75, makes this clear. Based on this, I would suggest that their route from here was up Soda Canyon, over the mountains, and down El Capitan Canyon and Dripping Springs Wash.

Pages 135–37. Pattie's trip with Allen is in *PN*, 57. For attempts to identify him, see Camp, *Yount*, 50–51, 254–55, and Weber, *Taos Trappers*, 141n.

Page 137. Pattie, *PN*, 58, places the head of "Beaver River" in the south-

•

west, while the San Pedro heads in the southeast. Apparently, it is a misprint, for from the distances involved, and the description of the country, it could only be the San Pedro.

Page 137. If the party went as far west as the Sacaton Mountains, or even well short of it, Pattie failed to mention one of the most spectacular sights along the Gila—the Casa Grande ruin. The WPA guidebook *Arizona* (New York, 1940, 1966), 403, gives him credit for seeing it, but a careful check of the *PN* (p. 101) shows his only mention is of the town of Casas Grandes in Mexico. Indian country and the territorial limits are based on Grenville Goodwin, *The Social Organization of the Western Apaches* (Tucson: University of Arizona Press, 1969), 65.

Pages 138–39. Pattie's account of the battle is in *PN*, 58–61.

Pages 140–42. Pattie's account of the trip from the San Pedro back to the copper mines is in *PN*, 61–65. My choice of route—the San Pedro, across Aravaipai Valley, over the Grahams, to the Gila—is based on Pattie's description, a study of the appropriate maps, and on traveling the area. There are, again, some points that do not entirely fit, but they can be explained by either confusion or overdramatization on Pattie's part.

CHAPTER SEVEN
pp. 143–154

Pages 144–46. Pattie's account of the reception at the mines is in *PN*, 65–66; the trip up the Rio Grande and the return are found on pp. 66–67.

Page 146. The promissory note itself has disappeared. In 1828, however, it fell into the hands of Isaac McGirk, who in trying to collect wrote his lawyer, Abiel Leonard, and in the course of the letter quoted both the original note and Pattie's endorsement on the back. See Isaac C. McGirk to Abiel Leonard, St. Louis, Missouri, November 29, 1828, Leonard Collection, State Historical Society of Missouri, Columbia, Missouri.

Page 147. Pattie quote is in *PN*, 67.

Pages 147–49. Pattie's account of the activities around Santa Rita is from *PN*, 66. I have filled it out with other accounts, although the historiography of Santa Rita is almost as dark a labyrinth as the early mine itself. Beyond the general accounts, there is material in Fayette A. Jones, *New Mexico Mines and Minerals* (Santa Fe: The New Mexico Printing Company, 1904), 27–32; A. C. Spencer and Sidney Paige, *Geology of the Santa Rita Mining Area of New Mexico* (Washington, D.C.: U.S. Department of the Interior, 1935); John Schilling, *Silver City-Santa Rita-Hurley, New Mexico* (Socorro, New Mexico: State Bureau of Mines and Mineral Resources, 1959); and H. A. Thorne, *Mining Practices at the Chino Mines* (Washington, D.C.: Department of Commerce, 1931). There are also two articles devoted to the mines: John M.

•

Sully, "The Santa Rita Copper Mine," *Old Santa Fe* 3 (January 1916): 133–49; and T. A. Rickard, "The Chino Enterprise," *Engineering and Mining Journal Press* 116 (1923): 753–58, 803–10, 981–85, 1113–21. I have relied most heavily on Sully and Rickard, particularly for mining techniques, for both were experienced mining men, and Sully made an extensive report on the mine and was there when many of the early artifacts were found. Contemporary descriptions of the mine are based on the above sources, but particularly on the accounts of Emory, 58–59, and John R. Bartlett, *Personal Narrative* (1854; reprint, Chicago: Rio Grande Press, 1965), 1:231–36.

Pages 150–52. Pattie's account of the Apache is in *PN*, 68–72. The description of the Apache on p. ooo is from Emory, 61, while the mention of Mangas Coloradas is from Johnston, in Emory, 578–79. For general material on the Mimbres Apache's early life and their leaders, see Dan L. Thrapp, *Victorio and the Mimbres Apaches* (Norman: University of Oklahoma Press, 1974), 3–25.

Page 152. Bartlett's comments are in his *PN*, 1:230. The other member was T. H. Webb, who is quoted in Bartlett, 1:179.

Pages 152–53. Pattie's general description of the days after the peace was made is in *PN*, 72–73. The use of the term "farce" is on p. 72, as is the quote concerning the priest. The story of Mocho Mano and the priest is on p. 73.

Page 154. The trip to the salt mines is in *PN*, 73–74. For details on the salt lake near Zuñi, including the fact that it was used by the Apache as a supply of salt, see Matilda Coxe Stevenson, *The Zuñi Indians* (Washington, D.C.: U.S. Government Printing Office, 1904) 354–61. There is a picture of the lake facing p. 356. As usual, there are minor inconsistencies in Pattie's account, but again the general description fits well enough.

CHAPTER EIGHT
pp. 155–171

Pages 157–58. The best attempt to straighten out the various parties passing through Santa Rita in the fall of 1826 is Weber, *Taos Trappers*, 118–20, which also contains the basic sources. See also Joseph Hill's two articles, "New Light on Pattie and the Southwest Fur Trade," *SWHQ* 26 (April 1923): 243–54, and "Ewing Young and the Fur Trade of the Far Southwest, 1822–24," *OHSQ* 24 (March 1923): 1–35; and Thomas Maitland Marshall, "St. Vrain's Expedition to the Gila in 1826," *SWHQ* 19 (January 1916): 251–60. Marshall's article contains the full text of Baird's letter.

Pages 158–59. Pattie's story of the offer by Onis, his argument with his father, and the specific quote, are all in *PN*, 74.

Page 159. Pattie does not specifically name the Frenchman as Robidoux. For that identification, see Hill, *SWHQ* 26 (April 1923): 244–45.

•

Material on Robidoux's background is from Merril J. Mattes, "Joseph Robidoux," *MMFT* 8:287–314.

Pages 159ff. For reasons that will become clear in the text, I have followed Pattie's account in *PN*, 74–82, without editorial comment, at least for the moment. One point needs a brief mention. There is considerable confusion on the tribe of Indians that attacked the Frenchmen. Pattie (*PN*, 76) called them Papawars, obviously meaning Papago. Stephen C. Foster, who obtained his story from Nat Pryor, said they were Maricopa; see *HSSCP* (1887), 30. George Yount, who was on the scene soon afterward, said it was a combined band of Pima and Maricopa. See Camp, *Yount*, 31–33. To complicate the issue further, a later anthropologist identifies them as either Western Apache or Southeastern Yavapai. See Clifton Kroeber, ed., "The Route of James O. Pattie on the Colorado in 1826. A Reappraisal by A. L. Kroeber," *Arizona and the West* 6 (Summer 1964): 124.

Page 165. "Now they were all dead" is based on Pattie's assumption that only he and two others survived. Foster, however, in *HSSCP* (1887), 30, indicates there were other survivors. He said, "They struck south into the desert, and after great suffering reached Tucson."

Page 167. Yount's version of the massacre is in Camp, *Yount*, 31–32.

Page 168. For Ewing Young's background, see Harvey L. Carter, "Ewing Young," *MMFT* 2:379–401. Pattie's comment on Young is in *PN*, 82.

Pages 168–70. Smith's story is well told in "Sketches from the Life of Peg Leg Smith," *Hutchings California Magazine* 5 (1860–61): 147–55, 198–206, 318–21, 334–36, 420–21. The specifics of the hunt are on pp. 320–21 and 334.

CHAPTER NINE
pp. 173–189

Page 174. Pattie (*PN*, 83) describes a trapping trip up the Black River. If my theory that he was with Young all the time is correct, this trip would have taken place before, not after, the time they reached the scene of the massacre. See Camp, *Yount*, 33.

Pages 174–78. Pattie's account of the trip along the Colorado River is in *PN*, 83–88. Yount's version of the same trip is in Camp, 33–36. I have checked both men's description of geography and Indian customs against Kroeber, *Arizona and the West* 6:119–36; Jack Forbes, *Warriors of the Colorado* (Norman: University of Oklahoma Press, 1965); and Leslie Spier, *Yuman Tribes of the Gila River* (Chicago: University of Chicago Press, 1933). I have, as usual, used the USGS 1:250,000 maps, in this case El Centro, Salton Sea, Needles, and Kingman.

Page 175. The relations of the Halchadhom with the Cocomaricopa are described in Kroeber, *Arizona and the West* 6:125–26. For Jede-

•

diah Smith's experiences among the Mohave, see Dale Morgan, *Jedediah Smith*, 199–200.

Page 176. Pattie's story and the specific quote are in *PN*, 86; Smith's story and his specific quote are in *Hutchings* 5:320.

Pages 176–77. Yount's story is in Camp, 35; Pattie's adaptation of it is in *PN*, 87.

Page 177. There is considerable material to verify a quarrel among the trappers. Yount mentions it in Camp, 38, and Tom Smith in *Hutchings* 5:334. Jedediah Smith heard of it from the Mohave; see Morgan, *Jedediah Smith*, 238–39. Even Pattie vaguely mentioned it, in *PN*, 88.

Pages 178–79. Pattie's highly confused account of the trip home appears in *PN*, 88–93. My reasons for placing him with Young and Yount, and for refusing to accept the story of the trip to the Yellowstone, appear in the text. Once those points are accepted, then certain things become obvious. Yount, in Camp, 36, indicates they made the decision to go home in the Mohave Valley, and therefore there was no point in continuing on up the Colorado. A years later (Camp, 54) Yount mentions leaving the Mohave villages directly for Taos. Probably they did the same in 1826. Yount, too, in Camp, 38, specifically mentions reaching the Zuñi villages. Even in the confusion of Pattie, *PN*, 89–90, there is at least vague substantiation of this if a rather simple correction is made. Pattie refers several times to the "Red River," and the automatic assumption is that he means the Colorado River. Yet, in the narrative, pp. 51 and 83, he twice refers to the upper waters of the "Red River" when he is clearly talking about not the Colorado, but the Little Colorado. If it is assumed that in this part he means the Little Colorado, and if much of the confusion leading up to the Yellowstone trip is ignored, then his account can be read in such a way that it agrees with Yount. A possible route would be south of the Grand Canyon to a point near Desert View, down into the canyon by way of what is now Tanner Trail, out of the canyon by way of the Little Colorado, then on to Zuñi. A careful analysis of Yount's description of the 1827 trip, and the place where Burr's furs were found, and a comparison with Pattie's story of the trappers who were killed on a stream leading into the Colorado lend considerable weight to this theory. See Camp, 54–55, and *PN*, 88.

Page 179. Reception at the Zuñi villages is in Camp, 38.

Page 180. The two best accounts of the return to Taos are in David Weber, *Taos Trappers*, 129–30, and Cleland, *Reckless Breed*, 219–20. Cleland includes a translation of a document from the New Mexican Archives that describes the attack on Cabeza de Vaca's home.

Page 180. Yount's quote is in Camp, 38; Pattie's is in *PN*, 93. This, too, thoroughly substantiates the claim that Pattie returned with Young and Yount.

•

Pages 181–82. The story of the trip is in *PN*, 93–102. The inconsistent and suspicious part, however, is all on p. 93. What I am suggesting is that a proper reading of the narrative would skip from the arrival in Santa Fe on p. 93 directly to the beginning of the Pecos trip on p. 105.

Page 182. The dates of Pattie's return to New Mexico: Ewing Young is listed in Weber, *Extranjeros*, 26–28, on a New Mexican treasury report as paying duty in January 1827, although he need not have been present at the time. Still, two other men identified as part of this expedition, Antoine Leroux and Maurice LeDuc, are clearly listed among a group of trappers who left for the Ute country in March 1827. Obviously, they had come back some time previously. See Janet LeCompte, "Maurice LeDuc," *MMFT* 6:230, and Forbes Parkhill, *The Blazed Trail of Antoine Leroux* (Los Angeles: Western Lore Press, 1965), 57. The list of trappers is in Weber, *Extranjeros*, 38. The documents concerning the confiscation of the furs are dated May and June 1827, but this refers to the discovery of them, and Young may well have hidden them weeks or even months before. See Weber, *Taos Trappers*, 129–30, and Cleland, *Reckless Breed*, 219–20.

Page 183. Thwaites's comment on this is in *EWT* 18:159; Quaife's is in his edition of the *PN* (Chicago: R. R. Donnelly and Sons, 1930), 181.

Pages 183ff. Pattie's account of the trip to the Pecos is in *PN*, 105–12. The specific quote is on p. 105.

Page 183. General material on Pecos can be found in A. V. Kidder, *An Introduction to the Study of Southwestern Archaeology* (rev. ed., New Haven: Yale University Press, 1962), 61–87. The specific description is from Josiah Gregg, *Commerce of the Prairies* 1:145.

Page 184. Pattie's pine trees and aspen again demonstrate that he is on the river above Pecos Pueblo. I have compared Pattie's account with Herbert E. Unganade, *Guide to the New Mexico Mountains* (Denver: Sage Books, 1965), and find that it holds up rather well.

Page 185. For material on the Mescalero Apache, see C. L. Sonnischen, *The Mescalero Apaches* (Norman: University of Oklahoma Press, 1958), particularly pp. 14–15. It goes a long way toward verifying Pattie. It is also worth noting that John Upton Terrell, in *Apache Chronicle* (New York: World Publishing, 1972), 158, after quoting Pattie's description of Apache, says of the *PN*, "There are good reasons for believing a large part of it."

Pages 186–88. The description of the Navaho raiders is based on Ruth Underhill, *The Navajos* (Norman: University of Oklahoma Press 1956), 76–78. Other material on Enemy Way and on the Navaho and their attitude toward death and ghosts has been drawn mainly from Clyde Kluckhohn and Dorothy Leighton, *The Navaho*, 184–87, 222.

Page 188. The settlement they reached was called Perdido, which Pattie correctly translates as meaning "lost." It is an appropriate name,

•

for it is impossible to find. A search through the list of New Mexican settlements of 1827, prepared by Governor Antonio Narbona and included in Carrol and Haggard, *Three New Mexico Chronicles,* produces nothing that even vaguely resembles Perdido. A few paragraphs later Pattie refers to Santa Fe as "San Tepec," although he clearly knew the name of the capital. There seems to have been some problem in transcription in this point in the narrative.

Page 188. Pattie's claim (*PN*, 111) that only 16 of 116 had survived is surely an exaggeration. Possibly only 16 were still in New Mexico. Pattie also mentions, at this point, the death of S. S. Pratte. That, clearly, is a later addition, for Pratte did not die until October 1827, by which time Pattie was on his way to California.

Page 189. The quote is from *PN*, 112.

CHAPTER TEN
pp. 191–205

Pages 192–93. Sylvester's life at the mines is from several comments in *PN*, 113–18.

Pages 193–94. Biographical material on Kirker is from McGaw, *Savage Scene;* that on Pryor from Kate Gregg, *Road to Santa Fe,* and Raymond W. Settle, "Nathaniel Miguel Pryor," *MMFT* 2:285–88. For the Pryors in Missouri, see *Goodspeed's History of Franklin et al.,* 619–22. Those who place Kirker and Pryor at the mines are J. J. Warner, "Reminiscences of Early California from 1831 to 1846," *HSSCP* 7 (1907–08): 183, and Foster, *HSSCP* (1887), 30. Warner mentions only Kirker and Pryor, while Foster mentions Pryor, Kirker, the two "Patys," and Richard Laughlin. Laughlin, who would soon accompany the Patties to California, was in his early twenties, and I suspect worked there but was not a partner.

Page 194. Pattie's return to Santa Rita is in *PN*, 112–13. The description of the country along the Mimbres is mainly from Bartlett, *Personal Narrative* 1:221–23. Bartlett spent some time camped on the river.

Page 195. The mention of thirty thousand dollars is in *PN*, 119. Other comments on the general subject are in Hardy, *Travels,* 412, 462–63; Emory, *Notes,* 58–59; and Wislizenus, *A Tour,* 57–58.

Pages 195–96. His attitude toward the superintendent and clerk is in *PN*, 113.

Page 196. The trip to El Paso and the specific quotation are also on p. 113. The individual whom Pattie talked to may well have been John Hawkins, a relative of the famous gunmakers in St. Louis. There is a biographical article by Janet LeCompte in *MMFT* 4:137–45, but it says nothing about his whereabouts before 1828. Still, he was a gunsmith, and the article does establish he was associated with Paul Anderson, who was in El Paso shortly before Pattie arrived. See *MMFT* 3:37.

•

Pages 196–97. Pattie's version of the lost money and the lost opportunity is in *PN*, 118–20.

Pages 197–98. Pryor's version of losing the mines is in Foster, *HSSCP* (1887), 30. Material on McKnight is in Rex Strickland's "Robert McKnight," *MMFT* 9:259–68, and "James Baird," *MMFT* 3:27–37. For additional material on Courcier, see McGaw, *Savage Scene*, 79–81; Wislizenus, *A Tour*, 57–58, 62–63; and *Diccionario Porrua de Historia, Biografía y Geografía de México* (Mexico, D. F.: Editorial Porrua S.A., 1964), 541.

Page 198. Pattie's specific comments are in *PN*, 119.

Pages 198–99. Pattie and Glenn's permit, dated August 19, 1827, is in Museum of New Mexico, New Mexican Archives (photocopy, Bancroft Library). My interpretation of Pattie's movements at this time does not agree with his dates, which are thoroughly confused. I had no choice but to go with the original document.

Page 199. Sylvester Pattie's permit is also in the New Mexican Archives. There is a translation, by James Pattie, in *PN*, 121. It is relatively accurate, although he has combined the wording of his own permit with that of his father. He also gives the date as September 22, 1829, clearly a misprint for 1827. Beyond that, the rest agrees entirely with the original permit, and thus Pattie, at least temporarily, is again accurate in his dates.

Page 199. For Isaac Slover, see Andrew Rolle, "Isaac Slover," *MMFT* 1:367–71, and Harry S. Stevens, "A Company of Hands and Traders: Origins of the Glenn-Fowler Expedition of 1821–22," *NMHR* 46 (1971): 181–221.

Pages 200ff. Pattie's account of the trip down the Gila is in *PN*, 121–25. This expedition, however, is covered by several sources other than the *PN*. See Foster, *HSSCP* (1887), 30–33; Warner, *HSSCP* 7:183–84; *Alta California*, July 2, 1865, the most important part of which is quoted in Cleland, *Reckless Breed*, 194–95; Camp, *Yount*, 43–46; and the testimony of Manual Hurtado and José Garcia in New Mexican Archives (photocopy, Bancroft Library). For a translation, see Weber, *Taos Trappers*, 138.

Pages 201–2. Pattie's analysis of the problems of a trapping expedition is in *PN*, 122–23.

Page 203. The agreement and the comment on shooting deserters is in *PN*, 122.

Pages 203–4. Pattie's version of the division of the party is in *PN*, 124–25. All the sources cited above also give a version, and although there is disagreement on many specifics, all but Warner agree that the split occurred on the Gila before they reached the Colorado. The specific claim that a majority of trappers lost faith in Sylvester Pattie is in *Alta California*, July 2, 1865. See Cleland, *Reckless Breed*, 194–95.

Page 204. For the names of those who went to California, see *St. Louis Times*, July 7, 1829. Yount's comment on the division is in Camp, 45.

•

353

The trip that follows is covered not only by Pattie, but also by Nathaniel
Pryor, whose version is in *HSSCP* (1887), 30–35. The tendency
has been to accept Pryor as automatically accurate and Pattie as
automatically inaccurate, particularly because of Pryor's comment on the *PN*, "most of which is false, and has the same relation to the true narrative that Robinson Crusoe had to the journal
of Andrew Selkirk." Yet, except for a story Pattie tells of the
Yuma Indians and the attitude toward Californians, the two versions agree quite closely. Also, Alfred Ferdinand Morris, in his
"Journal of a Crazy Man," *CHSQ* 15 (1936): 103–35, provides
still a third version that he obtained from Jesse Ferguson. It is
both more specific and closer in time to the events than Pryor,
and in many cases it agrees more closely with Pattie than with
Pryor.

Page 208. Pattie (*PN*, 126–27) tells a story of how the Yuma ran off their
horses and how a battle followed it. I have ignored it, for no other
source mentions it. Also, Pattie is clearly using it as an interven-
tion of fate that forces them to go to California. All other versions
indicate that decision was made before the parties split. Besides,
according to Pryor, they had already traded their horses to Yount.

Page 209. Pattie's version of the trip down the Colorado is in *PN*, 128–31.
Pryor's account is more general, but the description of their life
is almost identical.

Pages 209–10. The description of the Cocopa is in *PN*, 132–35. Pattie is
reasonably accurate and locates them correctly, but he claims the
feast was made up of dog meat. Spier, in *Yuman Tribes*, 73, says
they did not eat dog meat. They did, however, eat jackrabbit, and
Pattie may well have mistaken one for the other. Besides, a dog
meat story was a virtual necessity for any traveler writing of his
visit to the Indians.

Page 210. Pattie's story (*PN*, 136) that it felt as if he was on a high ridge
may sound like another tall story. Godfrey Sykes, however, in
The Colorado Delta (n.p.: American Geographical Society of
New York, 1937), 15, says "A sense of being upon an elevation,
is very noticeable in the Colorado delta as one emerges from the
densely wooded region . . . into the comparatively open country."
Sykes, in this careful study of the region, not only accepts Pattie's
description but also shows considerable respect for the Lower
Colorado portions of the narrative.

Pages 211–12. The story of being flooded out is told by Pattie in *PN*,
137–38, and Pryor, *HSSCP* (1887), 31, with only minor differences. For a modern view of the effect of tides on the mouth of
the Colorado, see Sykes, *Colorado Delta*, 49–50.

Page 212. Pattie and Pryor agree on the essentials of the retreat upriver,

•

including the burying of the furs and even what they carried in their packs. The only real difference is that Pryor indicates they buried the furs near the mouth of the river, while Pattie has them retreat well upriver. Eight years later, Morris (*CHSQ* 15:109) was shown the site by Ferguson. His location bears out Pattie.

Pages 213–15. The description of the Indian village and the specific quotations are in *PN*, 141–44. My reasons for suggesting Pattie may be the man who stripped are in the Prologue, p. 19.

Pages 215ff. Pattie's account of the trip from the Indian village to Santa Catalina is in *PN*, 144–51. Pryor, *HSSCP* (1887), 31, said, "They did not find water until the third day, and suffered terribly from thirst." Again, there is no essential disagreement, for Pattie only vividly demonstrates what Pryor mentions in passing.

Pages 216–19. The route from the salt plain to Santa Catalina was probably that which leads through Agua Caliente and El Portazuela. In tracing it I have used the material, maps, and photographs in Sykes, *Colorado Delta*, and Peveril Meigs, *The Dominican Mission Frontier of Lower California* (Berkeley: University of California Press, 1935).

Page 219. Pattie's account of the arrival at Santa Catalina as well as the various quotations are all in *PN*, 151–52. Meigs, 119–25, accepts Pattie's statement that the herds had all been run off by Indians and provides additional information on the raids that eventually caused abandonment.

Pages 219–21. Pattie (*PN*, 152–55) describes his life at San Vicente, which he erroneously calls "San Sebastian." At the same time Pryor takes the party directly from Santa Catalina to Ensenada, then to San Diego. Pattie, however, gives too accurate a description of the mission and the route to ignore. Both Meigs and Alexander S. Taylor, "Historical Summary of Lower California," in J. Ross Browne, *Resources of the Pacific Slope* (San Francisco: H. H. Bancroft and Company, 1869), accept Pattie's claim to have been at San Vicente. His description of the ocean (*PN*, 155) also goes far toward verifying the claim. See particularly plate seven in Meigs.

Page 221. For the governor's order, which is dated Santa Barbara, March 22, 1828, see Dept. Rec. 6: 194, Bancroft Library, or the translation in Bancroft, *HC* 3:163.

CHAPTER TWELVE
pp. 223–238

Page 224. The arrival in San Diego is a combination of Pattie and Pryor, who complement each other. Pattie mentions the *Franklin* in port, Pryor the sailors standing in the crowd. The major point of disagreement concerns the disarming of the eight men. Pattie says it happened before they reached town, Pryor that they were still carrying their rifles when they marched into San Diego and

•

were disarmed later. I have accepted Pattie's version because of the governor's order. Pattie had no way of knowing of it, but the conversation with a corporal that Pattie reports (*PN*, 157) reflects that order exactly. Also, I doubt that a man ordered to disarm the trappers would have allowed them to march through San Diego in full sight of the governor carrying their rifles on their shoulders.

Page 224. Description of San Diego is from Charles F. Carter, trans., "Duhaut-Cilly's Account of California in the Years 1827–28," *CHSQ* 8 (September 1929): 218. Duhaut-Cilly was in San Diego at the same time as Pattie but does not mention him.

Pages 225–26. Echeandia's character is drawn mainly from Bancroft, *HC* 3:9–11, 244–45. Bancroft also reported the rumor of the young lady, but for evidence that it was common gossip at the time Pattie was there, see Duhaut-Cilly, *CHSQ* 8:219.

Pages 226–28. Material on Jedediah Smith and Governor Echeandia is well covered by Morgan, *Jedediah Smith*. The first meeting is on pp. 204–6; the second, pp. 246–55.

Pages 228–30. Pattie's account of the interview is in *PN*, 158–60, and all the quotations are included therein. Pattie said the meeting took place on March 25, but he is apparently wrong. Letters in Dept. Rec., 6: 197–98, Bancroft Library, show that Echeandia was in Santa Barbara as late as March 30, and in San Diego by April 10.

Pages 230–31. Pattie's version of the postconference events and also his fear for his father are in *PN*, 160. Pryor's account of Sylvester's illness is in *HSSCP* (1887), 32.

Pages 231–33. Pattie's description of his mental attitude is in *PN*, 160–62.

Pages 233–34. Pattie never identifies the sergeant by name. Later, however (*PN*, 189), he calls his sister "Miss Peak," and this, plus the fact that José Pico was the only sergeant in San Diego at the time (*HC* 2:543), makes the identification clear enough. For material on various members of the Pico family, see *HC* 4:776–79, and Arthur P. Botello, trans., *Don Pio Pico's Historical Narrative* (Glendale: Arthur H. Clark Company, 1973). However memorable these events were to Pattie, they made little impression on Pio Pico, who was in San Diego at the time, for he passes over them in silence.

Page 234. That the ship *Franklin* was in port, and that Bradshaw and Perkins interested themselves in Pattie's case, is established by several contemporary records. See particularly the *St. Louis Times*, July 7, 1829. It is quoted in Ann Hafen, "James Ohio Pattie," *MMFT* 4:246–47. Pattie will have later dealings with Bradshaw and Perkins and more sources will be developed at that time.

Page 235. Pryor's comments are in *HSSCP* (1887), 32. A third version, as told by Jesse Ferguson, is in Morris, *CHSQ* 15:109, 133. I have consulted but not used it, for in bitterness it outdoes Pattie and some of the claims are demonstrably false.

Page 235. The story of Sylvester's writing the letter is in *PN*, 165; "miserable republican despot," p. 163; and "fickle and infirm," p. 171.

Pages 235–36. Pryor's story is in *HSSCP* (1887), 32–33. There is no clear record to either confirm or deny Sylvester's deathbed conversion. I have indicated my reasons for accepting the story in the text. See particularly the conversation with "Miss Peak," *PN*, 167.

Page 237. Pattie gives the date of his father's death as April 24, the *St. Louis Times* on July 9, 1829, gives it as May 24. Since that story is based on a letter written immediately after the death, and since Pattie shows signs of being confused in his dates again, I consider the May date the most logical.

Page 238. Pryor's account is in *HSSCP* (1887), 33; Pattie's, *PN*, 168–69.

Page 238. Pattie's description of the immediate change is in *PN*, 169.

CHAPTER THIRTEEN
pp. 239–253

Page 240. Pattie (*PN*, 169) mentions the three ship captains, but not their ships. He is accurate, for all three captains can be placed in San Diego Bay at the time. For each man's ship, see *HC* 3:145–46. The *Clio* and *Andes* are placed in San Diego by Duhaut-Cilly's account, *CHSQ* 8:331. The *Courier* is placed there by "The Log of the Courier," MS in Peabody Library, microfilm copy in Bancroft Library.

Pages 240–41. Pattie's claim that he served as an interpreter for Echeandia would seem to be another example of his overdeveloped self-importance if it were not for the existence of a document (Dept. Rec., 6: 73, Bancroft Library) that says, "Dice el Americano James Ohio Pettis, que sirvio de interprete." See also *HC* 3:134.

Pages 241ff. Pattie begins his version of the *Franklin* affair on *PN*, p. 173, and continues, with a few interruptions, to p. 184. The question —which also plagued Bancroft—is how seriously to take this. In answering it, the following points are worth considering: (1) The document cited above clearly verifies Pattie's service as interpreter. Once that is accepted, it puts him in a position to know the things he claims to know. (2) The dates, with only minor discrepancies, can be easily established by Duhaut-Cilly, *CHSQ* 8:331–34; *HC* 3:132–34; and the material in Dept. Rec., 6:28, 32, 56, 59, 63–68, 72–73, 200, Bancroft Library. (3) Pattie stretches the events out and makes them culminate in September. If, however, his specific dates are changed from September to July, then his daily dates fit easily into the pattern of events. (4) Pattie, as usual, enhances his own importance. If all this is taken into account, then Pattie's eyewitness account of the affair agrees reasonably well with the other evidence.

•

Pages 242–44. Pattie's description of his relations with the governor during this period is in *PN*, 170–75.

Page 245. Pattie on board the ship is in *PN*, 175.

Pages 245–46. The arrangements for retrieving the furs are in *PN*, 176–77.

Page 246. Pattie offers no description of the route to San Luis Rey. Instead, it comes from Duhaut-Cilly, *CHSQ* 8:225–26, and Alfred Robinson, *Life in California* (Santa Barbara: Peregrine Publishers, 1970), 15–17. Both men visited the mission about the same time as Pattie. See also *HC* 2:554.

Pages 247–48. Pattie's account of his talk with Peyri is in *PN*, 177–79. He does not mention Peyri by name, but his description fits Peyri and no one else. For biographical material on Peyri, see Maynard Geiger, *Franciscan Missionaries in Hispanic California* (San Marino: The Huntington Library, 1969), 192–96, and *HC* 3:621–22. One clear indication that the decision was made in July rather than September is the article in the *St. Louis Times*, July 7, 1829. It is based on information obtained by Bradshaw and Perkins. Since they left in July and did not return, the information can be no later than that. In the letter they clearly state that Echeandia has already given the trappers permission to return to the river.

Page 249. Promissory note is James O. Pattie to Jesse Ferguson, MS, n.d., n.p., Bancroft Library.

Page 249. Pattie mentions writing the letter to "Mr. Jones," the "consul at Wahu" in *PN*, 181. The *St. Louis Times* story clearly establishes that such material was received. The fact that Congressman Coleman was notified will be documented in a later chapter.

Pages 249–51. Pattie's account of the final days of the *Franklin* affair is in *PN*, 183–84. It fits well enough into the basic accounts given by Duhaut-Cilly and the various records. Specifically, for the *Franklin*'s running out of port, see Dept. Rec., 6: 32, 72–73; and Duhaut-Cilly, *CHSQ* 8:334. The closeness of Pattie's description of the damage to Duhaut-Cilly's revised estimate is noted in the text. The accuracy of Pattie's account establishes not only that he could be a good observer when he wanted, but also contradicts his claim that he was locked in prison. Certainly, he needed to be where he could see in order to assess the damage so accurately.

Pages 251–52. Pattie's testimony is in Echeandia to Subtiente Zamorano, July 23, 1828, Dept. Rec., 6: 72–73, Bancroft Library. Pattie's portion of the testimony is in *HC* 3:134.

Page 252. Pattie's story of his treatment in San Diego is in *PN*, 184.

Page 253. The story that the furs were rotten and unsalvageable is corroborated by Pryor in *HSSCP* (1887), 33, and by Ferguson in *CHSQ* 15:109.

Page 257. Passports for the five men who went for the furs are in Dept. Rec., 6: 13, Bancroft Library.

Pages 257–58. Pattie's version of the Lang affair is in *PN*, 190–92; Bancroft's is in *HC* 2:139. The latter is very sketchy and without dates and I have filled out the account with material from Dept. St. Papers, Ben. Mil., liii, 90–92, and lxix, 10–13, Bancroft Library.

Pages 258ff. Pattie's story of smallpox begins on *PN*, p. 185 and continues, with some interruptions, to p. 200. The best and most careful analysis of the story is Sherburne F. Cook, "Smallpox in Spanish and Mexican California, 1770–1845," *Bulletin of the History of Medicine* 7 (February 1939): 153–91. See also Rosemary K. Valle, "Pattie and the 1827–28 Alta California Measles Epidemic," *CHSQ* 52 (Spring 1973): 28–36.

Pages 259–60. Rosemary Valle, in the article cited above, argues that Pattie's whole story was manufactured from this epidemic. Because of the time factor, and because of the presence of smallpox, as noted in the text, I do not find this argument convincing.

Page 260. Smallpox at Santa Clara and San Jose is noted by Cook, 178; the arrival of the *Baikal* with vaccine is in *HC* 3:146, 168. Echeandia's letters to Peyri and Sanchez are in Dept. Rec., 7: 58 and 60.

Page 260. For the three foreigners, see *HC* 2:725 (Borris); 2:757 (Chapman); and 5:694 (Richardson). Richardson's medical qualifications are mentioned in Dept. St. Papers, Ben. Mil., lxvi, 2.

Page 261. Pattie's request for a travel pass, dated February 17, 1829, is in Dept. Rec., 7: 86, and the *carta de seguridad*, dated February 28, 1829, is in 7: 89. There is a translation of the latter document in *HC* 3:168.

Page 261. Pryor's mention of the route to Los Angeles is in *HSSCP* (1887), 32–33. Based on various records his dates seem to be as unreliable as Pattie's, and thus his separation of this into two trips need not be taken too seriously.

Pages 261ff. Pattie's account of the trip to Los Angeles and intervening descriptions is in *PN*, 194–96.

Pages 262–63. For information on Barona and Zalvidea, see Geiger, *Missionaries*, 26–28, 266–69.

Pages 263–64. Pattie's description of Los Angeles and the tar pits is in *PN*, 196. For Rocha, see *HC* 5:699. See also Marion Parks, "In Pursuit of Vanished Days," *HSSCP* (1928), 181–82, and "A Brief History of Rancho La Brea," *HSSCP* (1914), 254.

Page 264. For the later careers of the three Americans, see Bancroft, *HC* 3:736 (Ferguson); 4:708–9 (Laughlin); and 4:785 (Pryor).

Pages 264–65. Pattie's story of the two missionaries is in *PN*, 196. Other material on Altamira and Ripoll is in Geiger, *Missionaries*, 6–10,

·

207–8; and *HC* 3:93–95. Duhaut-Cilly's version is in *CHSQ* 8:328.

Page 266. A list of foreigners in San Diego at this time is in *HC* 2:545. Additional material on each man can be found in the alphabetical "Pioneer Register" at the end of volumes 2 through 5 of *HC*. There is further material on Fitch in *HC* 3:140–42.

Page 266. San Gabriel and Los Angeles foreigners are listed in *HC* 2:558, and those in Santa Barbara in 2:573. Alfred Robinson's experience is from his journal, in Adele Ogden, "Alfred Robinson, New England Merchant in Mexican California," *CHSQ* 23 (September 1944): 193–218.

Page 267. Pattie's description of Santa Barbara is in *PN*, 196–97.

Pages 267–68. The vague summary of the trip north is in *PN*, 197. In it La Purísima Concepción is ignored, Santa Cruz and "St. John Bapistrano" (actually, San Juan Bautista) are moved too far south, and San Antonio de Padua too far north. Pattie's description of going to sea, misplaced as I suggest, is in *PN*, 202.

Page 268. The *Baikal* was in San Diego December 10–17, 1828, and again on February 12, 1829. See Adele Ogden, *The California Sea Otter Trade* (Berkeley: University of California Press, 1941), 174.

Pages 269–70. Pattie's trip with the "Coriac" Indians and his account of Fort Ross is in *PN*, 198–200. For another view, as well as a drawing of the Russian settlement at the time, see Duhaut-Cilly, *CHSQ* 8:323–27. Duhaut-Cilly was there in June 1828, Pattie about a year later. There is also a summary of material and sources for Fort Ross during this period in *HC* 2:628–52.

Pages 270–72. Pattie's description of these events and the document itself are in *PN*, 200–202. For Estenega and Cabot, and their locations in 1829, see Geiger, *Missionaries*, 32–34, 78–81. The three documents referred to are: the permit at Santa Fe, New Mexican Archives (photocopy, Bancroft Library); *carta de seguridad*, Dept. Rec. 7: 89; and the passport, Dept. Rec., 4: 9.

Page 272. For Slover and Pope's later careers, see Andrew Rolle's biographical articles in *MMFT* 2:275–76 (Pope), and 1:367–71 (Slover).

Pages 272–74. Pattie divides his description of Monterey into two separate parts, *PN*, 197 and 202ff. The first, however, is so brief and general it can be easily tied to the rest. Additional material has been drawn from Robinson, *Life in California*, 8–9.

Page 274. Background on Solis and Gomez is in *HC* 3:16.

Pages 274ff. Pattie's account of the revolution is in *PN*, 202–10. Bancroft's version, backed by documents, is in *HC* 2:69–86. Pattie's dates are wrong again, but beyond that, his general account fits well into other versions except for certain key points that are noted in the text. Bancroft, *HC* 3:82–83, assesses Pattie's account and calls it "absurdly inaccurate." He is, however, specifically discussing the story of the capture of Solis and, as noted, that is indeed "absurdly inaccurate."

Page 276. The Scots doctor quoted is Dr. Stephen Anderson, and the state-

•

ment may be found in his letter to John Rogers Cooper, Vallejo Documents, Bancroft Library, 30: 7. See also *HC* 3:81.

Page 278. Pattie's conversation with Jones and his preparations for making a claim are in *PN*, 210–11; the letter to his companions is mentioned on p. 217.

CHAPTER FIFTEEN
pp. 279–303

Page 280. Pattie (*PN*, 210) mentions the arrival on March 29, 1830, of a ship with Jones on board, but does not mention its name. For that, and for the dates of the *Volunteer* in various ports, see Ogden, *California Sea Otter Trade*, 175, and *HC* 3:149, 170.

Page 280. From here until he reaches home, Pattie can be frequently checked against outside sources. As noted in the text, his dates are accurate except that he has somehow gained a day and is consistently one day off.

Page 281. Pattie's account of the meeting with Echeandia is in *PN*, 211–14.

Pages 281–82. Pattie's mention of Hinckley and the description of the festival at San Carlos are in *PN*, 214–15. Additional material on Hinckley can be found in *HC* 3:785–86.

Page 283. Pattie and his rifle is in *PN*, 216.

Pages 283–84. Pattie's attitude toward California is in *PN*, 216–17.

Page 284. The passport is in Dept. Rec., 4: 9, Bancroft Library. It is dated May 7, 1828, which is incorrect. The date, of course, should be May 7, 1830, as indicated by Pattie and by the fact that the passport immediately preceding this in the records is dated March 10, 1830, while that immediately following is August 2, 1830.

Page 284. Pattie's account of the voyage to San Blas is in *PN*, 217–18. Jones's comments on the same trip are in John C. Jones to [J.B. Cooper?], Oahu, August 17, 1830. Vallejo Documents, 30:109, Bancroft Library.

Pages 284–86. Pattie's description of the trip from San Blas to Tepic and beyond is in *PN*, 218–19. It is brief and general and I have used Basil Hall, *Extracts of a Journal* (Edinburgh: Archibald Constable and Company, 1824), 2:183–231, both as a check on Pattie and to fill in details on the country.

Page 286. Pattie mentions the customs search in *PN*, 219. G. F. Lyon, *Journal of a Residence and Tour in the Republic of Mexico in 1826* (1828; reprint, Port Washington: Kennikat Press, 1971), describes the rigors of the search at Guadalajara in 2: 18, and tells the story of the watch in 2:107.

Pages 286–87. Pattie gives his brief comments on Guadalajara in *PN*, 219. Additional material, including the threat of confiscation, is from Lyon, 2:18–41.

Pages 287–88. Pattie's conversation with the Mexican officer is in *PN*, 219–20. A law designed to tighten control of Americans in Texas

•

had passed on April 6, 1830. See George L. Rives, *The United States and Mexico* (New York: Charles Scribner's Sons, 1913), 1:197.

Page 288. Pattie's experiences at a *mesón* are in *PN*, 220. For a guide to various travelers' comments on the same subject, see G. Harvey Gardiner, ed., *Mexico, 1825–1828* (Chapel Hill: University of North Carolina Press, 1959). For cleaning out the room with a shovel, see Joel R. Poinsett, *Notes on Mexico* (1825; reprint, New York: Frederick A. Praeger, 1969), 25.

Page 288. Pattie mentions meeting the Englishman in *PN*, 220, but does not specifically name him as "Perry" until p. 229. The passenger list for the *United States* confirms that an Edward B. Perry, age twenty-nine, a merchant from Europe, was traveling with Pattie.

Pages 288ff. Pattie's description of events in Mexico City is in *PN*, 220–22. He places his arrival on June 10, but it was apparently a day earlier. Corpus Christi—the ninth Thursday after Easter—was on June 10, and Pattie arrived the day before. Again, it fits with his consistent misdating by one day.

Page 289. The Sociedad Grande is mentioned by Poinsett, *Notes*, 46; Lyon, *Journal* 2:126–27; and W. Bullock, *Six Months Residence and Travels in Mexico* (1824; reprint, Port Washington: Kennikat Press, 1971), 204–5.

Pages 289–90. For descriptions of the feast of Corpus Christi, see Gardiner, *Mexico, 1825–28*, 54–55; Lyon, *Journal* 2:115–18; and Fanny Calderon de la Barca, *Life in Mexico*, Howard T. Fisher and Marion Hall Fisher, eds. (Garden City: Doubleday and Company, 1966), 201–2, 275–76.

Pages 290–91. The best of several descriptions of the Alameda is in Gardiner, *Mexico*, 59, while the best of several descriptions of *léperos* is in Poinsett, *Notes*, 49. See also Calderon de la Barca, 168–69.

Pages 291–92. For a guide to various descriptions of the theater at this time, see Gardiner, *Mexico*, 70. I have also used Bullock, *Six Months*, 169–73, and Poinsett, *Notes*, 81. Lyon, *Journal* 2:110, who found so much smoking at the theater in Guadalajara, parts company with the others when he says he saw little in Mexico City.

Pages 292–93. Pattie's description of the Valley of Mexico and his only mention of his reading habits are in *PN*, 222. Viga Canal is described by many. See Poinsett, *Notes*, 82, and Gardiner, *Mexico*, 63–64, 115, for a good description of Popocatepetl.

Pages 293ff. Pattie's account of his experiences with Butler is partly in *PN*, 222. The rest is contained in a letter he wrote in Mexico City, June 14, 1830. See Vallejo Documents, 30:85, Bancroft Library. The letter is also reproduced in Cleland, *Reckless Breed*, 207–8.

•

Pages 293–94. The letter Butler received is Martin Van Buren to Anthony Butler, Washington, D.C., January 22, 1830. U.S. Dept. of State, Diplomatic Instructions, 1801–1906, National Archives, Record Group 59, M-77. The letters from Coleman, Buckner, and Taylor are not included but are summarized in this letter. There is a brief biography of Coleman in *Biographical Directory of the American Congress, 1774–1961* (Washington, D.C.: U.S. Government Printing Office, 1961), 721.

Page 294. Material on Butler's personality is drawn from Rives, *United States and Mexico* 1:234–36, and the supporting documents therein.

Pages 294–95. The two Butler letters concerning Pattie are both to Van Buren, from Mexico City, on April 10 and June 29, 1830. National Archives, Record Group 59, M-97.

Pages 295–96. At first glance Pattie's claim to have talked to Bustamente seems exaggerated. His description of the president and his report of the subjects they covered, however, fit well with other records. For Echeandia's replacement and later career, see *HC* 3:181–82, 244–45.

Page 297. Pattie's account of the meeting with the bandits is in *PN*, 224–25.

Pages 297–98. Almost every traveler in Mexico at the time gave a good description of Jalapa, Vera Cruz, and the road between. For a guide to all the descriptions, see Gardiner, *Mexico*, 20–26.

Pages 298–99. Material on Isaac Stone is from U.S. Department of State, Consular Dispatches from Vera Cruz, National Archives, Record Group 59, M-183. The description of the consul's house is in Poinsett, *Notes*, 113.

Page 299. Information on the movement of the *United States* during 1830 is from a "Report of Ships" in the consular dispatches cited above. Material on Creaghead's various commands is spread through volumes 2 and 3 of *Ship Registers and Enrollments of New Orleans, Louisiana* (University: Louisiana State University, 1942).

Page 300. The arrival of the *United States* in New Orleans is from National Archives, Record Group 36, M-259, Passenger Lists, New Orleans, August 2, 1830.

Pages 300–1. Pattie's problems in New Orleans are in *PN*, 226–29.

Pages 301–2. Material on Josiah Johnston and his family is from "The Johnstons of Salisbury, Conn.," a typescript in the Kentucky Historical Society, Frankfort, Kentucky. See also *Biographical Directory of the American Congress*, 1132.

Page 302. Material on the *Cora* is from *Ship Registers* 2:33. Pattie's description of ascending the river is in *PN*, 229.

Page 302. Pattie in Cincinnati is in *Cincinnati Advertiser and Ohio Gazette*, August 28, 1830.

Page 303. The final quote is in *PN*, 230. The italics are Pattie's.

•

Page 306. "Last day of August" is based on *PN*, 229. Confirmation of the date as well as material from the passenger list are from sources cited in the previous chapter.

Page 307. Ann and John Pattie's deaths were determined by their wills in Bracken County Will Book C, pp. 336–37 (John); and D, p. 497½ (Ann). Ann Pattie's trip to Frankfort is from her depositions in Bell, *Revolutionary War Pensions . . . Fayette County, Ky.* (1936), 38.

Page 307. The presence of various people is from the 1830 census and the yearly tax books of Bracken and Mason counties.

Page 308. Population of the area is based on statistics in Timothy Flint, *History and Geography of the Mississippi Valley* (Cincinnati: E. H. Flint and L. R. Lincoln, 1832), 2:247–49.

Page 309. *Lexington Reporter*, June 10, 1829; Flint, *History and Geography* 1:357–58.

Pages 309ff. The basic source for Pattie at Augusta College is William Waldo, "Recollections of a Septuagenarian," Missouri Historical Society, *Glimpses of the Past* 5 (April–June 1938): 80. As will soon be evident, I have serious reservations about much of what Waldo says. In this case, however, the circumstantial evidence— particularly the Pattie family's presence in Augusta and its tie to the old Bracken Academy—makes this entirely probable. Life at Augusta College is based on Rankins, *Augusta College*.

Page 310. John Pattie's will is in Bracken County Will Book C, pp. 336– 37. The inventory is in Will Book D, p. 6.

Pages 311–12. Information on the two editions is taken from the title page. Material on John H. Woods is from the *Cincinnati Directory of 1831*.

Page 312. *Cincinnati Mirror and Ladies Parterre*, 1 (May 12, 1832): 131.

Pages 312–13. Constantine Rafinesque, "Abrégé des Voyages de Pattie, Willard et Wyeth," *Bulletin de la Societé de Géographie* 3, ser. 2 (Mars 1835): 181–202. Obviously, I have not been able to search every magazine for a mention of Pattie or the *PN*. I have, however, used Nelson F. Adkins, ed., *Index to Early American Periodicals to 1850* (New York: Readex Microprint, 1964). It includes an index to book reviews in all the major national and western magazines, as well as a large number of minor, short-lived publications. Even the very minor mention of the *Cincinnati Mirror* is indexed—under Flint's name—but there is nothing else.

Page 313. Flint mentions his move to New York in the *Knickerbocker* 2 (October 1833): 242–63.

Page 313. Pattie is in the Bracken County, Kentucky, Tax Book for 1833 but not that of 1831. The tax book for 1832 is missing.

•

Pages 313–14. William Waldo, *Glimpses* 5:79–80. Material on the background of the Waldos is from James W. Goodrich, "In the Earnest Pursuit of Wealth," *MHR* 66 (January 1972): 155–84.

Page 314. The presence of both Waldo and Keeney in court is from the Osage County, Missouri, Deed Book B, p. 166. The tie between the Keeneys and Pattie was first pointed out to me by Anna Virginia Parker, who was using her grandfather's Bible in which he kept track of various members of the family. I confirmed it by carefully examining the 1850 census for Osage County, Missouri, in which the Keeney family appears.

Pages 314–15. The various comments by Waldo are spread throughout *Glimpses* 5, as follows: no diary or notes, 71; clearness of memory, 62; Boggs's story, 65; Pratte, 66; Le Grand, 90; Jedediah Smith, 84–88; and Pattie, 79–80.

Page 315. The manuscript version with the sentence that was later deleted is in the Missouri Historical Society, St. Louis.

Page 316. *History of Napa and Lake Counties, California* (San Francisco: Slocum, Bowen and Company, 1881), 549.

Pages 316–17. *HC* 3:171. The tie between Pattie and Norris is in Thomas Norris, *A Descriptive List* (Oakland: Holmes Book Company, 1948), although Sylvester is listed erroneously as Norris's grandfather rather than great-grandfather. A careful comparison of Nancy Pattie in the 1850 Osage County, Missouri, census with Nancy Norris in the 1880 Sonoma County, California, census will corroborate the claim. I have also checked various San Diego County records for Pattie and found nothing.

Page 318. The summary of the lives of John, Ann, John, Jr., and Leland Pattie is based on many records—tax books, will books, deed books, etc., in Bracken, Grant, and Ohio counties, Kentucky. James appears in none of these places after 1833. The naming of the grandson James O. Pattie is from a family history form filled out by this James O. Pattie and filed with the Missouri Historical Society in St. Louis. Some of the material on his ancestors is inaccurate, and he offers no clue concerning his namesake.

Page 318. The account of the brothers and sisters is pieced together from many records of Gasconade and Osage counties, Missouri. There is also material on the Patties, available nowhere else, in Everett M. King, *History of Maries County* (Cape Girardeau, Missouri: Ramfre Press, 1963). The exception is Jennie Collins. Material on her is from the letter from Anna Virginia Parker, the DAR *Lineage Book*, 120: 111, and the Hamilton County, Ohio, census of 1840.

Pages 320ff. General material on the arrival and spread of cholera in the United States is from Charles E. Rosenberg, *The Cholera Years* (Chicago: University of Chicago Press, 1962); and Edward Mansfield, *Personal Memories* (1879; reprint, Freeport, New York: Books for Libraries Press, 1970).

•

Page 321. Flint's statement is from "Reminiscences of a Recent Journey from Cincinnati to Boston," *Knickerbocker* 2 (October 1833): 243.

Pages 321ff. For the Kentucky cholera epidemic, see J. S. Chambers, *The Conquest of Cholera* (New York: Macmillan Publishing Company, 1938), particularly the chapter entitled "The Bluegrass," pp. 148–79. See also each week's entry in the *Niles Weekly Register*, from May through August, 1833.

Pages 322–23. Specific comments from *Niles* are: quote from *Maysville Eagle*, June 22, 1833, p. 265; letter from Maysville, June 29, p. 281; Flemingsburg, Eliza, and fleeing farmers, June 29, p. 281; letter from Lexington, June 22, 1831, p. 266; specific mention of cholera in Augusta, July 13, p. 321.

Page 323. Auction of property is in Bracken County Will Book D, p. 7.

Page 325. The long quotation is from George W. Ranck, *History of Lexington* (Cincinnati: Robert Clarke and Company, 1872), 325–26.

INDEX

•

•

•

•

•

•

•

•